HOW TO MAKE CLEAN COPIES FROM THIS BOOK

YOU MAY MAKE COPIES OF PORTIONS OF THIS BOOK WITH A CLEAN CONSCIENCE IF

- you (or someone in your organization) are the original purchaser;
- you are using the copies you make for a noncommercial purpose (such as teaching or promoting your ministry) within your church or organization;
- you follow the instructions provided in this book.

HOWEVER, IT IS ILLEGAL FOR YOU TO MAKE COPIES IF

- you are using the material to promote, advertise or sell a product or service other than for ministry fund-raising;
- you are using the material in or on a product for sale; or
- you or your organization are not the original purchaser of this book.

By following these guidelines you help us keep our products affordable.
Thank you,
Gospel Light

EDITORIAL STAFF

Senior Managing Editor, Sheryl Haystead • **Editor,** Mary Davis • **Contributing Editors,** Debbie Barber, Wes Haystead, Sherri Martin, Rich Smith, Kelly Steinbock • **Art Directors,** Lenndy McCullough, Christina Renée Sharp, Samantha A. Hsu • **Designer,** Rosanne Moreland

Founder, Dr. Henrietta Mears • **Publisher,** William T. Greig • **Senior Consulting Publisher,** Dr. Elmer L. Towns • **Senior Consulting Editor,** Wesley Haystead, M.S.Ed. • **Senior Editor, Biblical and Theological Issues,** Bayard Taylor, M.Div.

Scripture quotations are taken from the *Holy Bible, New International Version*®. Copyright © 1973, 1978, 1984 by International Bible Society. Used by permission of Zondervan Publishing House. All rights reserved.

© 2006 Gospel Light, Ventura, CA 93006. All rights reserved. Printed in the U.S.A.

Contents

LESSON TOPICS AND TITLES

How to Use This Book

IF YOU ARE THE CHILDREN'S PASTOR OR DIRECTOR,

1. Read "Schedule and Options" on page 7 to get an understanding of ways to use *The Big Book of Wild and Wacky Bible Presentations*.

2. If *The Big Book of Wild and Wacky Bible Presentations* will be used as a regular feature of an ongoing program, you may want to recruit a coordinator several months before the program begins. Provide the coordinator with this book and plan regular check-ins with him or her. Be available for practical support and encouragement.

3. If individual teachers will use these presentations to supplement an existing curriculum, provide them with copies of the appropriate presentations.

IF YOU ARE THE COORDINATOR OF AN ONGOING PROGRAM,

1. Read "Schedule and Options" on page 7 to get an understanding of ways to use *The Big Book of Wild and Wacky Bible Presentations*.

2. In conjunction with the children's pastor or director, recruit the appropriate number of adults needed: an emcee or large-group leader, a presenter or presenters and small-group leaders. (One emcee or large-group leader is needed for each lesson. One presenter is needed for each lesson. You may choose to have the same presenter for all lessons, alternate two different presenters or rotate multiple presenters. One adult small-group leader is recommended for every four to eight children in a small group.)

3. Use a calendar to schedule the lessons. (Note: Each lesson stands alone, so lessons may be used in any order.)

4. Prepare ahead of time the materials needed for each lesson. (You may wish to recruit a supply coordinator to prepare lesson materials for small-group leaders as well as a drama coordinator to gather costumes and props in cooperation with presenters. Some presenters may prefer to prepare their own costumes and props.)

IF YOU ARE A LARGE-GROUP LEADER,

1. Read each lesson's material ahead of time so that you are familiar with the schedule and the presentation.

2. Greet students as they enter and gather into their small groups, helping any who are new with questions, registration, etc.

3. As timekeeper and facilitator, be aware of the time. Have fun using a variety of ways to signal students that Small-Group Warm-up time is over (perhaps relating the signal to the day's visiting character).

4. Help students make the transition to the Large-Group Presentation, to the Small-Group Discussion and then back for the Grand Finale large-group time.

IF YOU ARE A PRESENTER,

1. Read "Presentation Tips" on page 10 to find helpful suggestions for preparing and presenting each character sketch.

2. In conjunction with the coordinator, plan your presentation dates. Determine ahead of time whether you, the coordinator or the drama coordinator will gather props and costumes for the lessons you present.

3. Be sure you have photocopies of the lessons you will present so that you have ample time to make your own outline, "cheat sheet" or other prompt to help you present smoothly and effectively.

IF YOU ARE A SMALL-GROUP LEADER,

1. Read "Schedule and Options" on page 7 to get an understanding of ways to use *The Big Book of Wild and Wacky Bible Presentations*.

2. Read the following articles: "You: The Small-Group Leader!" and "Leading a Child to Christ" found on pages 8 and 11, respectively.

3. Prepare materials as needed and lead small-group activities for each lesson. Ahead of time, read the lesson's presentation and the questions used during Small-Group Discussion time and mark Bible verses with Post-it Notes as needed.

Schedule and Options

The lessons found in *The Big Book of Wild and Wacky Bible Presentations* are intended for students ages 8 to 12. These lessons can last anywhere from 30 to 50 minutes, depending on the length of time spent in small-group study. The dramatic presentations will vary in time from 5 to 10 minutes.

OPTIONS FOR USING THE LESSONS FOUND IN THIS BOOK:

As an occasional supplement. To supplement Sunday School, a second-hour session, midweek program, church retreat or other class, photocopy the entire session for the presenter in preparation for giving the dramatic presentation.

Photocopy the session's Discussion Sheet for each small-group leader as well. The sheet guides the small-group leader through the group's discussion; making a copy for each student may also be useful.

As an ongoing program based on this book. After planning the order of the lessons (see "How to Use This Book"), photocopy and put into a notebook all of the dramatic presentations planned. Give this to the presenter or presenters so that he or she is able to prepare well in advance. If you have a drama coordinator, create a prop and costume list (or photocopy the first page of each session used) so that he or she can easily gather needed items.

TO EXTEND THE LESSONS FOUND IN THIS BOOK:

• Add a recreational game time

• Add a snack time (some presentations already suggest a snack)

• Add a service project time

• Add a Bible memory practice game

SAMPLE SESSION SCHEDULE

Small-Group Warm-up	5-10 minutes
Large-Group Presentation	5-10 minutes
Small-Group Discussion	10-20 minutes
Grand Finale	5-10 minutes

YOU: THE SMALL-GROUP LEADER!

A small-group leader's job is a bit like that of shepherding a small flock of sheep: Because the responsibility isn't overwhelming, you can focus more on individual relationships and less on the problems of large-group management. Leading a small group gives you the chance to create a community where each person feels known and valued. Tracking attendance and prayer needs becomes second nature as you grow in relationship with each student, getting to know each one as an individual. You are the person whose consistent attention and care will increase each member's understanding and level of comfort in sharing his or her thoughts.

ASKING GOOD QUESTIONS

When your small group gathers, use the Small-Group Warm-up questions found in the session to set the stage for thinking about the presentation to come. But when using those questions, spark lively responses by remembering these points.

• Good questions are open-ended; that is, they are questions that don't have yes-or-no kinds of answers, such as "What do you think . . .?" "What is the best about . . . ?" "What would you tell a kid who . . . ?" Questions that can't be answered in one word awaken minds far better than ones for which a student will provide a one-word answer.

• Good questions may give rise to more questions from your students. Congratulations! You are accomplishing the goal of a small-group leader: to motivate thinking that will help your group be built up in their faith. If a question is beyond your scope, give yourself permission ahead of time NOT to know every answer!

• When you have no answer for a question, say, "That is a good question. And I don't know the answer. Let's both look for the answer and talk about it next time." Keep your promise and do your research, even play "Stump the Pastor"! Your honesty about what you don't know is a positive example that contributes to growth among your students!

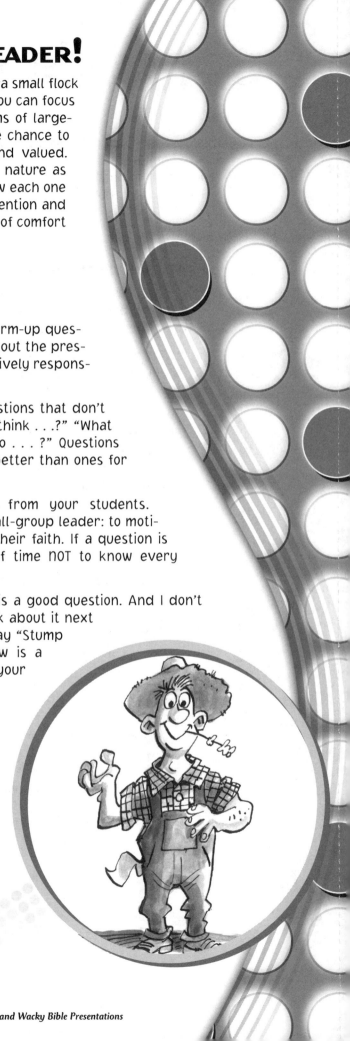

CUSTOMIZING LESSONS FOR YOUR GROUP

As you look at the Discussion Sheet for a session, take a moment to think about the skills needed and the level of understanding required for the kids in your group to successfully discuss the questions. Then consider ways you can best adapt the questions and discussion to your particular group.

TIPS FOR BETTER BIBLE DISCOVERY

To help keep your group focused on the Bible content to be discussed, consider ways to help your group members successfully find Bible verses:

• Ahead of time, find each verse and mark it by placing a Post-it Note beside it at the outer margin. Group members pass the marked Bible to take turns reading verses.

• Assign easy-to-find verses to students (from the Gospels or Psalms, for example). Find more difficult ones yourself and then hand your opened Bible to a student to read aloud.

• Before Small-Group Warm-up time, write out each reference on a Post-it Note. Assign a verse or two to each student to find before you meet during Small-Group Discussion time.

• Demonstrate and practice using a Bible's Table of Contents.

• Pair a member with weak Bible study skills with a more skilled one.

• If there is a long passage to read, each student reads one verse aloud.

Use the Key Verse Cards in a variety of ways to help your students memorize the verses! Students may cut out cards and then:

• Collect cards in a scrapbook or use them to decorate a book cover.

• Stamp or color a card when they have memorized that verse.

• Hole-punch cards to add to a ring or key chain for easy reference.

• Accumulate cards as "points" or vouchers to use toward a class prize, party, etc.

If members of your small group are not good at writing or are burned out on written homework, increase participation by using variety.

• Rather than working on individual sheets, discuss questions as a group to build teamwork and increase each group member's understanding.

• Write each Bible reference on a Post-it Note for a group member to find and then discuss answers as a group, adding answers to individual sheets as desired.

• Rather than expect individual note-taking, appoint a scribe for the group (one who *likes* to write!). This person may take notes on the Discussion Sheet or on other paper and then photocopy them for group members, e-mail them to group members, or give them to you to use for next week's review.

• For a change of pace, provide art materials so that students may create an art piece (sculpt, make a collage, etc.) and then describe the art as a way to answer a question.

Adapting your small-group times to your students' needs and personalities ensures that all students participate successfully. More than that, it tells each student: "You are important. We all help each other. We learn better together. We're all part of the same family!" It is a powerful way to model the loving, Christlike attitudes and actions you want your students to learn and show!

PRESENTATION TIPS

There you are, holding a notebook full of dramatic presentations. Someone asked if you would give a dramatic presentation and you agreed—NOW WHAT?

Don't panic. These skits are funny and easy to prepare. The presentations will get the attention of even the most resistant kid in the crowd. (Remember, kids love to see adults act in unpredictable ways!)

THE SCRIPT

Each character has a fairly vivid personality with which to begin. At least one prop or costume piece is listed (and more are often added) to help you create the character. You might also think of other props or characteristics to add!

Notice that the script is broken into sections with headings. These are provided as a way for you to outline for yourself the main points of the presentation. You may wish to create an outline from these headings or you may wish to memorize the whole presentation. Whatever you do, the key to success is to enjoy portraying the character! (Note: For variety, you may occasionally have someone interview the main character.)

ENTRANCES AND EXITS

Presentations contain stage directions for entrances and exits. However, your unique situation will most likely require adaptation. Some presentations work best with the character already sitting at a desk, etc., but most characters can simply walk into the room.

APPROPRIATE CONTENT

Most presentations found in *The Big Book of Wild and Wacky Bible Presentations* are intended for use with 8- to 12-year-olds. However, some presentations are more appropriate for upper-elementary through middle-school ages. Read each presentation ahead of time to be sure the content is appropriate and relevant to your group's age and understanding level.

MAKING A POINT

One minor caution: Some of us natural "hams" are easily able to embellish on a character. But have the point of the presentation firmly in your mind ahead of time so that embellishments reinforce (not obscure!) the point of the presentation.

LEADING A CHILD TO CHRIST

Many adult Christians look back to their childhood years as the time when they accepted Christ as Savior. As children mature, they will grow in their understanding of the difference between right and wrong. They will also develop a sense of their own need for forgiveness and feel a growing desire to have a personal relationship with God.

However, the younger the child is, the more limited he or she will be in understanding abstract terms. Children of all ages are likely to be inconsistent in following through on their intentions and commitments. Therefore, they need thoughtful, patient guidance in coming to know Christ personally and continuing to grow in Him.

PRAY

Ask God to prepare the students in your group to receive the good news about Jesus and prepare you to communicate effectively with them.

PRESENT THE GOOD NEWS

Use words and phrases that students understand. Avoid symbolism that will confuse these literal-minded thinkers. Remember that each child's learning will be at different places on the spectrum of understanding. Discuss these points slowly enough to allow time for thinking and comprehending.

a. God wants you to become His child. Do you know why God wants you in His family? (See 1 John 3:1.)

b. You and I and all the people in the world have done wrong things. The Bible word for doing wrong is "sin." What do you think should happen to us when we sin? (See Romans 6:23.)

c. God loves you so much, He sent His Son to die on the cross for your sins. Because Jesus never sinned, He is the only One who can take the punishment for your sins. (See 1 Corinthians 15:3; 1 John 4:14.) On the third day after Jesus died, God brought Him back to life.

d. Are you sorry for your sins? Tell God that you are. Do you believe Jesus died to take the punishment for your sins? If you tell God you are sorry for your sins and tell Him you do believe and accept Jesus' death to take away your sins, God forgives all your sin. (See 1 John 1:9.)

e. The Bible says that when you believe that Jesus is God's Son and that He is alive today, you receive God's gift of eternal life. This gift makes you a child of God. This means God is with you now and forever. (See John 3:16.)

Give students many opportunities to think about what it means to be a Christian; expose them to a variety of lessons and descriptions of the meaning of salvation to aid their understanding.

TALK PERSONALLY WITH THE STUDENT

Talking about salvation one-on-one creates the opportunity to ask and answer questions. Ask questions that move the student beyond simple yes or no answers or recitation of memorized information. Ask open-ended, what-do-you-think questions such as:

• "Why do you think it's important to . . . ?"

• "What are some things you really like about Jesus?"

- "Why do you think that Jesus had to die because of wrong things you and I have done?"

- "What difference do you think it makes for a person to be forgiven?"

When students use abstract terms or phrases they have learned previously, such as "accepting Christ into my heart," ask them to tell you what the term or phrase means in different words. Answers to these open-ended questions will help you discern how much the student does or does not understand.

OFFER OPPORTUNITIES WITHOUT PRESSURE

Children normally desire to please adults. This characteristic makes them vulnerable to being unintentionally manipulated by well-meaning adults. A good way to guard against coercing a student's response is to simply pause periodically and ask, "Would you like to hear more about this now or at another time?" Loving acceptance of the student, even when he or she is not fully interested in pursuing the matter, is crucial in building and maintaining positive attitudes toward becoming part of God's family.

GIVE TIME TO THINK AND PRAY

There is great value in encouraging a student to think and pray about what you have said before making a response. Also allow moments for quiet thinking about questions you have asked.

RESPECT THE STUDENT'S RESPONSE

Whether or not a student declares faith in Jesus Christ, there is a need for adults to accept the student's action. There is also a need to realize that a student's initial responses to Jesus are just the beginning of a lifelong process of growing in faith.

GUIDE THE STUDENT IN FURTHER GROWTH

There are several important parts in the nurturing process.

a. Talk regularly about your relationship with God. As you talk about your relationship, the student will begin to feel that it's OK to talk about such things. Then you can comfortably ask the student to share his or her thoughts and feelings, and you can encourage the student to ask questions of you.

b. Prepare the student to deal with doubts. Emphasize that certainty about salvation is not dependent on our feelings or doing enough good deeds. Show the student places in God's Word that clearly declare that salvation comes by grace through faith. (See John 1:12; Ephesians 2:8-9; Hebrews 11:6; 1 John 5:11.)

c. Teach the student to confess all sins. This means agreeing with God that we really have sinned. Assure the student that confession always results in forgiveness. (See 1 John 1:9.)

It's Only Proper

TOPIC
Attitude toward unbelievers

CHARACTER
Anita Allgood, Miss Manners-type etiquette expert

SUMMARY
Anita Allgood shares her (self-righteous) opinions about those who are not good Christians like she is.

KEY VERSE
Romans 5:6-8
"At just the right time, when we were still powerless, Christ died for the ungodly. Very rarely will anyone die for a righteous man, though for a good man someone might possibly dare to die. But God demonstrates his own love for us in this: While we were still sinners, Christ died for us."

PROPS
Notebook or pad of paper, pen

OPTIONAL PROPS
Clipboard, fluffy dress (especially good for curtsy demonstrations)

PREP POINTERS
This character's fussy and self-righteous quality should show clearly.

SCHEDULE
Small-Group Warm-up (5-10 minutes)
Large-Group Presentation (5-10 minutes)
Small-Group Discussion (10-20 minutes)
Grand Finale (5-10 minutes)

SMALL-GROUP WARM-UP
Meet, greet and discuss the following questions in your small group:
- **What is one thing your family considers to be bad manners?**
- **Who is a person you think has very good manners?**
- **Why do you think people care about manners?**

IT'S ONLY PROPER

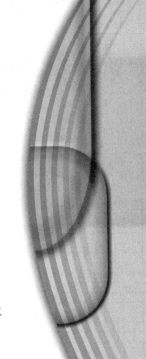

LARGE-GROUP PRESENTATION

(ANITA *enters, patting hair, shaking hands with random individuals, etc.*)
Good evening. How ARE you all this evening? I'm VERY pleased to be with
you tonight. Allow me to introduce myself. My name is Anita Allgood—
and I am ALWAYS good! I always HAVE been. You see, I LOVE proper etiquette. I love to know JUST what fork to use. I am delighted to know
when one should shake hands or when one should curtsy. (*Demonstrates
a curtsy.*) I know EXACTLY the proper attire for ANY occasion.

As a child, I did extremely WELL in school. My teachers all LOVED me and
my grades were EXEMPLARY—nearly flawless! Since I am SO well-versed in
being proper and correct, I am PLEASED to give you the BENEFIT of my vast
knowledge!

APPROPRIATE APPAREL

Now FIRST of all, I see that nearly all of you are wearing casual attire. For this setting, that would be entirely APPROPRIATE. However, it does NOT forgive some of the
horrendous POSTURE I am seeing. (*Claps sharply.*) All of you! We need to be poised at
all times—time to sit up nice and straight! Please keep your back from touching your
chair. Fold your hands and rest them on your laps. MUCH better! And if you DO choose
to rest arms on the table, remember—absolutely NO elbows!

And, ladies, be aware. If we choose to cross our legs, they must be crossed at the ankle
and NEVER with a foot on the thigh, although this is quite acceptable for a gentleman—but
ONLY when he is in casual attire.

(*Looks around, beaming.*) Oh, you are all looking more PERFECT already! I can see that SOME of
you will take more time than others, but no matter. Onward.

Now, those of you who are sitting CORRECTLY, please IGNORE those who aren't—or won't. Some are
either unable or unwilling to understand the FINER points of stately behavior. Many people just
don't GET it. One could become absolutely CRAZY trying to explain what is right and proper to SOME
people.

APPROPRIATE ATTITUDE?

Take, for instance, my fourth-grade Sunday School class. When the teacher explained that we are all sinners, I had to think VERY hard to find ANY sin in MY life. But then I realized that I OCCASIONALLY did not
tuck in the sheets as I should have when I made my bed. My mother had instructed me on the fine art of
bed making and had shown me the RIGHT way to do it, but I didn't always take the time to DO it in JUST
the way she showed me. So that DID make me guilty of poor bed making and hasty disobedience.

At any rate, the teacher told us how Jesus had made a way to heaven for us by dying on the cross
to take the punishment for our sins and that to receive the gift of eternal life, we had to ask Jesus
to forgive our sins and ask to become part of His family. Of course, I was the FIRST to pray. But SOME
heard the same message I heard and yet STILL didn't pray. And at school, SOME children didn't
believe in Jesus, even when I TOLD them about Him. So I decided that SOME people love being bad
SO much that they just WILL NOT follow Jesus . . . or maybe they are just too mean or stupid.

JUST MY KIND

Of course, I STILL go to Sunday School. It is ENJOYABLE to be with others who believe as I do. We even have HOMEWORK—although SOME people don't always FINISH theirs! But I usually do MINE on Monday, far ahead of time. Mine is always the neatest, as well! In fact, let me read this assignment's questions for you: (Clears throat, opens workbook and takes out pen. She murmurs the answers to the questions below, not writing them down.)

1. Are you BETTER than other people because you're a CHRISTIAN?
Oh dear me, I would have to say so. They're all—PAGANS!

2. Is there anyone that God doesn't love?

Hm. Well, the Bible DOES say that God loves everyone . . . but CERTAINLY not in the way He loves ME!

3. Is there anyone God cannot bring to salvation?
Well, there are a few I might RECOMMEND that He did NOT!

4. What should our attitude be toward non-Christians?
Hm . . . you know, THAT is a rather DIFFICULT question. I'm going to work on this by myself while you work together on these questions. We'll check our answers when we're finished. See you in a few minutes! (Exits.)

SMALL-GROUP DISCUSSION TIME

Provide one "It's Only Proper" Discussion Sheet (p. 16) to each student. Invite students to find verses and discuss answers to questions on the sheet. Invite interested students to talk more with you about joining God's family (see "Leading a Child to Christ" on p. 11).

GRAND FINALE

(ANITA returns, somewhat subdued, fanning herself with her workbook.)
Goodness, could it BE? I've had a self-righteous, snooty attitude! Thinking I'm better than others is NOT part of being a Christian! IMAGINE that! The Bible is quite clear: Jesus loves everyone. He even loved me BEFORE I became a Christian. I am humbled. I need to ask God to FORGIVE me and give me HIS love for people who don't know Him.

God wants me to love others even BEFORE they are Christians. That's the VERY way they will KNOW I am part of GOD'S family! Even as we grow AWAY from wanting to sin, we should also grow to LOVE people who are still IN sin. The most GRACIOUS thing we can do is simply to tell them about the Savior! NO one is too bad, mean or stupid to hear about God's love. I don't have to love their sin but I DO need to love and accept them for who they are—God's special creations that need to know HE loves them! Indeed! Loving unbelievers—THAT would be the PROPER thing to do! (Exits.)

Leader invites a student to read Romans 5:6-8 from the Key Verse Card. **It's comfortable for us to meet together as Christians and think we are all doing well. But God asks us to obey Him in everything. That means He wants us to love every person in ways that show His love, no matter what. It takes God's power to do that!**

Close in prayer, asking God to help students be humble and thankful for what He has done for them so that they are willing and ready to show God's love to others and tell them about God's gift of eternal life through Jesus.

It's Only Proper

DISCUSSION SHEET

Does being a Christian make you better than people who are not Christians?
Find 1 Corinthians 1:26-31.

Is there any person whom God does not want as part of His family?
Find 2 Peter 3:9.

Is there anyone God cannot save?
Find Mark 10:24-27.

What should our attitude be toward people who don't know Jesus?
Find Matthew 5:43-48.

How should Christians act when they live among non-Christians?
Find 1 Peter 2:11-17.

How should non-Christians affect us?
Find 2 Peter 3:17-18.

How will non-Christians know that we follow Jesus?
Find John 13:35.

KEY VERSE CARD

Romans 5:6-8
"At just the right time, when we were still powerless, Christ died for the ungodly. Very rarely will anyone die for a righteous man, though for a good man someone might possibly dare to die. But God demonstrates his own love for us in this: While we were still sinners, Christ died for us."

Digging for the Truth

TOPIC
Biblical accuracy

CHARACTER
Idaho Smith, Indiana Jones-type archaeologist

SUMMARY
Idaho Smith lets us in on some of the archaeological evidence for believing the accuracy of Scripture.

KEY VERSE
2 Peter 1:20-21
"Understand that no prophecy of Scripture came about by the prophet's own interpretation. For prophecy never had its origin in the will of man, but men spoke from God as they were carried along by the Holy Spirit."

PROPS
Bible, Indiana Jones-type hat and duffel bag containing notebook, at least one archaeology-related tool (such as a small hammer, paintbrush, dental pick, etc.), all of it dusty

OPTIONAL PROPS
Pickax or small shovel to lean on

PREP POINTERS
To make the presentation humorous, stuff the duffel bag with unneeded items that you remove and display as you search for what you need!

SCHEDULE
Small-Group Warm-up (5-10 minutes)
Large-Group Presentation (5-10 minutes)
Small-Group Discussion (10-20 minutes)
Grand Finale (5-10 minutes)

SMALL-GROUP WARM-UP
Meet, greet and discuss the following questions in your small group:
- **Why do you think the Bible is true?**
- **What would you tell a person who didn't think the Bible is really true?**
- **What is something in the Bible that you know is true because of what has happened to you?**

DIGGING FOR THE TRUTH

LARGE-GROUP PRESENTATION

(ARCHAEOLOGIST *enters, carrying bag, shaking hands with random individuals, looking around as if missing something.*)
Greetings, all! My name is Idaho Smith. I'm an archaeologist. I was just looking around to see if I could POSSIBLY find any ancient artifacts in here! (*To an older lady.*) No, not you, ma'am. You are STILL too young to qualify.

DIGGING TO DISCOVER

Pardon my appearance, but I just came in from an archaeological dig. Does anybody here know what an archaeologist DOES? (*Listens as audience answers.*) Have any of you ever found anything OLD and INTERESTING? Something you couldn't EXPLAIN? Archaeology is exciting because you get to find things that help you understand the way things were MANY years ago.

I haven't found anything TOO significant yet. A few years ago, I dug up a strange pink rock. But I had it analyzed. It turned out to be a wad of REALLY old, hard bubble gum. Then another time, I thought I'd discovered a rock with hieroglyphic writing on it! But it turned out to be part of an old Oreo cookie. But even though I haven't made any great discoveries yet, many other archaeologists HAVE made exciting discoveries.

AN ANCIENT SOURCE

What do you think could help people like me learn about ancient cultures when we dig up really old stuff? Aha! I see some of you have a VERY valuable primary SOURCE for ancient archaeology right in FRONT of you—a rendering of an ancient text! Hold it up if you have one! That's right—it's the Bible. (*Finds Bible in duffel bag; holds it up.*) This book, the BIBLE, is VERY valuable to ANYONE who studies the ancient cultures that are found in the cradle of civilization. That's the area we call the Middle East!

Now some think that a book that began to be written about 3,500 YEARS ago just could NOT be completely accurate. After all, did you know that the Bible took about 1,500 YEARS to ASSEMBLE? That it had 40 different AUTHORS? That it was written in 3 different LANGUAGES?!

Besides that, the books of the Bible were written LONG before there were printing presses or photocopiers! In those days, when they needed new copies, a scribe had to copy every jot and tittle to make a new book by hand. How could a book stay EXACTLY the same under those conditions? The funny thing is that archaeologists have NEVER made any discoveries that have shown the Bible to be inaccurate in anything it says. It is a most amazing thing! Very exciting!

AN ACCURATE SOURCE

For instance, you know the first five books of the Bible? What are they named? (*Listens to audience's answers.*) Well, those books were supposed to have been written by Moses, right? THAT would mean that they were written around 1400 B.C. Well, until 1964, historians believed that civilizations had NO written languages until MUCH later. So they were sure there was no way that MOSES could have written those books. But here's the exciting part.

On an archaeological excavation in 1964 in Northern Syria, the diggers found an old city named Ebla. And in those ruins, they found about 17,000 clay tablets with cuneiform writing on them! And get this: Those tablets were PROVED to have been written no later than 2250 B.C. That means that there was a very sophisticated form of writing almost 1,000 years before Moses did his writing!

There is something ELSE those tablets told us. Before this, there had never been proof outside of the Bible that the cities of Sodom and Gomorrah ever existed. Many people said the cities and the story were just MADE UP. But right there on those Ebla tablets, the names of those cities were mentioned! Just another PROOF of the accuracy of the Bible!

A BIG DISCOVERY

Here's another discovery that was even MORE exciting. In 1947, a young Bedouin shepherd in the Judean Desert entered a cave where he found many clay jars. Those jars held ancient SCROLLS—thousands of them! Among them was a scroll of the book of Isaiah. These scrolls were about 1,000 years OLDER than any other copy. So of course, they COMPARED these newly discovered manuscripts with the old manuscripts they already had. And guess WHAT? The words were virtually UNCHANGED! Aside from a few minor spelling differences, the manuscripts were IDENTICAL.

Scientists were astounded. HOW could the contents have stayed so accurate through all those years? I know—why don't you do some archaeological fact-finding of your own? Check out what the prophet Isaiah wrote. Then find out if his prophecies came true by reading in the New Testament! (Exits.)

SMALL-GROUP DISCUSSION TIME

Provide one "Digging for the Truth" Discussion Sheet (p. 20) to each student. Invite students to find verses and discuss answers to questions on the sheet. Invite interested students to talk more with you about joining God's family (see "Leading a Child to Christ" on p. 11).

GRAND FINALE

(ARCHAEOLOGIST *returns, holding Bible.*)
Archaeology ALONE cannot prove that God exists or that everything in the Bible really happened. BUT the more we learn about the people and places and times written about in the Bible, the more we find that the Bible is amazingly historically accurate! That's EXCITING!

Can you trust the Bible? I certainly do! And not just for information about history or archaeology. Trusting in the Bible means I believe that Jesus really died for our sins and really was raised from the dead. I know we really ARE sinners and need Jesus to be our Savior. In order to spend eternity in heaven with God, we really DO need to believe and trust in Jesus as our Savior! It's either true or it's not true. So, because there's never been evidence otherwise, I DO believe it's true!

Well, I've got to get back to the field! There's a whole lot more to be discovered! Maybe I'll dig up Moses' stone tablets or Joseph's Egyptian prison! Maybe, just maybe, I'll find the bones of Jonah's big fish! I know they exist—it's all right here in the true Word of God! *(Picks up bag and exits.)**

Leader invites a student to read 2 Peter 1:20-21 from the Key Verse Card. **The few archaeological findings we have heard about are only the beginning. God's Word has not been proven wrong by any archaeological find. In fact, many finds in the Middle East confirm the truth of the accounts we read in Scripture.**

Close in prayer, asking God to help students to both believe and to obey His true and accurate Word.

*Information for this presentation taken from Josh McDowell, *Evidence That Demands a Verdict* (San Bernardino, CA: Here's Life Publishers, 1972), pp. 56-58, 68, 1D.

Digging for the Truth

DISCUSSION SHEET

Check out these prophecies from the book of Isaiah!
After you have read **Isaiah 40:3,** find **Matthew 3:1-2.** What happened?

You don't want to miss **Isaiah 53:8!**
Now find out what happened 700 years later!
Find Matthew 27:1-2.

After you know what **Isaiah 53:7** says, fast-forward to find **Matthew 27:12-14.** What was promised? What happened?
Find Isaiah 53:12 and Matthew 27:38.

This one's a biggie!
Find Isaiah 53:5. And then find Acts 13:38.

As a matter of fact, there are more than 50 major prophecies about Jesus in the Old Testament that are accurately fulfilled in the New Testament. Not one of those prophecies was wrong!
Why have the Scriptures been preserved so accurately?
Find John 20:31.

KEY VERSE CARD

2 Peter 1:20-21
"Understand that no prophecy of Scripture came about by the prophet's own interpretation. For prophecy never had its origin in the will of man, but men spoke from God as they were carried along by the Holy Spirit."

Honestly!

TOPIC
Cheating and honesty

CHARACTER
Referee

SUMMARY
The ref blows the whistle on dishonesty.

KEY VERSE
Philippians 4:8
"Finally, brothers, whatever is true, whatever is noble, whatever is right, whatever is pure, whatever is lovely, whatever is admirable—if anything is excellent or praiseworthy—think about such things."

PROPS
Referee's shirt, whistle (Note: A real referee's whistle will be very loud indoors!)

OPTIONAL PROPS
Clipboard

PREP POINTERS
"Authoritative" is the word!

SCHEDULE
Small-Group Warm-up (5-10 minutes)
Large-Group Presentation (5-10 minutes)
Small-Group Discussion (10-20 minutes)
Grand Finale (5-10 minutes)

SMALL-GROUP WARM-UP
Meet, greet and discuss the following questions in your small group:
• **When have you seen a situation where someone was caught cheating?**
• **Why do you think people lie or cheat?**
• **Why do you think telling the truth is important or not important?**

HONESTLY!

LARGE-GROUP PRESENTATION

(REFEREE *enters, blows whistle, makes a referee-like signal and yells.*) HALFTIME! *(Blows whistle again; addresses audience.)* It's been a ROUGH GAME so far—and it's only halftime! Don't get me wrong, I LOVE football—the spirit of competition, the drive for excellence, the desire to WIN—it's all GREAT! But I've got to admit, NOBODY loves the REF. At least HALF of the people think I'm wrong EVERY time I make a call! If the call goes against the team YOU'RE rooting for, you're just POSITIVE that I've made a mistake. Am I RIGHT? I'm RIGHT!

INSULTED

I've been called the most INTERESTING things. I've been told I'm as blind as a bat. I've had my intelligence insulted. I've EVEN been told my mother DRESSES me funny! But I'm JUST doing my job.

Look at it this way. IF the players played by the RULES all the time, if they never tried to GET AWAY with doing things they're not supposed to do, then I WOULD NOT be a necessary part of the game! But they DO try to get away with breaking the rules. I'm out there to keep things SAFE and FAIR. Am I RIGHT? I'm RIGHT!

IMPORTANT

Have you ever been playing a game and the person you're playing with cheats to win? How about at school? Have you ever known someone who CHEATED on homework or on a test? If you THINK about it, you'll probably remember a time when YOU cheated—or were TEMPTED to cheat or lie. Am I RIGHT? I'm RIGHT!

I've seen people CHEAT—and then LIE about it! Like the time I heard, "Really, Ref, I didn't pull on the guy's face mask! He just HANDED me this piece of his broken helmet—honest." HONEST? Give me a BREAK! Am I RIGHT? I'm RIGHT!

Honesty. Does it really MEAN anything anymore? Why should WE be honest if so many OTHER people get away with being DISHONEST all the time? Well, halftime's over. I've got to get back out on the field. Why don't you take a look into this honesty thing for me? See you after the game. *(Exits.)*

SMALL-GROUP DISCUSSION TIME

Provide one "Honestly!" Discussion Sheet (p. 24) to each student. Invite students to find verses and discuss answers to questions on the sheet. Invite interested students to talk more with you about joining God's family (see "Leading a Child to Christ" on p. 11).

GRAND FINALE

(REFEREE returns.)

OK, game's over. According to the FANS, I need to get GLASSES. According to one of the COACHES, I need to read the RULEBOOK, which I happen to know by HEART. And according to my MOM, I need to wash my UNIFORM!

But according to GOD, cheating, lying, stealing and using foul language are ALL WRONG—not things He wants us to do! They hurt other people and they end up hurting us, too. That's why doing them is SIN. You know, I'm not perfect. Every once in a while, I don't see a foul and so a player gets away with playing unfairly. But just because I didn't SEE it doesn't mean it wasn't SEEN. Just because you or I get away with a LIE or a bad WORD doesn't mean it wasn't HEARD.

The Bible tells us that God sees and hears everything we DO and SAY and THINK. And if we want the ultimate WIN—a win for God—we need to please HIM!

Here's my hope for us all: that when God looks at us, He doesn't need to toss a FLAG on the play we're making. I pray that we make Him smile, and maybe even say, "TOUCHDOWN!"*(Exits.)*

Leader invites a student to read Philippians 4:8 from the Key Verse Card. **It's easy to think that no one sees or hears us do what is wrong. But God does. He wants to see us make touchdowns in our lives—times we obey Him and please Him with our honesty.**

Close in prayer, asking God to help students be honest and obey His rules of the game for honesty and cheating.

Honestly!

DISCUSSION SHEET

What did God say about cheating others by changing measures and weights?
Find Proverbs 20:10.

What does God say about lying?
Find Ephesians 4:25 and Proverbs 12:22.

What is God's rule about stealing?
Find Ephesians 4:28.

How does God feel about bad language and telling dirty jokes?
Find Ephesians 4:29 and Ephesians 5:4.

Who does Jesus call the "father of lies"?
Find John 8:43-44.

No one will ever be perfect. What can we do when we've blown it?
Find 1 John 1:9.

KEY VERSE CARD

Philippians 4:8
"Finally, brothers, whatever is true, whatever is noble, whatever is right, whatever is pure, whatever is lovely, whatever is admirable—if anything is excellent or praiseworthy—think about such things."

Ticket to Paradise

TOPIC
Choosing heaven

CHARACTER
Vacationer to Hawaii

SUMMARY
The vacationer tells about how the unexpected results of the Hawaiian vacation have caused serious thought about an eternal destination.

KEY VERSE
Psalm 84:10-12
"Better is one day in your courts than a thousand elsewhere; I would rather be a doorkeeper in the house of my God than dwell in the tents of the wicked. For the LORD God is a sun and shield; the LORD bestows favor and honor; no good thing does he withhold from those whose walk is blameless. O LORD Almighty, blessed is the man who trusts in you."

PROPS
Hawaiian shirt, lei, bandage around head, arm in a sling

OPTIONAL PROPS
Crutches

PREP POINTERS
Practice hobbling!

SCHEDULE
Small-Group Warm-up (5-10 minutes)
Large-Group Presentation (5-10 minutes)
Small-Group Discussion (10-20 minutes)
Grand Finale (5-10 minutes)

SMALL-GROUP WARM-UP
Meet, greet and discuss the following questions in your small group:
- **When have you gone on a vacation?**
- **Why did you go on this trip?**
- **What did you like about the vacation? What did you not like?**

TICKET TO PARADISE

LARGE-GROUP PRESENTATION

(VACATIONER *enters, hobbling or on crutches.*)

Hi! I just got back from my vacation. I went to Hawaii! When I first decided to take a vacation, I didn't know where I wanted to go. The travel agent told me about two trips: one was to the Sahara Desert and the other to Hawaii. Now the Sahara is a blistering hot desert. Hawaii is a tropical island. I chose Hawaii.

The travel agent booked my trip and I was off! Paradise on Earth, here I come!

SURPRISING PARADISE

But I've got to be honest: Hawaii wasn't EXACTLY what I expected! When I first stepped off the plane, someone put some flowers around my neck. Unfortunately, I turned out to be ALLERGIC to them. My face started swelling up like a balloon and I had to go to a doctor for an allergy shot!

Then I decided to do some hiking. Now, Hawaii is made of volcanic rock. All that rock can make the ground pretty rough. Wouldn't you know it—I stumbled, twisting my ankle and cutting my knees BADLY on those sharp rocks!

So I decided to do something a little SAFER: I took a hula lesson. But THAT turned out to be more dangerous than I expected! My grass skirt got stuck on a palm tree. And when I tried to pull it loose, it shook the tree. And THEN guess what? A COCONUT fell on my head! WHUMP! I kind of staggered down to the beach. I remember seeing an outrigger canoe pulled up on the shore but then I PASSED OUT!

When I came to, I realized I had fainted right INTO that canoe. And as I stepped out, I fell right into the water! The canoe had drifted out into the ocean while I was out cold! Of course, I heard some creepy music, so I turned around. Sure enough, there was a SHARK coming right FOR me! I kicked him in the nose and then swam as FAST as I could for the shore. Amazingly, I made it ALIVE!

When I got to the shore, all I wanted was to go back to my hotel room and LIE DOWN. So I asked a guy in a jeep to give me a ride. That guy drove like a MANIAC! I was hanging on for dear life! When we got to the hotel, he stopped SO quickly that I went flying OVER the windshield and landed on the pavement. I got to LIE DOWN, all right—in the HOSPITAL! I had PLENTY of time to lie there and WONDER if I should have chosen a DIFFERENT destination!

TRIP CHOICE

Frankly, I don't remember too much else about my trip, except this—I ALMOST DIED!! Not just once, but LOTS of times! Being so CLOSE to DEATH made me think a LOT more about my choice of an ETERNAL destination. I know my life won't last forever here on Earth. So just like the travel agent gave me two choices for my vacation, I ALSO have been given two choices for where I spend eternity. I've got to find some answers before NEXT year's vacation. My travel agent wants to send me to Aruba or Afghanistan! So find out what you can about heaven for me, will you? I need to find some more aspirin. (*Exits.*)

SMALL-GROUP DISCUSSION TIME

Provide one "Ticket to Paradise" Discussion Sheet (p. 28) to each student. Invite students to find verses and discuss answers to questions on the sheet. Invite interested students to talk more with you about joining God's family (see "Leading a Child to Christ" on p. 11).

GRAND FINALE

(VACATIONER returns.)

My Hawaiian vacation may not have been heaven on Earth, but that's OK. I can always decide to take another vacation somewhere else—OR I could get a new travel agent! But for my ETERNAL life, I'd better make sure, since the Bible is so clear about God's long-term plans for us!

God lets me choose where I will spend eternity. If I choose heaven, then I need to do what it will take to get there: to join His family and then live my life the way He wants me to, according to His Word. No one can make THAT choice for me—not my pastor, not my parents, not my teacher or small-group leader. I have to make my own choice. And if I say that I REFUSE to choose, then I'm actually choosing to reject God—and I don't even want to THINK about where THAT leads!

You know what? I choose God. I want to be part of His family and be able to know He is with me every day. And since THIS vacation is for eternity, well, I'd be CRAZY to choose anything but God! We all have to make our own choices. What will you choose? *(Exits.)*

Leader invites a student to read Psalm 84:10-12 from the Key Verse Card. **There is nothing more valuable than knowing where you will spend eternity. As our vacationer said, it's the individual choice of every person here.**

Close in prayer, asking God to help students understand the importance of choosing heaven as their eternal destination.

Ticket to Paradise

DISCUSSION SHEET

What is heaven like?
Find 2 Peter 1:10-11, Revelation 21:3-4 and Revelation 21:22-27.

Does God want some people to go to hell?
Find 2 Peter 3:9.

What does the Bible say we need to do to go to heaven?
Find Romans 10:9-10.

Do we really have to make the choice?
Find John 3:17-18.

KEY VERSE CARD

Psalm 84:10-12
"Better is one day in your courts than a thousand elsewhere; I would rather be a doorkeeper in the house of my God than dwell in the tents of the wicked. For the LORD God is a sun and shield; the LORD bestows favor and honor; no good thing does he withhold from those whose walk is blameless. O LORD Almighty, blessed is the man who trusts in you."

A Prescription for Compassion

TOPIC
Compassion

CHARACTER
Dr. Ima Meaney

SUMMARY
Dr. Meany realizes that his humor lacks compassion and hurts those around him, giving him "cancer of compassion."

KEY VERSE
Psalm 103:13-14
"As a father has compassion on his children, so the LORD has compassion on those who fear him; for he knows how we are formed, he remembers that we are dust."

PROPS
White medical coat, doctor's bag, large toy injection needle

OPTIONAL PROPS
Stethoscope (for self-diagnosis), pill bottle (when talking about prescription)

PREP POINTERS
The doctor habitually rubs his hands together or slaps his knee when talking about his humor.

SCHEDULE
Small-Group Warm-up (5-10 minutes)
Large-Group Presentation (5-10 minutes)
Small-Group Discussion (10-20 minutes)
Grand Finale (5-10 minutes)

SMALL-GROUP WARM-UP
Meet, greet and discuss the following questions in your small group:
- **What do you think the word "compassion" means?**
- **Who is someone you know who shows compassion?**
- **What makes people like that person? How does that person show compassion?**

A PRESCRIPTION FOR COMPASSION

LARGE-GROUP PRESENTATION

(DR. MEANY *enters, cheerful and whistling.*)
Good evening. I'm Doctor Ima Meany. I didn't realize there would be quite so MANY of you, but I think I might have *(Looks into bag.)* . . .yes, I have JUST enough vaccine for EVERYONE. Now, if you'll all roll up your SLEEVES, I'll prepare the NEEDLES.

JUST TEASING

(Sees audience response.) What? What's the matter? Would you rather have the shot in your . . .? *(Points to posterior and then slaps leg, laughs.)* RELAX, everyone! I was just KIDDING. I'm not here to give you all shots—UNLESS you make me mad. I'm just TEASING!

I ENJOY teasing people. For example, I had a patient named Mrs. Trout. She had to have her spleen removed. I told her to be very careful in the weeks following her surgery NOT to eat foods that start with the letter S or her stomach would fall into the space left by the removed spleen! I'm SUCH a joker! *(Slaps knee; chuckles.)* She was calling me every other day, asking me questions like, "Can I have SLICED cheese? Is a hamburger considered a SANDWICH? What about lettuce? When is lettuce a SALAD?" It was so AMUSING! But when I finally told her I had been KIDDING, she was ANGRY. You know, some people have NO sense of humor.

NOT FUNNY

At any rate, Mrs. Trout and a few OTHER unhappy patients recently REPORTED me to the Medical Association, complaining about my teasing. ONE guy got mad because I told him he looked like a GOONY BIRD when he tried to travel on crutches!

But now I have been ordered to take a class in "Bedside Manners." I supposedly need to learn to be more CARING and COMPASSIONATE to my patients. I'm SURE this will be a COMPLETE waste of time. It's just MY WAY of adding a little HUMOR to everyone's day. But I'm not allowed to order any more blood tests until I've completed the course. So be good enough to help me out, would you? After all, I just LOVE to draw blood! See what you can find out about kindness and compassion—STAT! *(Exits.)*

SMALL-GROUP DISCUSSION TIME

Provide one "Prescription for Compassion" Discussion Sheet (p. 32) to each student. Invite students to find verses and discuss answers to questions on the sheet. Invite interested students to talk more with you about joining God's family (see "Leading a Child to Christ" on p. 11).

GRAND FINALE

(DR. MEANY returns.)

You know, I have a SELF-diagnosis to make. I have CANCER—cancer of COMPASSION. I never thought my teasing and joking were MEAN—I thought it was everyone ELSE'S fault that they didn't appreciate my HUMOR. But I guess that's just it. I never stopped to THINK about how my patients actually FELT. I was too busy trying to be FUNNY.

You know, God CREATED our sense of humor. He has one Himself! After all, who do you think created the ARMADILLO? But comedy should NOT be at someone else's expense, causing PAIN or suffering. There is a time and place for TRUE humor. But apparently it doesn't involve hurting people's feelings! Perhaps the best cure for my cancer of compassion would be to THINK about other people's feelings BEFORE I make a joke. That's going to require some serious HUMOR SURGERY.

But I think that with GOD'S help, my condition will not be TERMINAL. The first step to recovery is to ask God to forgive me for being UNKIND to His creations. Then the NEXT step is to APOLOGIZE to everyone whose feelings I have hurt. THAT'S not going to be easy—there are a LOT of them! But it's what I must do.

Next, I prescribe for MYSELF a dose of daily Bible reading and lots of prayer. The Bible says that if I draw near to God, He will draw near to me. THAT makes my prognosis for a full recovery look pretty good!

(Chuckles.) So in my NEW spirit of COMPASSION, I'll only charge you all HALF-PRICE for this house call! *(Chuckles.)* I'm only KIDDING!!! Compassion: It's just what the Great Physician ordered! *(Exits.)*

Leader invites a student to read Psalm 103:13-14 from the Key Verse Card. **Compassion is something we all love to receive. But it's sometimes harder to give than we expect! Even the TV shows we laugh at usually are funny because they are making fun of someone—and it doesn't usually show how hurt that person might be. Let's ask God to help us do some exploratory surgery on our own sense of humor.**

Close in prayer, asking God to help students to see ways they might be hurting others by their humor and to change the kinds of humor they show so that others are not hurt by the students' words and actions.

A Prescription for Compassion

DISCUSSION SHEET

What kinds of actions does God want us to show to others?
Find Micah 6:8, Colossians 3:12-14 and Ephesians 4:32.

How can we show compassion to others?
Find Matthew 7:12 and Philippians 2:1-4.

What actions and words are not compassionate?
Find Proverbs 26:18-19, Proverbs 28:27 and Ephesians 4:31.

How much compassion does God have?
Find Psalm 144:8 and Lamentations 3:22-23.

What does God do to show compassion to us?
Find Isaiah 40:24-31 and John 3:16.

KEY VERSE CARD

Psalm 103:13-14
"As a father has compassion on his children, so the LORD has compassion on those who fear him; for he knows how we are formed, he remembers that we are dust."

The Hunt for Happiness

TOPIC
Contentment in Christ

CHARACTER
Crocodile hunter (script is written for a female croc hunter)

SUMMARY
The croc hunter tells about the search for true happiness.

KEY VERSE
Matthew 6:33
"But seek first his kingdom and his righteousness, and all these things will be given to you as well."

PROPS
Bible, Australian outback crocodile hunter-type clothing and hat

OPTIONAL PROPS
Dollar bills; pictures of sports car, beach house, valentine (to represent love)

PREP POINTERS
Use the optional props as you describe these things.

SCHEDULE
Small-Group Warm-up (5-10 minutes)
Large-Group Presentation (5-10 minutes)
Small-Group Discussion (10-20 minutes)
Grand Finale (5-10 minutes)

SMALL-GROUP WARM-UP
Meet, greet and discuss the following questions in your small group:
- **When have you hunted for something?**
- **What was it? Was it easy or hard to find?**
- **What do you think people might do to search for happiness?**

The Hunt for Happiness

Large-Group Presentation

(CROC HUNTER *enters, stopping to greet individuals with "G'day, mate!"*)
G'day, mates! I come from the land down under. That's Australia to you blokes who don't know geography! Now, I hunt crocodiles. They're such cute, cuddly little creatures. I really ENJOY takin' one down. And croc meat? It's my FAVORITE on the barbie! One of the BEST for Christmas dinner!

Now, I wasn't ALWAYS a croc hunter. There was a time when I was hunting something MUCH more important. And it was much harder to get HOLD of than a CROC! I was on a hunt for true happiness. Let me tell you about it.

OFF I GO

You see, one morning a few years back, I asked myself, "Am I HAPPY?" I had my family and a home. I had friends and chores and playtime, but I wasn't sure I was really HAPPY. So I asked my parents for my college funds. I told them I wanted to go out and find TRUE HAPPINESS. They handed me the money and sadly watched me go.

At first, I thought that MONEY would bring happiness. I bought everything I SAW—a car, clothes, a house on the beach. I enjoyed those things, but having them DIDN'T make me happy.

Maybe I would be happy if I had people to share all my stuff with, I thought. So I invited lots of people to parties. I hung out with people who were popular and trendy. I BOUGHT them LOTS of things and they all seemed to like me very much! But I still wasn't happy.

And what do you think happened next? Yep. I RAN OUT of money. So all those "friends" went away. I had to sell my car and then my house. Soon all of THAT money was gone, too. I tried to BORROW money, but no one would loan me any!

MAKE ME HAPPY?

So every day, I sat on the beach. I had no home and just sat there looking toward the ocean, wondering where I would EVER find true happiness.

One day, a very attractive man came jogging down the beach. He was friendly and quite cute! We started spending time together and really ENJOYED each other's company. Before long, we decided to get MARRIED!

I looked in his eyes and said, "I'm so GLAD to find someone who will LIVE to give me TRUE HAPPINESS. Happiness IS finding true love—right?"

"WAIT a minute," he said. "I thought YOU wanted to live YOUR life to give ME true happiness!"

"Nope," I replied. "I'm looking for true happiness for ME." So—we broke up.

That was it. I was CRUSHED. I cried and cried. I had FAILED. I HADN'T found true happiness in money or stuff. I hadn't found true happiness in friends or popularity. I hadn't found true happiness even in LOVE.

When I thought about it, I realized that I HAD been HAPPY at home! I had a warm bed, my family and friends. I started to think about going back home. I was afraid my parents would be upset because of my bad decisions, but I decided it was worth the risk. I picked up my tuckerbag and headed home.

WELCOME HOME?

I was NERVOUS when I knocked on the door. My father opened it. But he didn't start lecturing me about my bad decisions! He just took me in his arms and gave me a tremendous HUG. You should have seen my mom—laughing and crying and hugging me! She called up all my friends and relatives to tell them I had returned. We had a HUGE party! Shrimp and croc on the barbie for everyone! I was SO GLAD to be home!

Later, Dad asked if I had ever FOUND true happiness.

"No, Dad. I never did." I answered. "Do YOU know where I could find true happiness?" I asked.

I bet you'll NEVER guess what he told me! Go ahead, see if you can guess. *(Waits for audience answers.)* I'll give you a hint *(Holds up a Bible.)* The ANSWER is in here! So why don't you start YOUR hunt for true happiness right now? I'm off to wrestle down a croc—just a small one—so we can have a SNACK! *(Exits.)*

SMALL-GROUP DISCUSSION TIME

Provide one "The Hunt for Happiness" Discussion Sheet (p. 31) to each student. Invite students to find verses and discuss answers to questions on the sheet. Invite interested students to talk more with you about joining God's family (see "Leading a Child to Christ" on p. 11).

GRAND FINALE

(CROC HUNTER returns.)

Well, now YOU'VE learned some of what I found out about true happiness. It doesn't come from money or popularity or even love. It begins with being with God. We humans were MADE for that. But we LOST that closeness when Adam and Eve got kicked out of the Garden of Eden. But because Jesus took the punishment for our sin, we can join God's family and know that one day, we'll have PERFECT true happiness—in heaven!

In the meantime, we can have true happiness through spending time with God. Because God loves us, He takes care of us. He sees to our needs. That doesn't mean He gives us everything we want—that would lead to STUFF making us happy instead of HIM!

NOW, I'm REALLY happy—because I'm content in Christ. Life's not perfect, but someday it WILL be. And right now, I know I'm on the RIGHT TRACK to finding TRUE HAPPINESS. Let's all HUNT IT DOWN together, shall we? G'day! *(Exits.)*

Leader invites a student to read Matthew 6:33 from the Key Verse Card. **Well, our croc hunter friend surely has hunted up some keys to true happiness! We hear all the time that money or stuff or love will make us happy. But God's Word says that if we seek God and His kingdom first, He will give us EVERYTHING else we need—even happiness!**

Close in prayer, thanking God for His gifts and the contentment that comes from being part of His family and spending time with Him.

The Hunt for Happiness

DISCUSSION SHEET

What makes a person happy?
What do we need to know about money and true happiness?
Find 1 Timothy 6:9-10.

What's better than money? Why?
Find Proverbs 16:16 and Proverbs 20:15.

Will a special person be able to love you more than Jesus does?
Find John 15:13.

What's the secret to happiness?
Find Psalm 16:11.

What kind of life will lead to happiness?
Find Proverbs 3:5-6 and Matthew 6:33.

KEY VERSE CARD

Matthew 6:33
"But seek first his kingdom and his righteousness,
and all these things will be given to you as well."

Back in Time

TOPIC
Creation

CHARACTER
Time-traveling scientist (like "Doc" from the film *Back to the Future*)

SUMMARY
The scientist takes us on a tour of creation and some theories of origin.

KEY VERSE
Romans 1:20
"For since the creation of the world God's invisible qualities—his eternal power and divine nature—have been clearly seen, being understood from what has been made, so that men are without excuse."

PROPS
Lab coat, wild wig, pencil, clipboard

OPTIONAL PROPS
Flip chart, or blackboard, and appropriate drawing tools

PREP POINTERS
This character can be a little crazy, but he or she must seem credible!

SCHEDULE
Small-Group Warm-up (5-10 minutes)
Large-Group Presentation (5-10 minutes)
Small-Group Discussion (10-20 minutes)
Grand Finale (5-10 minutes)

SMALL-GROUP WARM-UP
Meet, greet and discuss the following questions in your small group:
- **What ideas have you heard about how Earth got here?**
- **Where have you heard these ideas?**
- **What do you think makes sense about these ideas?**
- **What do you think does not make sense?**

Back in Time

Large-Group Presentation

(TIME TRAVELER enters, staggering a little and looking around as if dazed.)
What YEAR is this? *(Waits for audience's response.)* Oh, thank goodness. On my LAST trip I only got back as far as 1975. I thought I would be stuck there, wearing polyester leisure suits for the rest of my LIFE!

TRAVELING BACK

I'm Zebulon Pike, by the way. I'll bet you're wondering where I've BEEN. *(Holds up pencil.)* See this pencil? This morning I took this brand-new pencil out of my notebook. I began to wonder, *Where did this pencil come from?* It's mostly WOOD, so it came from a tree—but where was that tree GROWING? And how did it GET there?

I've always asked a lot of questions. In fact, my insatiable CURIOSITY led me to invent my . . . *(Whispers loudly.)* Can you keep a secret? I don't want word to get out, but I've invented—a TIME MACHINE! *(Louder.)* It works pretty well, too—except for getting stuck in the DISCO era. I've been able to travel back in time to learn a LOT!

PENCIL QUEST

For instance, back to this PENCIL: The wood came from a tree in the state of Washington. The SEED that tree grew from came from a tree that was once SAT under by a member of the Lewis and Clark Expedition. And the seed that began THAT tree was home to a family of screech owls for hundreds of years! WOW!

I've been to all SORTS of places in my time machine. I've been to the signing of the Declaration of Independence . . . THAT was interesting. I've been to the Battle of Midway . . . THAT was just plain SCARY. I've been to the SIXTH wedding of Henry the EIGHTH . . . THAT was just plain WEIRD.

So far, I haven't been able to get my time machine to travel any farther back than the time of ancient Egypt. But I'm working on modifications to go back even farther, because I REALLY want to know how Earth and the universe GOT here!

THE BIGGER BANG

Most scientists today explain how the universe was created by a theory called "The Big Bang." When scientists used telescopes to look at the stars in the night skies, they noticed that stars were clustered into galaxies and that these galaxies were all moving away from each other. Since all the galaxies were moving AWAY from each other, scientists figured at one time they must have all been TOGETHER, at the same place. With all the stuff that makes up the universe in just one place, it would have been under tremendous pressure and have been very hot. Most scientists regard THAT time as the beginning of the universe (space and time) and call it "The Big Bang."

BIGGER QUESTIONS

But scientists have no idea about what WAS before that time or why all the material was in that ONE PLACE to start with. They do think Earth formed as the original material when the Big Bang expanded and cooled and condensed together to form stars and planets like our sun and the earth. I've been working on my time machine for years now to get BACK to that time, because this Big Bang Theory still leaves me with so many MORE QUESTIONS! Where did the "stuff" come from to make the Big Bang? Is there anything ELSE in the universe? How could the Big Bang result in Earth, our big, beautiful planet that's just right for us to live on and enjoy?

Do YOU have any idea how Earth got here? Why don't you talk about that while I run out for a snack—time travel makes me HUNGRY! *(Exits.)*

SMALL-GROUP DISCUSSION TIME

Provide one "Back in Time" Discussion Sheet (p. 40) to each student. Invite students to find verses and discuss answers to questions on the sheet. Invite interested students to talk more with you about joining God's family (see "Leading a Child to Christ" on p. 11).

GRAND FINALE

(TIME TRAVELER returns.)

I always wanted to go back in my time machine to see Earth being created. But maybe I don't NEED to. I know that however the earth was made, GOD created it. God existed before the earth was made—in fact, before the universe or time or space existed. GOD made EVERYTHING! It takes faith to believe that, but it makes my purpose on Earth very clear: I am here to enjoy God and His creation and to build a relationship with Him that will last FOREVER! I know that whatever happens to me throughout my life, God is here (or there, or wherever!) with me, loving me. My FUTURE lies with God—I DON'T need a time machine to see that!

I think that this wonderful planet shows us what an amazing Creator we have. *(Opens Bible and reads.)* "In the beginning, God created the heavens and the earth." I'm putting my faith in God!

But if I can get my time machine to go into the FUTURE, I can see how I'll LOOK in 20 years! *(Runs hand through hair.)* On SECOND thought, maybe I don't want to know! *(Exits.)*

Leader invites a student to read Romans 1:20 from the Key Verse Card. **This has been quite an adventure! Although people who believe the Bible have different ideas about how creation might have happened, evidence everywhere points to God the Creator! Let's thank Him for His love in making this beautiful world for us.**

Close in prayer, thanking God for His creativity in making Earth and for His love for us wherever we go.

Back in Time

DISCUSSION SHEET

How does the Bible say Earth got here?
Find Genesis 1:1-2 and John 1:1-5.

Both the Big Bang and Genesis indicate a beginning: Genesis focuses on God's careful preparation in creating a home for us, while the Big Bang theory looks for Earth's starting point. How does Genesis compare to the Big Bang?
Find Isaiah 40:25-26,28 and Colossians 1:16-17.

(Scientists wonder how the natural world works. Scientists who believe in God want to know how God created what exists. Those who don't believe in God just want to know how it happened.)

Is there more to this world than material stuff?
Find Romans 1:20 and Ephesians 1:3.

What does it take for people to believe that God created Earth?
Find Hebrews 11:3.

What is faith?
Find Hebrews 11:1.

What happens when we put our trust in God?
Find Proverbs 3:5-6.

KEY VERSE CARD

Romans 1:20
"For since the creation of the world God's invisible qualities—his eternal power and divine nature—have been clearly seen, being understood from what has been made, so that men are without excuse."

Surely You Jest

TOPIC

Dishonesty (being two-faced)

CHARACTER

Jester

SUMMARY

The two-faced jester helps us understand why we need to be pure in heart.

KEY VERSE

Proverbs 13:15-16

"Good understanding wins favor, but the way of the unfaithful is hard. Every prudent man acts out of knowledge, but a fool exposes his folly."

PROPS

Face paint in two colors, cold cream, tissues

OPTIONAL PROPS

Jester hat or costume

PREP POINTERS

Draw a line down the center of your face and then paint one side one color and the other side a contrasting color. (Red and blue are used in the presentation to keep the concept clear.) Practice turning one side of your face to the audience as you speak the words of one personality or the other.

SCHEDULE

Small-Group Warm-up (5-10 minutes)
Large-Group Presentation (5-10 minutes)
Small-Group Discussion (10-20 minutes)
Grand Finale (5-10 minutes)

SMALL-GROUP WARM-UP

Meet, greet and discuss the following questions in your small group:
- **When have you known a person that others said was two-faced?**
- **What do you think the term really means? How does a two-faced person act?**
- **What kinds of things does a two-faced person do?**

SURELY YOU JEST

LARGE-GROUP PRESENTATION

(JESTER enters, weaving through the group and turning from one side to the other so that everyone sees the dual-colored face. Turns red side to audience, smiling.)
Hi! I'm SO happy to be here! I LOVE to come here! This is my FAVORITE time of the week. I learn so much and have SUCH a great time. *(Turns blue side of face to audience, looking bored.)* Hey, guys. Here we are AGAIN. I don't really LIKE it all that much. I just come to make my folks happy.

(Turns red side to audience, smiling.) I really LOVE to learn more about God. I try my BEST to be a good Christian. *(Turns blue side of face to audience, looking bored.)* Actually, I get pretty TIRED of always hearing about God and Jesus. I only believe in them because my parents do. Religion is just a bunch of RULES.

TWO FACES AT SCHOOL

(Turns red side to audience, smiling.) I was talking with some kids at school today about their beliefs. I told them what I believe and what we learn here. I even invited some of them to come with me! *(Turns blue side of face to audience, smirking.)* Then there were some OTHER kids I was talking to. One guy told a dirty joke. It was HILARIOUS! Then I told them one I had heard. They laughed their heads off!

(Turns red side to audience, smiling.) My teacher is so nice. She explains things well. I never really understood about dividing fractions, but she took the time to explain it to me! Now I don't have ANY problems with dividing fractions. *(Turns blue side of face to audience, looking a little less bored.)* Of course, the kids all make FUN of her. She's not very pretty. AND she dresses funny. When her back was turned today, I drew a picture of her. It looked like a horse in a bag lady outfit. I showed it to everyone and they all laughed!

(Turns red side to audience, smiling.) At lunchtime, I sat with another kid who goes to church here. We talked about stuff we like to learn about God. She said, "God bless you," when we got up. I said it back to her. *(Turns blue side of face to audience, smirking.)* Then I saw her again at recess. I was with some other friends who don't like her. So when she said, "God bless you" again, I just IGNORED her. Some of my other friends called her a geek. I laughed along with them.

(Turns red side to audience, looking sad.) The yard-duty lady saw us laughing. She said we were being unkind. So I said, "You're right, I'm sorry." I felt bad. *(Turns blue side of face to audience, smirking.)* Yeah, I felt bad—bad that I got CAUGHT! That yard-duty lady always sees me being nice. I guess she doesn't expect ME to be mean.

TWO FACES TO FRIENDS

(Turns red side to audience.) There's one very popular girl who I want to be friends with but she cusses a lot. She lies, too. Come to think of it, she doesn't obey very often, either. I wanted to be her friend. But I don't like the way she acts. *(Turns blue side of face to audience.)* Of course, I TRIED to be her friend WITHOUT being LIKE her. BUT it was really CLEAR that she ONLY liked me if I acted like HER. So now I swear and tell lies sometimes. It's NOT like I'm as BAD as SOME people. If I'm so BAD, why doesn't God STRIKE me with a lightning bolt? Anyway, now I have a POPULAR friend—so THERE!

(At this point, JESTER gets personalities confused, shows the wrong side of the face for the character first portrayed. Turns red side to audience.) We were at the mall together. I saw my friend steal a pair of earrings. It's OK. I didn't do it! But I MIGHT. After all, it's the STORE's fault. If

things weren't so EXPENSIVE, I could afford to BUY them. *(Turns blue side of face to audience.)* My mom has a new pair of really pretty earrings. I told her how nice they looked on her.

(Turns red side to audience.) She looks nice for an old lady! But she's a real dinosaur. She has NO idea what's going on. Sometimes I even yell at her. *(Realizes the mix-up and then tries to correct it, becomes defensive. Turns red side to audience.)* Oh. No. Uh . . . I mean, I would NEVER yell at my mother. That's DISOBEDIENT! I know God doesn't want us to disobey our parents. And uh, I didn't really LIE about yelling at her, I just sometimes wish I COULD . . . I mean, I could if I WANTED to. No one can STOP me. I can do anything I WANT to do. *(Turns blue side of face to audience, talking to self.)* I don't want THEM to think I'm some kind of goody-goody . . . *(Turns red side to audience, talking to self.)* And I DON'T want THEM to think I'm some sort of bad girl. Oh, man. I'm in a REAL mess. I've been CAUGHT trying to be TWO DIFFERENT people! I feel like a FOOL.

(Faces audience.) Why do we DO that two-faced thing when we feel pressured to act like other people even though we know it's WRONG? What do YOU think the right thing is to do? *(Turns blue side of face to audience.)* I'm SUPPOSED to be a Christian. I don't want to be a FOOL. But how can I keep from being two-faced? *(Exits.)*

SMALL-GROUP DISCUSSION TIME

Provide one "Surely You Jest" Discussion Sheet (p. 44) to each student. Invite students to find verses and discuss answers to questions on the sheet. Invite interested students to talk more with you about joining God's family (see "Leading a Child to Christ" on p. 11).

GRAND FINALE

(JESTER returns, turning both sides of face while speaking.)
Okay, let's look at BOTH sides of this question. You might be like me—a person who has gone along with doing wrong in the past. But now you really want to please God instead of people. What can you say to tell someone that even though you have said and done wrong things before, you don't want to do them anymore?

These are hard questions to answer, aren't they? It comes down to first choosing whether you care more about pleasing your friends or pleasing God. It's one thing to KNOW the right answer and SAY the right answer, but it's ANOTHER thing to DO what is right. It is not always as easy as talking!

(JESTER applies cold cream and removes makeup while speaking.) God says that Christians are new creations. I'm TIRED of being two-faced. I don't want to act in different ways to please the person I am with. If I'm a NEW creation, I'm going to please GOD. I can ask HIM to give me the words to say if people make fun of me for obeying HIM. *(Smiles at audience, showing clean face.)* That's IT! ONE face from now on—honest! *(Exits.)*

Leader invites a student to read Proverbs 13:15-16 from the Key Verse Card. **We all have times when we are tempted to be two-faced. It's hard to think when other people pressure us to do wrong. But the Bible makes it clear that people in God's family need to be different! God wants us to be honest in the way we act. And He promises to help us do what is right.**

Close in prayer, asking God to help students obey Him and trust Him to help them when they feel pressured to do wrong.

Surely You Jest

DISCUSSION SHEET

How should we react when we see other Christians acting in wrong ways? What should we say?
Find Galatians 6:1.

What if it's you that has done wrong? When you are corrected, how should you respond to another Christian who points out your un-Christlike behavior?
Find Proverbs 10:17.

What did Paul say about being ashamed of being a Christian?
Find Romans 1:16.

Will people always like us because we're Christians?
Find John 15:18-19.

Who should we try to please most? Why?
Find Galatians 1:10.

What can happen to us if we keep trying to lead a double life?
Find Proverbs 11:3.

KEY VERSE CARD

Proverbs 13:15-16
"Good understanding wins favor, but the way of the unfaithful is hard. Every prudent man acts out of knowledge, but a fool exposes his folly."

Build on the Rock

TOPIC
Firm foundations

CHARACTER
Construction worker

SUMMARY
The construction worker helps us understand the importance of having the proper foundation for life.

KEY VERSE
Psalm 127:1
"Unless the Lord builds the house, its builders labor in vain. Unless the Lord watches over the city, the watchmen stand guard in vain."

PROPS
Construction worker's clothing, hard hat, tool belt and lunch box

OPTIONAL PROPS
Model houses (built of linking blocks or logs, for demonstration purposes)

PREP POINTERS
Toy hard hats are often available at party supply stores or online.

SCHEDULE
Small-Group Warm-up (5-10 minutes)
Large-Group Presentation (5-10 minutes)
Small-Group Discussion (10-20 minutes)
Grand Finale (5-10 minutes)

SMALL-GROUP WARM-UP
Meet, greet and discuss the following questions in your small group:
- **What is something you have helped build?**
- **What is something you have seen being built?**
- **What is the first thing that is done when constructing a building?**

BUILD ON THE ROCK

LARGE-GROUP PRESENTATION

(CONSTRUCTION WORKER *enters, clamping hard hat onto head.*)
Hello there. Oh, hey, you know that this is a construction zone, right? Where are your hard hats? Well, from the looks of it, you've all got pretty hard HEADS, so maybe you'll be OK.

BUILDING WHAT?

My name's Reggie, by the way. I'm a construction worker, a builder of buildings. You heard of the Eiffel Tower? I DIDN'T build that. But you know the Empire State Building? I didn't build THAT, either. Surely you've heard of the Taj Mahal? So have I. But I didn't build IT, either.

But I DID help build the shopping center down the road. It has a burger place, a coffee place and a home improvement store. Right now I'm working on a new shopping plaza. When it's completed, it will have a burger place, a coffee place and a home improvement store. Come to think of it, the last six construction projects I've done have included a burger place, a coffee place and a home improvement store. Must be a pattern there!

SOLID BUILDING

Anyway, I've been in construction for 23 years now, so I know a thing or two about how to construct a good, solid building. I don't usually give away trade SECRETS, but I'll let you in on the MOST important part of constructing a building that will stand the test of time. The SECRET is having a strong FOUNDATION. If you don't get the foundation right, the building will NEVER be structurally sound.

Some guys on the crew are IMPATIENT about getting the foundation laid so that they can get to the walls and the roof. Those are the parts that people see. The average person looking at a building will say, "Nice walls!" or "Fancy roof." But NO one ever says, "Awesome foundation!" Because once the building is up, you never SEE the foundation again! But believe you me, you'll KNOW if it's a good one when the tornadoes come or the hurricanes blow or the earth quakes. Yessiree, when things get ROUGH, that firm foundation is mighty IMPORTANT!

SOLID LIVES

Something else I've noticed is how a firm foundation is JUST as important in our LIVES as it is in BUILDINGS. When difficulties and hard times come into people's lives—and they happen to EVERYONE—the quality of a SPIRITUAL foundation shows RIGHT up! Yep, the foundation may be weak or strong, but it's a little LATE to find out when hard times hit.

Instead, I have to ask myself BEFORE the storms hit, "Reggie, how firm is that SPIRITUAL foundation?" It's a question we're all wise to ask before things get rough.

But hey, if there's one thing I like better than BUILDING, it's taking a LUNCH break. So I'll just be over here expanding my PHYSICAL foundation while you all see what you can find out about the SPIRITUAL kind. *(Exits.)*

SMALL-GROUP DISCUSSION TIME

Provide one "Build on the Rock" Discussion Sheet (p. 48) to each student. Invite students to find verses and discuss answers to questions on the sheet. Invite interested students to talk more with you about joining God's family (see "Leading a Child to Christ" on p. 11).

GRAND FINALE

(CONSTRUCTION WORKER returns.)

Well, now you know the biggest secret of construction: a good foundation. And you also know the biggest secret to LIFE: a strong spiritual foundation. When times are good and everything is calm, a foundation doesn't seem to matter. But when storms and hard times come—sickness, tragedy, trouble of any kind—THAT'S when a firm foundation means EVERYTHING.

Jesus did HIS part. He IS our firm foundation. But those Bible verses you read were saying that you are like a building, like a holy temple for God, right? So you gotta ask yourself, "Self, how's the spiritual foundation? And hey, what's going on with the construction of that spiritual temple?"

Is your life like a well-built temple for the Holy Spirit or is He living in a place like a rickety shack? Jesus deserves a GREAT place to live in our lives! So people, roll up your sleeves. Time to lay STRONG foundations and build SOLID temples for the Holy Spirit! *(Exits.)*

Leader invites a student to read Psalm 127:1 from the Key Verse Card. **There are lots of ways to build our lives, but unless they are built on Christ, our ideas and plans won't stand. Take a moment to think of one way you can check your spiritual foundation this week and then do some foundation building or repair so that your spiritual temple is stronger.**

Close in prayer, asking God to help students to build their lives firmly on Jesus.

Build on the Rock

DISCUSSION SHEET

Who does the Bible say should be the spiritual foundation of our lives?
Find Ephesians 2:19-21.

If we are becoming a holy temple, who lives in it?
Find Ephesians 2:22.

How do we build our spiritual temple to be strong?
Find Luke 6:46-49.

How do we know if we have a well-built spiritual temple?
Find 1 Corinthians 3:10-11.

What does God say about His spiritual temples?
Find 1 Corinthians 3:16.

KEY VERSE CARD

Psalm 127:1
"Unless the Lord builds the house, its builders labor
in vain. Unless the Lord watches over the city, the
watchmen stand guard in vain."

What's Forgiveness All About?

TOPIC
Forgiveness

CHARACTER
Bad Bart, Western gunslinger

SUMMARY
Bad Bart, a former member of the Hole in the Heart Gang, tells about how he learned about God's forgiveness—and about forgiving others.

KEY VERSE
Ephesians 4:31-32
"Get rid of all bitterness, rage and anger, brawling and slander, along with every form of malice. Be kind and compassionate to one another, forgiving each other, just as in Christ God forgave you."

PROPS
Cowboy shirt, hat, kerchief, jeans

OPTIONAL PROPS
Stick horse, stuffed rooster

PREP POINTERS
If using the optional props, consider entering on the stick horse and using the rooster to represent Jehosephat.

SCHEDULE
Small-Group Warm-up (5-10 minutes)
Large-Group Presentation (5-10 minutes)
Small-Group Discussion (10-20 minutes)
Grand Finale (5-10 minutes)

SMALL-GROUP WARM-UP
Meet, greet and discuss the following questions in your small group:
- **What is the meanest thing you have ever heard of a kid your age doing?**
- **Why do you think (making fun of someone) is mean? How does it make a person feel?**
- **What is the kindest thing you've ever seen a kid your age do? What happened as a result of the way that kid acted?**

What's Forgiveness All About?

Large-Group Presentation

(BART enters.)

I'm gonna tell you all a story about an outlaw named BAD BART—who USED to be ME. Now, I was a mean and ORNERY little cuss. I used to hang around with some other little OUTLAWS called the Hole in the Heart Gang. We were always up to some sort of mischief or another. We stole the chickens out of Mrs. Cooper's yard and threw rocks at windows. We put Farmer Miller's barn door up on his ROOF a dozen times before we turned 10!

THE GANG

Things just went from bad to worse as we got older. People in town would see us coming and run off lickety-split to avoid our meanness. If you had asked me then why we were so mean, I'd say, "We're just havin' fun. People around here just ain't got no sense of HUMOR!"

But one day I saw old Farmer Miller at the Feed and Seed store. I snickered, "Hey, Farmer Miller, SORRY about that barn door on your roof!"

"That's OK," said Farmer Miller. "I FORGIVE you, Bart." I was STUNNED. He FORGAVE me? I didn't know WHAT to think!

It wasn't but another week later that we'd once AGAIN put Farmer Miller's barn door on his roof—and wouldn't ya know it, I saw Farmer Miller AGAIN!

I sort of chuckled, "I'm right SORRY about that barn door, Farmer."

"Well, alright then, I FORGIVE you!" Farmer Miller just GRINNED at me. I was plumb dumbfounded. Why did he keep FORGIVING me?

I thought about this for a LONG time. Finally, I couldn't STAND it. I HAD to know why he was FORGIVING me! So I rode my horse over to Farmer Miller's, in broad daylight. He was out fixing the barn door, as usual!

I asked, "Farmer Miller, WHY do you keep forgiving me?"

"Well," he replied, "you keep apologizing. You don't SEEM all that sorry, but y'see, I'm a Christian. God tells me to forgive YOU in just the same way that the Lord Jesus has forgiven ME. And Jesus has forgiven me for a LOT!"

Farmer Miller went on to tell me all about Jesus Christ. And because Farmer Miller had showed me so much of the grace and kindness of God, I UNDERSTOOD Jesus' love for me. I just up and knelt right there in the barnyard and asked Jesus to be my Savior! It was nothin' short of a MIRACLE!

NEW DOIN'S

Well, after I became a Christian, some things had to CHANGE. For ONE thing, I stopped runnin' with the Hole in the Heart Gang and bein' a part of all their wrongdoings. After all, Jesus' LOVE had filled up my heart—I didn't WANT to do those things anymore!

Now the REST of the gang thought it was just a hoot and a holler that I had up and "got religion." So THEY started playing their mean PRANKS on ME!

I'd be sippin' sarsaparilla and they'd sneak CHILI POWDER into it! Then the other day, I was sittin' against a tree, readin' my Bible when they snuck up and TIED me to the tree. They knew I'd have to WAIT for somebody who was no longer AFRAID of me to come along and untie me! Gotta say, I DID get a lot of readin' done!

But today, BOY HOWDY am I MAD! See, I got me a pet rooster called Jehosephat. Since I quit the gang and all, Jehosephat's been real good company. But LAST night was the LAST STRAW—er, feather! The Hole in the Heart Gang snuck into my yard, grabbed Jehosephat and plucked out every lasted ONE of his tail feathers! That poor bird is the most pathetic-looking creature you ever laid eyes on. I'm FURIOUS!

NOW WHAT?

The PROBLEM is, now I'm a CHRISTIAN. HOW am I supposed to respond to this most DESPICABLE act of feather pluckin'?

I TELL ya, I FEEL LIKE takin' my six shooters and makin' those varmints DANCE like marionettes to avoid the BULLETS I'd send flyin' their way! But I had a feeling that this wasn't the CORRECT response for a Christian! So I went and told Farmer Miller the whole sad story. He said God's Word would help me figure out the best thing to do and gave me some Bible verses to read. Would ya read them so's to help me figure out what to do? I'd sure be obliged—and it MIGHT save the lives of those feather-pluckin' scoundrels! *(Exits.)*

SMALL-GROUP DISCUSSION TIME

Provide one "What's Forgiveness All About?" Discussion Sheet (p. 52) to each student. Invite students to find verses and discuss answers to questions on the sheet. Invite interested students to talk more with you about joining God's family (see "Leading a Child to Christ" on p. 11).

GRAND FINALE

(BART returns.)
I listened from outside while you all read them verses. Those Bible verses really DID help! Now I think I got a pretty good idea of what to DO with that Hole in the Heart Gang! I'm gonna FIND 'em, CONFRONT 'em—and then FORGIVE 'em! FORGIVENESS will FIX 'em good! Thank you kindly for your help. Adios, amigos! *(Exits.)*

Leader invites a student to read Ephesians 4:31-32 from the Key Verse Card. **Forgiving others isn't always the easiest thing to do—even if you ARE a Christian. But how much has God forgiven YOU? He has sure forgiven ME a whole lot! And He tells us that because HE has forgiven His kids ALL of our sins, He wants us to be LIKE Him—in the way we forgive others freely, showing them grace and kindness. When we forgive others, they notice that God is in our lives. Forgiving others shows them what God is like. And it takes a BIG load of unhappiness off our shoulders!**

Close in prayer, thanking God for helping us to forgive each other as He has forgiven us.

What's Forgiveness All About?

DISCUSSION SHEET

What does "forgiveness" mean? Write some of the answers you come up with so that you can share them with the others in your group—and tell Bart, too!
Find Matthew 18:21-35.

Who does the master represent in the parable?
Who are the servants?
What did the master do about the first servant's debt?
What did the master expect that servant to do about the other servant's debt?
What should we do when we want revenge? Why? What should we do instead?
Find Romans 12:19-21.

How should Bart treat the Hole in the Heart Gang—and why?
Find Matthew 6:14-15.

What are some steps we can take when someone says or does something that hurts us?
Find Matthew 18:15-17, James 1:19 and James 5:16,19.

KEY VERSE CARD

Ephesians 4:31-32
"Get rid of all bitterness, rage and anger, brawling and slander, along with every form of malice. Be kind and compassionate to one another, forgiving each other, just as in Christ God forgave you."

Yodel-ay-ee-who's a Good Friend?

TOPIC
Friendship

CHARACTER
A Swiss Alpine yodeler

SUMMARY
The yodeler helps us discover what it takes to be a good friend.

KEY VERSE
John 15:13-15
"Greater love has no one than this, that he lay down his life for his friends. You are my friends if you do what I command. I no longer call you servants, because a servant does not know his master's business. Instead, I have called you friends, for everything that I learned from my Father I have made known to you."

PROPS
Swiss Miss-type costume (for female) or lederhosen (for male), cup (imaginary cocoa), paper sealed in an envelope (letter)

OPTIONAL PROPS
Blond wig with pigtails (for female), Swiss flag, cocoa mix, carafe of hot water, cups (to share cocoa during Small-Group Discussion time)

PREP POINTERS
You will need to practice yodeling—it doesn't come naturally! Audio examples are available on the Internet.

SCHEDULE
Small-Group Warm-up (5-10 minutes)
Large-Group Presentation (5-10 minutes)
Small-Group Discussion (10-20 minutes)
Grand Finale (5-10 minutes)

SMALL-GROUP WARM-UP
Meet, greet and discuss the following questions in your small group:
• **Think of a friend. Why do you like to be around that person?**
• **What would you say makes that person a good friend?**
• **What people do you know who are good friends to each other? How would you describe the way they treat each other?**

YODEL-AY-EE-WHO'S A GOOD FRIEND?

LARGE-GROUP PRESENTATION

(YODELER enters, stopping often to yodel loudly while moving to front of group.)
Oh, hi. I'm Heidi (or Franz). I am from Switzerland, ya. I am here on vacation. What I miss most about Switzerland right now is da yodeling. You hear it everywhere in my village! I learned to yodel when I was only a small child. I LOVE to yodel! *(Demonstrates.)*

CALLING A FRIEND

You know yodeling, ya? Yodeling is da way we call each other in my country. We live where there are big mountains, the Alps. We yodel to call our goats and cows. We yodel to each other across the deep valleys.

My very best friend Helga (or Sven) lives on the next mountain. We only get to see each other once a week when we go into the village with our parents for church. Since we missed being together during the week, ya, we learned to yodel across the valley between our homes. The yodel echoes all the way to Helga's house and when I hear Helga yodel back to me, it makes me feel good to know she is there. Friends should always try to be there for each other, don't you think? I do, ya.

NO ANSWER

That is why I have been so UPSET. Last week, Helga didn't answer my yodel—not one time, no! I had just found out that my family was coming here to your country for a super vacation to visit my Uncle Schweitzer—and I was excited, ya! So I wanted to tell Helga about my trip. I yodeled in the morning but I got no answer, no. I yodeled again after lunch and still no answer. So that evening, I tried some of my SPECIALTY yodels. I yodeled high like a soprano singer. *(Demonstrates.)* It's LOUD, ya? No answer.

Then I yodeled my special goat-calling yodel. *(Demonstrates.)* It's even LOUDER, ya? But again, no answer.

Finally, I tried my BEST yodel of all—my Broadway musical GRAND FINALE yodel! *(Demonstrates.)* It's REAL-LY LOUD, ya? And do you KNOW what I heard from Helga? NOTHING! Not one little warble did I hear from Helga.

UNHAPPY TRAILS

So here I am on vacation, ya? I am trying to have a good time. But I am still so angry. Why did my good friend ignore me? Is this how you treat friends here in your country? What does it mean to be a good friend, anyway? Will you find these answers for me? I will be out looking for a cup of good Swiss cocoa, ya. *(Exits.)*

SMALL-GROUP DISCUSSION TIME

Provide one "Yodel-ay-ee-who's a Good Friend?" Discussion Sheet (p. 56) to each student. Invite students to find verses and discuss answers to questions on the sheet. Invite interested students to talk more with you about joining God's family (see "Leading a Child to Christ" on p. 11).

GRAND FINALE

(YODELER returns, draining contents of cocoa cup while walking to front.)
I have something to tell you, ya. While I was drinking my cocoa, a letter was delivered to me. It is all the way from my homeland. GUESS who sent it? *(Listens to audience's guesses.)* Ya! It is from Helga! Shall I read it? OK.

"My dearest Heidi, I hope you are having a wonderful time on vacation. I wanted to wish you a good trip, but I have been sick with a bad cold and LARYNGITIS. I am feeling better now, but the doctor says it will be a WHILE before I can yodel again. I miss you and am praying for you. Have a wonderful time. Love, your friend Helga.

P.S. It was GREAT to hear you do ALL your yodels before you left. It cheered me up while I was sick!"

(Puts down letter thoughtfully.) Oh, ya, I should have known something was wrong. How could I have doubted my dearest friend? I am so sorry. While I have been angry, she has been praying for me. I feel just awful, ya. I was surely not a very good friend. When I return to my homeland, I will ask for her forgiveness. And I will pray that she continues to get better, my poor little friend. God is good to give me such a friend. And ya, it is true, God has much to tell us about being a good friend. I am so happy now, I feel like yodeling! *(Demonstrates.)* It's LOUD, ya? Try it! It's fun!
(Exits, yodeling loudly, encouraging others to yodel.)

Leader invites a student to read John 15:13-15 from the Key Verse Card. **Sometimes it's hard to show love to our friends. But when they don't do things the way we expect, we should take time to listen to them. We should pray for them and help them do what is right. Those are ways to be really good friends—even if we can't yodel!**

Close in prayer, asking God to help students put the friendship principles learned in this session into practice.

Yodel-ay-ee-who's a Good Friend?

DISCUSSION SHEET

What makes friendship a good thing?
Find Ecclesiastes 4:9-12.

Here are some ways to be a good friend. Can you find out what they are?
Find Proverbs 17:17.
Find Galatians 6:2.
Find Ephesians 4:32.
Find James 5:16.

What should you be aware of with non-Christian friends?
Find Psalm 1:1-2.

KEY VERSE CARD

John 15:13-15
"Greater love has no one than this, that he lay down
his life for his friends. You are my friends if you do
what I command. I no longer call you servants, because
a servant does not know his master's business. Instead,
I have called you friends, for everything that I learned
from my Father I have made known to you."

Touring the Future

TOPIC
Future events

CHARACTER
Tour guide

SUMMARY
The tour guide gives a (self-guided!) tour of the future, since the museum has no exhibits to see.

KEY VERSE
Jeremiah 29:11
"'For I know the plans I have for you,' declares the LORD, 'plans to prosper you and not to harm you, plans to give you hope and a future.'"

PROPS
Uniform shirt or jacket, clipboard

OPTIONAL PROPS
Sign reading "Gift Shop" placed near set

PREP POINTERS
This tour guide should seem EXTRA efficient at first, to make up for the fact that there is NOTHING to SEE in this museum!

SCHEDULE
Small-Group Warm-up (5-10 minutes)
Large-Group Presentation (5-10 minutes)
Small-Group Discussion (10-20 minutes)
Grand Finale (5-10 minutes)

SMALL-GROUP WARM-UP

Meet, greet and discuss the following questions in your small group:
• **What is one thing you think will be different about the world in 10 years?**
• **Why do you think this will change?**
• **What do you think the world will be like when you are a grandparent?**

TOURING THE FUTURE

LARGE-GROUP PRESENTATION

(TOUR GUIDE bustles into the room, checking clipboard, nodding and smiling to individuals in the audience.)
Welcome to the Museum of Tomorrow. My name is Bertha (or Bert) and I'll be your tour guide. As you probably know, MOST museums display historical objects from the past. This is a wonderful way to learn about events that happened long ago. But here at the Museum of TOMORROW, our focus is not on the past but on the FUTURE. *(Gestures at empty space.)* Which is why you don't see any DISPLAYS! It's difficult to have displays of events that have not yet taken place.

CURIOUS QUESTIONS

How, you may ask, can you have a museum about the future, when you don't know what the future holds? EXCELLENT question. This museum was begun because we found that most people have a GREAT deal of CURIOSITY about the future. People want to know what's going to happen. Will things be like what we see in the movies? Will aliens from outer space invade Earth and take over our brains and make us all wear tube socks? *(Gets more agitated with each question.)* Will the ice caps melt and cause water to cover the whole world so that we'll have to try to stay alive while sailing along on boats made out of scrap metal and DUCT TAPE? Will an evil villain REALLY come and build a Death Star? *(Sighs.)* Just WHAT, exactly, does the future HOLD?

REAL ANSWERS?

Well, here at the Museum of Tomorrow, we have attempted to find some answers to our questions about the future. Based on our exhaustive research, the logical source was to investigate the words of prophets. Prophets are people who make predictions about the future. As we expected, not ALL prophets are TRULY prophets. There are plenty of fakes. Some may have guessed close once or twice, or mentioned some similarity, but for the most part, MOST prophets have been completely wrong.

ONE RELIABLE SOURCE

But as I said, our research has been EXHAUSTIVE. Therefore, we were able to find one source whose HISTORIC prophets were 100-percent accurate. That means that these prophets predicted things that have already come true in history. THIS gives us a basis for expecting that the prophecies of events that have not YET taken place will ALSO be accurate! The writings of THESE prophets are in the VERY Book in front of most of you—the Bible. In fact, you can use your own Bibles to read about our exhibits. Feel free to take our self-guided tour! Excuse me, I need to check on the next tour group. *(Exits.)*

SMALL-GROUP DISCUSSION TIME

Provide one "Touring the Future" Discussion Sheet (p. 60) to each student. Invite students to find verses and discuss answers to questions on the sheet. Invite interested students to talk more with you about joining God's family (see "Leading a Child to Christ" on p. 11).

GRAND FINALE

(TOUR GUIDE returns, checking clipboard, faces audience and sees discussion sheets.)
I can see that you have taken your self-guided tours in small groups. That's very good! There is fascinating information about the future in the Bible, isn't there? It can sometimes seem a little strange to us—there IS a lot of descriptive language that is a bit difficult for us to picture. But then—it IS the future! It's hard to picture things none of us have SEEN yet! Nevertheless, the prophecy of Scripture has been proven to be accurate and trustworthy.

Whatever the future holds, there is one thing that we are CERTAIN of: None of us knows how many "tomorrows" we have. If there was a museum about YOUR life, what would the exhibits show? What would the tour guide say about YOU? Just thinking about this makes me want to NOT WASTE one single day that I have been given!

We may not know exactly what the future holds for us, but God does. We can trust the future to Him and make the MOST of each "today."

Well, that COMPLETES our tour of the Museum of Tomorrow. Thank you for visiting—and oh, don't forget to visit our gift shop on the way out! They have a great special on a CD by the hottest new group—10 years from now. Of course, the group members are only in kindergarten right now! *(Waves.)* Good-bye! *(Waves and exits.)*

Leader invites a student to read Jeremiah 29:11 from the Key Verse Card. **What a great thing to remember! God has good plans for us. For that reason, we never need to worry about the future. Our tour guide made a good point: We need to remember that whatever the future holds, God gives us only one day at a time. We need to make the most of this day!**

Close in prayer, asking God's help to make the most of every "today" He gives us and to trust His care for the future.

Touring the Future

DISCUSSION SHEET

What did Jesus say would be the signs of the end times?
Find Matthew 24:3-14.

What can Christians expect during this time?
Find 2 Peter 2:1-2.

What must happen before Christ returns?
Find 2 Thessalonians 2:1-4.

What will God eventually do?
Find Revelation 21:1-4.

What will happen then?
Find Matthew 16:27 and John 5:24-29.

Do we know when all this will happen?
Find Matthew 24:36 and 1 Thessalonians 5:1-3.

Should we be afraid about all this?
Find Psalm 23:4-6.

KEY VERSE CARD

Jeremiah 29:11
" 'For I know the plans I have for you,' declares
the LORD, 'plans to prosper you and not to harm
you, plans to give you hope and a future.' "

Giving from the Heart

TOPIC
Generosity

CHARACTER
Elderly widow from New Testament times

SUMMARY
The widow of the "Widow's Mite" story gives her perspective about generosity.

KEY VERSE
2 Corinthians 9:13
"Because of the service by which you have proved yourselves, men will praise God for the obedience that accompanies your confession of the gospel of Christ, and for your generosity in sharing with them and with everyone else."

PROPS
Bible-times woman's clothing, walking stick, two small copper coins (pennies will do)

OPTIONAL PROPS
Small sack and bottle to represent grain and oil; pieces of fruit

PREP POINTERS
Perfect a hobbling walk for this character.

SCHEDULE
Small-Group Warm-up (5-10 minutes)
Large-Group Presentation (5-10 minutes)
Small-Group Discussion (10-20 minutes)
Grand Finale (5-10 minutes)

SMALL-GROUP WARM-UP
Meet, greet and discuss the following questions in your small group:
• **Tell about a time you saw someone give a surprising gift.**
• **What made the gift surprising? How did the receiver respond?**
• **Was it a generous gift? Why or why not?**

GIVING FROM THE HEART

LARGE-GROUP PRESENTATION

(WIDOW enters, leaning on stick and hobbling a little.)
Oi! The walk from the Temple to home seems to get a little LONGER every time I make it. *(Looks up.)* God, You couldn't make the bones last a little LONGER in Your creation? Not that I'm not thankful for the YEARS—just not for the RHEUMATISM.

(To audience.) I can't IMAGINE how poor Methuselah must have ACHED on the day HE died! Nine hundred sixty-nine years, now that's a LONG TIME to grow old!

RICH WOMAN

But let me tell you what happened at the Temple today! It was a very interesting thing. You see, two days ago I was talking with the young wife of one of the Temple priests. Before we parted, she gave me two *leptas*. This is not MUCH money, less than a penny to you, but still, I was touched by her kindness. When you're an old widow like me, you soon learn that it's the kindness of others that will keep you from STARVING!

But THEN, just yesterday, a neighbor lady was VERY kind. She gave me some wheat and oil—that means food for days and DAYS! THEN, a vendor in the marketplace let me have some fruit that was too bruised to sell. So TODAY, I was so FULL of food and happiness, I just HAD to go to the Temple. I wanted to give those two *leptas* back to God! He had faithfully provided for me AGAIN! I was eager to give something back to Him and share His gifts with others.

GLAD WOMAN

Well, as I waited to enter the Temple, there were many rich ones ahead of me. They put in large amounts of money, streams of coins, WADS of money! What ELSE could a person do with SO MUCH?!

As I approached the offering box, I noticed several young men watching the people putting in their offerings. As I passed by the box and dropped my money in, one of these young men turned to the others. He said, "I tell you truly, this poor widow gave more than all the others. They all gave out of their WEALTH. But SHE gave out of her POVERTY. She put in EVERYTHING—all she had to live on."

I can tell you, I was startled! Imagine that He should say such a thing! How can ANYONE think that I put in more than all the WEALTHY ones? But in one way, He is right: I HAVE no more money! But what I DO have is the love of God, who sustains me every day. He ALWAYS takes care of me!

WISE WOMAN

I must say, I was intrigued by this young man's words. So I stayed around longer, just to listen to Him. He speaks such WISDOM! So I began to ask people what they knew about Him. You know what they SAY? Some say He is a prophet. And that young priest's wife, the one who gave me the *leptas* to begin with? She says He is the MESSIAH, the chosen one—that He is not like anyone else in the world!

Come to think about it, what He said about my gift was certainly wise. After all, does the God of the UNIVERSE need my MONEY? I think NOT! He is kind enough to allow me to be PART OF what He is doing. He lets all of us SHARE in His work—I regard this as a privilege! Maybe it's a good time to find out what else the Scriptures have to say about giving to God. You do that. I'm going to rest my aching legs! *(Exits.)*

SMALL-GROUP DISCUSSION TIME

Provide one "Giving from the Heart" Discussion Sheet (p. 64) to each student. Invite students to find verses and discuss answers to questions on the sheet. Invite interested students to talk more with you about joining God's family (see "Leading a Child to Christ" on p. 11).

GRAND FINALE

(WIDOW returns.)

I have thought much about the things this Jesus said. I think that tomorrow I will return to the Temple to see if He is teaching again. I want to hear MORE! Well, I will go again tomorrow if God WILLS it—and if these old bones will CARRY me there and back again! *(Looks up.)* Oh God, would it be TOO much trouble to ask that the road to the Temple be SHORTER tomorrow? You have done greater miracles! *(To audience.)* Such wisdom in this Jesus! Shalom! May God be with you all! *(Exits, waving.)*

Leader invites a student to read 2 Corinthians 9:13 from the Key Verse Card. **We often think that giving to God is something we HAVE to do. But the Bible makes it clear that God wants our giving to come from hearts of thankfulness, like our visitor showed today! Generosity is not about how much you have or how much you give. What matters is that you give what you have to God from a grateful heart.**

Close in prayer, thanking God for the privilege of giving to Him to show that we are thankful for His gifts.

Giving from the Heart

DISCUSSION SHEET

What's the original story on this little old lady?
Find Mark 12:41-44.

Who really owns everything?
Find 1 Chronicles 29:11-12.

God wants us to excel in WHAT?
Find 2 Corinthians 8:7.

What should our attitude be about giving to God?
Find 2 Corinthians 9:7-8.

What will be the result of giving to God's work?
Find 2 Corinthians 9:13.

If you give Jesus a little, what can He do with it?
Find Matthew 14:15-21.

In what way does God give in return for what you give?
Find Luke 6:38.

KEY VERSE CARD

2 Corinthians 9:13
"Because of the service by which you have proved yourselves, men will praise God for the obedience that accompanies your confession of the gospel of Christ, and for your generosity in sharing with them and with everyone else."

Father Knows Best

TOPIC

God, our perfect Father

CHARACTER

Grumpy old person

SUMMARY

A slightly grumpy old person helps us learn more about God's perfect Fatherhood.

KEY VERSE

Romans 8:15-17

"For you did not receive a spirit that makes you a slave again to fear, but you received the Spirit of sonship. And by him we cry, 'Abba, Father.' The Spirit himself testifies with our spirit that we are God's children. Now if we are children, then we are heirs—heirs of God and co-heirs with Christ, if indeed we share in his sufferings in order that we may also share in his glory."

PROPS

Old person-type clothing, remote control

OPTIONAL PROPS

TV, afghan

PREP POINTERS

Feel free to be humorously cranky at the beginning; dramatically soften the character toward the end.

SCHEDULE

Small-Group Warm-up (5-10 minutes)
Large-Group Presentation (5-10 minutes)
Small-Group Discussion (10-20 minutes)
Grand Finale (5-10 minutes)

SMALL-GROUP WARM-UP

Meet, greet and discuss the following questions in your small group:
- **What characteristics do you think would make a perfect parent?**
- **Who is your oldest living relative?**
- **What do you like about visiting that relative? What do you not like?**

Father Knows Best

LARGE-GROUP PRESENTATION

(OLD PERSON *is sitting as if watching television. Speaks to TV.*)
Oh, this show is just RIDICULOUS. I don't know why I even WATCH it. I'm too OLD to waste what time I have left!

(*To audience.*) This show is called "The Grady Group." It's about a family with a whole bunch of kids. The RIDICULOUS part is the FATHER. (*Points remote at TV.*) See there? His kids wanted a swing set but he couldn't AFFORD it. So he took a second job at night to earn MONEY to buy them one.

Then, just when he'd SAVED enough money, someone STOLE the money. So the KIDS did chores for neighbors to earn the money AGAIN. Then when they didn't have ENOUGH to buy the swing set, the father used the money to buy materials to BUILD a swing set all by HIMSELF. HUMBUG! Like THAT would ever happen!

NOT MY DAD

(*Looks away, reminiscing, speaking more softly.*) I wanted a swing set once. But MY father wasn't around enough to even ASK him. (*Sighs.*) I wish I could have KNOWN him better. The kids down the street had a dad like that Grady dad. He PLAYED with them, showed them AFFECTION. My dad wasn't like that. I've wished my whole LIFE that he HAD been. Just to have gotten piggyback rides or to have built a tree fort together—I think those things would have made my life different.

(*Snapping into reality.*) HUMBUG. It really doesn't MATTER anymore. Who knows? Maybe my DAD'S dad didn't show HIM any love. (*Sighs.*) Dad never WAS a very happy person. But it DOES make me wonder: What is it like to KNOW the love of a GOOD father? How IS a father supposed to treat his kids? You find out about that. I've got to go drink my Metamucil. (*Exits.*)

SMALL-GROUP DISCUSSION TIME

Provide one "Father Knows Best" Discussion Sheet (p. 68) to each student. Invite students to find verses and discuss answers to questions on the sheet. Invite interested students to talk more with you about joining God's family (see "Leading a Child to Christ" on p. 11).

GRAND FINALE

(OLD PERSON returns.)

I heard some of the things you were reading and talking about just now. I heard someone say that God is the PERFECT Father—completely faithful, always kind, always loving and trustworthy. And I heard you say that He DISCIPLINES those He loves. That means He teaches us right from wrong. ANY good dad does that.

I can't change the way my dad was. I can't know WHY he was the way he was. Chances are, some of YOU don't have a "Grady Group" kind of dad, either. But now I realize that I DO have God as my HEAVENLY Father. *(Amazed.)* THAT is pretty wonderful! All along, I've had a REAL DAD who REALLY loves me—I just didn't realize it! I'm going to think about that some more. Amazing. A Father who is ALWAYS around. I can always trust Him, always talk to Him and know He CARES! Wow!

(Snaps back to being grumpy.) But don't think that will make me start SMILING all the time—smiling makes my DENTURES slip! I know, why don't you all come back next week? We can watch "The Grady Group" together. I guess it's NOT a dumb show after all. Now go away. I've got to take a nap. *(Exits.)*

Leader invites a student to read Romans 8:15-17 from the Key Verse Card. **None of us has a perfect dad. Even great dads are still human. But God is a perfect Father. He knows us, He loves us and He never forgets us. Let's thank Him.**

Close in prayer, thanking God for being our perfect Father who always loves us, and asking Him to help students to trust His goodness more each day.

Father Knows Best

DISCUSSION SHEET

According to the Bible, what is a father's job?
Find Ephesians 6:4.

Why are human fathers (and mothers) not perfect?
Find Romans 3:23.

What should our attitudes be toward our fathers (and mothers)?
Find Exodus 20:12 and Proverbs 1:8-9.

Do we have a perfect Father?
Find 1 John 3:1.

What are ways He shows us His love?
Find Psalm 145:17-19.
Find Hebrews 12:7-11.
Find 1 John 4:14-15.

What does our Heavenly Father want for us?
Find Jeremiah 29:11.

How can we please God, our perfect Father?
Find Romans 12:1-2 and 2 John 1:4.

KEY VERSE CARD

Romans 8:15-17

"For you did not receive a spirit that makes you a
slave again to fear, but you received the Spirit of sonship.
And by him we cry, 'Abba, Father.' The Spirit himself
testifies with our spirit that we are God's children. Now if
we are children, then we are heirs—heirs of God and co-
heirs with Christ, if indeed we share in his sufferings
in order that we may also share in his glory."

Happily Ever After

TOPIC
God's faithfulness

CHARACTER
Fairy-tale princess or prince

SUMMARY
The young royal discovers that the king's good plans are worth following.

KEY VERSE
Psalm 145:17-19
"The LORD is righteous in all his ways and loving toward all he has made. The LORD is near to all who call on him, to all who call on him in truth. He fulfills the desires of those who fear him; he hears their cry and saves them."

PROPS
Royal robe, scepter, crown

OPTIONAL PROPS
Advertisement or poster for a concert, shield, buffing cloth

PREP POINTERS
While talking about the knights, buff a shield to illustrate your point!

SCHEDULE
Small-Group Warm-up (5-10 minutes)
Large-Group Presentation (5-10 minutes)
Small-Group Discussion (10-20 minutes)
Grand Finale (5-10 minutes)

SMALL-GROUP WARM-UP
Meet, greet and discuss the following questions in your small group:
- **What is a project or activity you have done on your own?**
- **How did you feel about doing it alone?**
- **Tell about a time you did a project or activity with the help of others. Was it easy or hard to ask for help? How did it turn out?**

Happily ever after

LARGE-GROUP PRESENTATION

(PRINCESS or PRINCE enters, regally, shaking hands with random individuals.)
Hello. My name is Princess Regina (Prince Reginald). I'm a fairy-tale princess, though I'd guess you've never heard my story before. Everyone knows about Snow White and Beauty and the Beast, even the Princess and the Pea. But no one has ever heard MY tale, The Princess and the Unforsaking King. It begins the way all good fairy tales do—once upon a time.

TAKING LEAVE

Once upon a time, I lived with my father in the most beautiful castle in the most wonderful kingdom anywhere. One day, my father told me he had to go away for a while but that while he was gone, he would leave me with the swiftest messenger in the land. If I needed to tell him something, all I needed to do was to send the messenger.

He also gave me advisors to help me make decisions and guide me in running the castle and the surrounding kingdom. Although I was sad to see my father leave, I was excited to show him that I was capable of doing the tasks he was leaving me to do. After a tearful farewell, he was on his way.

TAKING TIME

Everything went well for the first few weeks. But one day I noticed that the knights' armor was a little dingy. I ESPECIALLY liked to see shiny armor, so I met with them to tell them I wanted them to polish up their armor.

The head knight explained that protecting our castle and kingdom took a lot of time and that it was important to have the knights use their time keeping things safe—MORE important than sitting around buffing their armor. However, I was VERY insistent. I was SURE that since I like shiny armor, my father did, too. He would be PLEASED to come home and see how shiny his knights looked! So the knights obeyed.

TAKING TROUBLE

But soon, one beautiful evening, a strong wind began to blow. The sky began to grow dark, as if clouds were overhead. But looking skyward, we realized that it WASN'T clouds—it was a vicious, fire-breathing DRAGON! The people fled inside to hide.

The fierce dragon flew across the skies for two weeks STRAIGHT while everyone stayed hidden. No one picked the corn or milked the cows. They wouldn't come out to deliver the bread. The corn in the fields had all been scorched into POPCORN by the dragon. The dragon sat in the field eating popcorn and breathing FIRE at anyone who dared to go outdoors!

Day after day, people begged me to HELP them—there was no milk for the children! No bread for their meals! But I was TERRIFIED. I wasn't sure WHAT to do. So I spent HOURS hiding in my room crying, wondering why this was happening to ME!

TAKING A MESSAGE

My advisors DID suggest that I send a message to my father. So that very day I sent the messenger. And in NO time, my father returned!

What chaos he found! It was pretty hard to MISS the huge fire-breathing dragon sitting in the cornfield! Those shiny knights were in the castle, too busy polishing their armor to go out and SLAY it! Things were a MESS.

TAKING RESPONSIBILITY

"Princess," my father asked, "why did you not send a message to me when you STARTED having trouble?"

I said, "I wanted to try to TAKE CARE of everything MYSELF so that you would be PROUD of me."

He answered, "Your intentions were good. But IF you had obeyed me, we wouldn't have all these problems now!"

I begged his forgiveness. I asked, "Is it too late to ask your help NOW?!"

My father kissed me on the forehead and said, "No. It is NEVER too late to ask my help. Now that we are TOGETHER, you have the help you need."

TAKING IT ON TOGETHER

So together, we went to slay the evil dragon. When we had rid the kingdom of that fierce beast, the people came out of their homes and returned to their duties. The children were fed and the corn was replanted. But STILL, the brave knights CONTINUED to polish their armor. By now it shone SO brightly that it HURT to LOOK at them!

Father asked me, "Which is more important, the way the knights LOOK or the WORK they do to protect the kingdom?"

I immediately understood the consequences of my actions. Had the knights not been so BUSY buffing and shining, they could have protected the kingdom from the DRAGON! Completely humbled, I asked my father to forgive me for failing to take care of the castle while he was gone.

He replied, "I NEVER expected you to do it alone. That's why I left a messenger! I set up everything in this kingdom. There is ALWAYS a reason why I have done it the way I have. EVERYTHING is designed so that when you ask for help, I can FREELY promise to always be available to help you."

Unlike MOST fairy tales, MY story has important lessons for YOU as well as for me. Let's see if you can figure out what they are! *(Exits.)*

SMALL-GROUP DISCUSSION TIME

Provide one "Happily Ever After" Discussion Sheet (p. 72) to each student. Invite students to find verses and discuss answers to questions on the sheet. Invite interested students to talk more with you about joining God's family (see "Leading a Child to Christ" on p. 11).

GRAND FINALE

(PRINCESS or PRINCE returns.)

I realize now how very much my father LOVES me. I was sorry I had tried to do everything MYSELF instead of trusting my father to help me! But I think I have learned my lesson. From that day forward, I've always tried to remember to ASK my father for help FIRST—no matter what the problem is! If I have a LITTLE problem, I try to talk to him FIRST, instead of waiting until it becomes DRAGON-SIZED! There are still times when I forget, but things have improved in the kingdom and—well, you know the rest: We live happily ever after! *(Exits.)*

Leader invites a student to read Psalm 145:17-19 from the Key Verse Card. **We certainly learned a great lesson from this fairy tale! If we ask God for His help every time we have a problem or don't know what to do, He PROMISES to help us, to give us wisdom and to be with us. We can trust His promises!**

Close in prayer, asking God to help students always ask for His help, no matter how small the problem or how confident they are that they can handle it alone.

Happily Ever After

DISCUSSION SHEET

Jesus often spoke in parables (told stories that had a point). Parables caused people to think. Let's do some thinking of our own about this parable:

Who do you think the king in our story represents?
Who do you think the princess or prince represents?
And who do the advisors represent?
The messenger?
How about the dragon?

The outward appearance of the knights was a big deal to the prince or princess. But what does God think about appearances?
Find 1 Samuel 16:7.

What does God want for us as we live our lives?
Find Romans 12:1-2.

Why are we smart to desire what God wants for us?
Find Isaiah 48:17.

What does God tell us to do when we don't know what to do?
Find James 1:5.

What can make us live happily ever after?
Find John 3:16.

KEY VERSE CARD

Psalm 145:17-19
"The Lord is righteous in all his ways and loving toward all he has made. The Lord is near to all who call on him, to all who call on him in truth. He fulfills the desires of those who fear him; he hears their cry and saves them."

An Apple a Day

TOPIC

God's Holy Spirit

CHARACTER

Farm kid

SUMMARY

The farm kid tells us about how the wind is like the Holy Spirit and how the apples are like the fruit of the Holy Spirit.

KEY VERSES

Galatians 5:22-23
"The fruit of the Spirit is love, joy, peace, patience, kindness, goodness, faithfulness, gentleness and self-control. Against such things there is no law."

PROPS

Farm clothes (overalls, flannel shirt, work dress, etc.), basket, apple, knife

OPTIONAL PROPS

Enough washed apples to cut up as snacks for the group

PREP POINTERS

Ahead of time, ask an adult to find John 14:15-17,25 in his or her Bible and be ready to read it aloud when asked during the Large-Group Presentation.

SCHEDULE

Small-Group Warm-up (5-10 minutes)
Large-Group Presentation (5-10 minutes)
Small-Group Discussion (10-20 minutes)
Grand Finale (5-10 minutes)

SMALL-GROUP WARM-UP

Meet, greet and discuss the following questions in your small group:
- **What fruit do you like best?**
- **Have you ever picked fruit? If not, what do you imagine you would like best about picking fruit?**
- **If you have picked fruit, how did you decide which (peaches) to pick?**
- **Did you pick every (peach) you saw? Why or why not?**

AN Apple a Day

LARGE-GROUP PRESENTATION

(FARM KID enters, carrying basket and whistling or singing. Pretends to pick up apples.)
Hi! My mom sent me out to gather apples. She's going to make apple pie. Yeah! Usually, I have to climb a big ladder to pick apples, but not today. The wind blew strong last night. All the ripest apples were BLOWN off the tree!

LIKE THE WIND

The wind sure made MY job easier. Now I don't have to drag that big old ladder out of the barn! *(Faces audience, puzzled.)* Have you ever seen the wind? What IS the wind? You've seen the EFFECTS of the wind, but no one can actually SEE wind. What are some ways you've experienced the wind? *(Waits for audience's answers.)*

ANOTHER force made my job easier, too. Know what it was? *(Waits for audience's answers.)* That's right! Gravity! If it weren't for gravity, those loose apples would float EVERYWHERE. I'd have to CHASE them all over the SKY—that would be MUCH harder than picking them up!

Have you ever seen GRAVITY? You've seen the EFFECTS of gravity, but can you actually SEE gravity? What are some ways we experience gravity? *(Waits for audience's answers.)*

INVISIBLE POWER

Now Christians know about ANOTHER invisible force. Do you know His name? He is at work in every Christian's life! Right—the Holy Spirit! In some ways, He is like wind and gravity: You can't see Him, but you know He is there—because of the effect He has on your life. *(Invites adult to read John 14:15-17,25 aloud.)*

When Jesus came to Earth in a human body, He came to be the sacrifice so that our sins could be forgiven. He took the punishment that we deserved to take for our sins. But in a human body, Jesus couldn't be everywhere. That's the reason He promised to send us His Holy Spirit when He returned to Heaven. He could then be with ALL of us who trust Him as our Savior—ALL of the time!

Now how about you all finding out more about the Holy Spirit and what He does, while I finish picking up these apples! *(Exits, pretending to pick up apples.)*

SMALL-GROUP DISCUSSION TIME

Provide one "An Apple a Day" Discussion Sheet (p. 76) to each student. Invite students to find verses and discuss answers to questions on the sheet. Invite interested students to talk more with you about joining God's family (see "Leading a Child to Christ" on p. 11).

GRAND FINALE

(FARM KID returns with basket full of apples.)
You all found some verses that tell us a lot about the Holy Spirit. I heard that God sent Him to be with us when we joined God's family. The Holy Spirit is here to help us do what God wants us to do. Just like the wind and gravity, we can't see Him physically. But His EFFECTS should show in our lives just the way you can see the effects of the wind loosening these apples and gravity making them fall! *(Bites into an apple.)*

FRUIT OF GOD'S SPIRIT

Ever heard the term "bad apple"? Some apples have disease or rot. Some get bugs or WORMS in them! Would you want THAT kind of apple in your apple pie? YUK!

Would you want to BE that kind of apple? DOUBLE YUK! But Jesus said that a good tree won't bear bad fruit and that a bad tree can't bear good fruit. So our words and our actions are kind of like fruit: What we say and do are the "fruit" on the outside that shows what's going on inside! If we are part of God's family but don't allow the Holy Spirit to work in our lives, then we can't grow the GOOD fruit that comes from the Holy Spirit. But the Holy Spirit will HELP us just as much as we will LET Him! When we remember to ASK His help instead of doing things our own way, we've made a good start toward growing good fruit!

(Cuts apple once horizontally.) Apples also remind me about the Holy Spirit in another way. Want to see? *(Shows star in center of apple.)* If you are a Christian, God's Holy Spirit is ALWAYS in you. Just like the star is in the center of the apple, He is right there, ready to help you! *(If providing snacks, FARM KID distributes apple pieces to students.)*

Well, I've got to get back home with these apples. I'm looking forward to some hot apple pie—full of GOOD FRUIT! *(Exits, whistling.)*

Leader invites a student to read Galatians 5:22-23 from the Key Verse Card. **Let's take a moment to think of one way each of us can bear the good fruit of the Holy Spirit in our lives this week. With the help of the Holy Spirit, we can grow good fruit— pleasing right down to the CORE!**

Close in prayer, asking God to help students remember that they can ask for help from His Holy Spirit to resist temptation and grow good fruit in their lives.

An Apple a Day

DISCUSSION SHEET

Who is the Holy Spirit?
Find John 14:16,26.

How do we discern right from wrong?
Find John 16:8.

How do we understand what is true?
Find John 16:13.

How do we know that the Holy Spirit is God's presence with us always?
Find John 14:16-17.

Who helps us pray? How?
Find Romans 8:26-27.

How does the Holy Spirit help us tell others about Jesus?
Find 1 Corinthians 2:13.

KEY VERSE CARD

Galatians 5:22-23
"The fruit of the Spirit is love, joy, peace, patience, kindness, goodness, faithfulness, gentleness and self-control. Against such things there is no law."

Hidden Treasure

TOPIC
God's real treasure

CHARACTER
Pirate

SUMMARY
aargh! A pirate discovers what kind of treasure Christians have!

KEY VERSE
Matthew 6:19-20

"Do not store up for yourselves treasures on earth, where moth and rust destroy, and where thieves break in and steal. But store up for yourselves treasures in heaven, where moth and rust do not destroy, and where thieves do not break in and steal."

PROPS
Bible marked at passages noted in script, toy sword or pistol, eye patch, pirate's hat (or kerchief tied around head), cloth bag for loot

OPTIONAL PROPS
Long jacket or vest, knee breeches, false moustache

PREP POINTERS
Brandish your weapon freely when you threaten your victims. Lay it down as you recognize that the treasure is different from what you expected.

SCHEDULE
Small-Group Warm-up (5-10 minutes)
Large-Group Presentation (5-10 minutes)
Small-Group Discussion (10-20 minutes)
Grand Finale (5-10 minutes)

SMALL-GROUP WARM-UP
Meet, greet and discuss the following questions in your small group:
- **What do you think a kid your age might say is the most valuable thing he or she owns? The least valuable?**
- **What is something you value that might surprise someone else?**
- **How do you take care of what you think is very valuable?**

HIDDEN TREASURE

LARGE-GROUP PRESENTATION

(PIRATE *enters, brandishing sword or pistol.*)
Aha! I've FOUND you! All right, you lily-livered landlubbers, hand over the TREASURE! That's right. You heard me. All yer TREASURE—just make big PILES of it right there! All yer silver and gold. All yer rubies and sapphires. All of those glittering, beautiful diamonds! Don't try to HIDE any of it, neither. A pirate can sniff out TREASURE like a CAT can sniff out a MOUSE. *AARGH!*

I've been sailin' the high seas and plyin' the pirate trade for nigh on 30 years now! And I've separated PLENTY of people from their valuables—and I've separated a FEW people from their HEADS! But THIS—this is the treasure I've been WAITING for. Aye, THIS is the BIG one!

Aye! After I steal all yer treasure, I'll be able to RETIRE from pirating. I've always dreamed of buying a castle in the south of France. Have people call me DUKE. Get me a pet dog. I've always WANTED one. I never HAD a pet dog. I was a poor, DEPRIVED child—so I took to pirating EARLY to get from others what I wanted!

AARGH! Me life hasn't been easy. Lost me eye in a sword fight. But by golly, now that I'm going to be RICH, I'll get a NEW patch, a blue velvet one, trimmed with lace. I can just IMAGINE how grandly I'll be livin' once I take all yer TREASURES!

Ya see, GUPPY-WITTED folk like you don't DESERVE yer riches! Look here! (*Picks up Bible.*) Even a SEA SLUG has got more brains than the lot of YOU! You left yer treasure map just LYIN' AROUND—that's right, I found yer MAP! (*Waves Bible.*)

BIG TREASURE

(*Brandishes weapon.*) So come on. I KNOW you've GOT IT. No more stallin'. Hand it ALL over. The gold, the jewels, the pieces of eight . . . don't just sit there and look all INNOCENT like! I KNOW you have the treasure!

(*Opens Bible.*) I read it in yer MAP. See? Right here in Isaiah 2:7 it says, "Their land is full of silver and gold; there is no END to their treasures." Read it for yourself! (*Flips through Bible.*) And here's another place, Proverbs 8:18. "With me are riches and honor, enduring wealth and prosperity."

So you see, yer secret is OUT! And since you each have yer own maps, you must ALL be this rich! All right. Better hand over some of this TREASURE or we're gonna have a little BLOODSHED! I'm fairly REASONABLE, as pirates go—what? You say it's some OTHER kind of treasure? Well, then. Ye'd best be lookin' in yer maps for a little more DIRECTION. But I'll be waitin' RIGHT HERE to see what ye come up with—*AARGH!* (*Sits down somewhere in the room and looks through Bible while small groups meet.*)

GRAND FINALE

(PIRATE *returns to front of group; speaks slowly.*)

So now I SEE it! This treasure you've got . . . it's NOT gold and silver and jewels. *(Holds up Bible.)* I must say, this is the most INTERESTIN' treasure map I've ever read. It says that you can have eternal LIFE in a place where PURE GOLD is mere PAVEMENT, like asphalt! To know God, to have His WISDOM and then to live forever with Him—what better TREASURE could there BE? Better than a dukedom in France, I'm tellin' ya, even with me own pet dog!

aaRGH! I believe I'm a CHANGED pirate, all new-like and DIFFERENT! I'm OFF to seek the GRANDEST treasure of them all—God's WISDOM! YE'VE got a treasure map, too; use it to KEEP ON seekin' the treasure! *aaRGH! (Exits.)*

Leader invites a student to read Matthew 6:19-20 from the Key Verse Card. **Well, THAT was a close one! It's a good thing that NO ONE can touch our most important treasures! Let's thank God for the treasure He has given us!**

Close in prayer, thanking God that we can have the great treasure of His wisdom and asking Him to help us search for His wisdom in every situation.

Hidden Treasure

DISCUSSION SHEET

What is the treasure you're hiding, you guppy-witted landlubber?
Find Proverbs 8:10-11.

What does the Bible say is the better treasure, wisdom or riches?
Find Proverbs 16:16.

Why is it better to get wisdom than riches?
Find Proverbs 3:13-18.

Where do we go to get this treasure called wisdom?
Find Proverbs 2:6.

How do we get God to give us this "wisdom" treasure?
Find James 1:5.

Why is wisdom such a great treasure?
Find Proverbs 2:9-12.

What do you need to do to join the hunt for God's treasure?
Find Proverbs 2:1-5.

KEY VERSE CARD

Matthew 6:19-20
"Do not store up for yourselves treasures on earth,
where moth and rust destroy, and where thieves
break in and steal. But store up for yourselves treasures
in heaven, where moth and rust do not destroy,
and where thieves do not break in and steal."

Don't Play with Matches

TOPIC
Gossip

CHARACTER
Firefighter

SUMMARY
An exhausted firefighter tells about how gossip is like a wildfire.

KEY VERSES
Proverbs 26:20-22
"Without wood a fire goes out; without gossip a quarrel dies down. As charcoal to embers and as wood to fire, so is a quarrelsome man for kindling strife. The words of a gossip are like choice morsels; they go down to a man's inmost parts."

PROPS
Firefighter's helmet and slicker (dirty and sooty), box of kitchen matches

OPTIONAL PROPS
Firefighter's axe or other equipment

PREP POINTERS
Smear black tempera paint across the firefighter's slicker to create a sooty effect.

SCHEDULE
Small-Group Warm-up (5-10 minutes)
Large-Group Presentation (5-10 minutes)
Small-Group Discussion (10-20 minutes)
Grand Finale (5-10 minutes)

SMALL-GROUP WARM-UP
Meet, greet and discuss the following questions in your small group:
- **What is good about fire? What is scary about fire?**
- **Tell about a time you lit a campfire or a fire in a fireplace. How many matches did you use?**
- **Have you ever seen a burning ember fly out of a fire? What happened?**

DON'T PLAY WITH MATCHES

LARGE-GROUP PRESENTATION

(FIREFIGHTER *enters while talking, apparently having just come from a fire.*) That fire was a tough one—we've been fighting it for 3 days now. We finally have it contained but 823 acres burned and 6 homes were destroyed. Countless animals dead or scattered. No loss of HUMAN life . . . that's one good thing. Man, fire can be scary. The heat is unbearable. The flames can reach so high—and spread so incredibly fast. And it doesn't always spread in the direction you EXPECT, either.

NOTHING LEFT

I feel awful for the folks who lost their homes. We did the best we could, but it's always so sad to see them when they come back to their burned-down homes. They just stand there in the ashes of the place where they lived and slept and ate and laughed. Sure, they can rebuild or get a new house—but some things that fire destroys can NEVER be replaced.

Know how this horrible fire got started? *(Opens matchbox, removes a match and lights it.)* All it took was one SINGLE match. That's it. That's all it took. One person used a match IRRESPONSIBLY—and it caused this HUGE disaster. *(Blows out match.)* There's only ONE other thing I know of that can spread as fast as a wildfire and cause JUST as much destruction—gossip.

REPUTATION REMOVAL

Let me tell you about just how much damage a few little WORDS, used IRRESPONSIBLY, can do. Here at the firehouse, we're all really close, like a family. We take group trips, coach each other's kids on sports teams, that sort of thing.

Not too long ago, one of our guys, Sam, was coaching his daughter Sarah's soccer team. Now, a boy named Danny had gotten into the habit of punching Sarah in the hallway at school nearly every day. Danny is actually the son of another firefighter. These kids have known each other since second grade, part of our firehouse family. But instead of telling Danny to STOP or even asking him WHY he was doing this, Sarah carried a grudge. And her grudge grew until it lit a little match of gossip.

One day at soccer practice, Sarah's team saw some racist graffiti on the wall by the soccer field. Because of her grudge against Danny, Sarah told her friends—and her friends told her dad, the coach—that she had heard Danny say racist things and that she bet Danny had done the graffiti.

Now some girls on Sarah's soccer team are ALSO part of our firehouse family. So it wasn't long before phones were ringing. Like hot embers blowing off a fire, the story spread—in all directions. Instant Messages flew like live SPARKS from computer to computer. Of course, Sam called Danny's dad about it, but he was at work at the time, so he couldn't check out the story. Soon, one little match of gossip had lit a roaring BLAZE—burning OUT OF CONTROL.

THE DAMAGE IS DONE

Sarah's mom questioned Sarah about what she'd said about Danny. Sarah stuck to her story, so Sarah's mom called Danny's mom and told her what Sarah had said. The two families had always been close, but this accusation seriously THREATENED the STRUCTURE of their friendship!

Needless to say, Danny's mom was REALLY upset! She went right upstairs to his room to confront him. Of course, Danny had NO IDEA what she was talking about. He DENIED everything, which made her even MADDER. She called Sarah's mom back and started yelling at HER! Now the damage was widespread.

Fortunately, Sarah's mom and Danny's mom calmed down. They decided some ACTION had to be taken to PUT OUT this fire! So they agreed to meet at the local burger place with Sarah and Danny RIGHT THEN. When the four of them met, Sarah and Danny were forced to tell the truth: That slowed down the FIRE at its CENTER, but by then, it had BLOWN so far and so much FUEL had been added to this fire, there was NO WAY to avoid DISASTER.

Some things can never be replaced. Even when Sarah apologized, the trust between Danny's family and Sarah's family just couldn't bear the damage. Other people didn't know what to believe. Some even thought Danny's family was racist! Soon, Danny's dad transferred to another station. Things were never the same at the firehouse. Most of us stopped going on trips together. This fire damaged something in us that can never be replaced.

Look, I'm exhausted. I'm going to get myself something cold to drink. Talk about this gossip business, will you? I'll be back. *(Exits.)*

SMALL-GROUP DISCUSSION TIME

Provide one "Don't Play with Matches" Discussion Sheet (p. 84) to each student. Invite students to find verses and discuss answers to questions on the sheet. Invite interested students to talk more with you about joining God's family (see "Leading a Child to Christ" on p. 11).

GRAND FINALE

(FIREFIGHTER returns.)

Tell me, how is the landscape different after a fire is out? *(Waits for audience's answers.)* What about after gossip has been spread? In both cases, the damage ALWAYS leaves a scar. Look, my best advice is this—don't play with matches. And DON'T EVER gossip. Like burning embers, your words scatter and create destruction far beyond where the fire started. Remember, only YOU can prevent wildfires! *(Exits.)*

Leader invites a student to read Proverbs 26:20-22 from the Key Verse Card. **It's very easy to assume that something we hear is true. But once gossip starts, it's nearly impossible to stop the damage. It's like flying embers from a wildfire. You'd be wise to post the questions from your Discussion Sheet somewhere else where you'll often see them. They can help you determine when not to talk, what to think about what others say and what to do about what you've heard. Remember, if you're not part of the problem or part of the solution, you have no business talking about it!**

Close in prayer, asking God to help students consider carefully what they say—before it becomes a wildfire.

Don't Play with Matches

DISCUSSION SHEET

The definition of gossip: Malicious (mean-spirited) chatter or rumors about other people; speaking about others to reveal secrets or intimacies.

What does God say about participating in gossip?
Find Leviticus 19:16.

If someone trusts you with a personal or private matter, what should you do?
Find Proverbs 11:13.

What can gossip do to friendships?
Find Proverbs 16:28.

Will there be gossip in heaven?
Find Psalm 15:1-3.

If we are people who praise God, how should our mouths not be used?
Find James 3:9-10.

What can we do about someone who gossips?
Find Proverbs 20:19.

THE GOSSIP TEST!
How do you know if what you're saying is gossip or not? ASK YOURSELF. . .
Do you know beyond a shadow of a doubt that it's true?
Are you saying something kind about the person?
Did the person give you permission to share what he or she has told you?
Will telling others be helpful?

KEY VERSE CARD

Proverbs 26:20-22
"Without wood a fire goes out; without gossip a quarrel dies down. As charcoal to embers and as wood to fire, so is a quarrelsome man for kindling strife. The words of a gossip are like choice morsels; they go down to a man's inmost parts."

And the Award Goes to . . .

TOPIC
Heavenly rewards

CHARACTER
Actress at the Academy Awards

SUMMARY
An actress recognizes her chance to gain unexpected awards.

KEY VERSE
1 Timothy 6:18-19
"Command them to do good, to be rich in good deeds, and to be generous and willing to share. In this way they will lay up treasure for themselves as a firm foundation for the coming age, so that they may take hold of the life that is truly life."

PROPS
Fancy clothes (for attending the Academy Awards)

OPTIONAL PROPS
Gold-painted statuette

PREP POINTERS
Play this actress as a very over-the-top character at the beginning!

SCHEDULE
Small-Group Warm-up (5-10 minutes)
Large-Group Presentation (5-10 minutes)
Small-Group Discussion (10-20 minutes)
Grand Finale (5-10 minutes)

SMALL-GROUP WARM-UP
Meet, greet and discuss the following questions in your small group:
- **When have you gotten an award?**
- **What did you like about getting an award?**
- **Why did you get the award? Did you think you deserved the award?**

AND THE AWARD GOES TO . . .

LARGE-GROUP PRESENTATION

(ACTRESS enters, patting hair, waving, shaking hands with random individuals.)

Good evening! Good evening to you ALL. I'd like to thank ALL my fans for coming out to SEE me as well as those at home who are cheering for me to win the Academy Award for BEST actress. I'd love to WIN, of course, but it's an honor just to be NOMINATED.

THE BEST

But I DO think my movie, *At Dawn the Hippos Grunt*, is a SUPERB film. I'm sure the OTHER nominees are proud of their films as well, but two of THEM have WON Academy Awards before. They should give someone ELSE a turn—someone like ME!

And of the other two actresses who are nominated, ONE has a super-rich and very famous husband. And he's quite HANDSOME—why does SHE need a trophy? The other actress is not a very NICE person. But for some reason she keeps getting these multi-million-dollar deals for blockbuster movies. She has a different boyfriend every month, probably because she's gorgeous—but I really think I deserve the award MORE than the others.

THE REST

Besides, if I win, I'll be on the COVERS of ALL the magazines. I'd get more movie deals and get paid more MONEY. I'd have 10 times as many fans as I do now—not that you're not all absolutely WONDER-FUL—but it would just be great to be RECOGNIZED wherever I went.

(Fans self.) Oh, I'm a nervous wreck! The show is about to start. Well, wish me luck. I really WANT to win. I know you can't come in with me, but you can THINK about how much this award would mean to YOU if you won it. Here I go . . . bye! (Exits.)

SMALL-GROUP DISCUSSION TIME

Provide one "And the Award Goes to . . ." Discussion Sheet (p. 88) to each student. Invite students to find verses and discuss answers to questions on the sheet. Invite interested students to talk more with you about joining God's family (see "Leading a Child to Christ" on p. 11).

GRAND FINALE

(ACTRESS returns, subdued.)

Well, you're probably DYING to know whether or not I WON. The truth is—I don't know! Instead of going in to the awards ceremony, I stayed just outside the door and listened to the verses you found. And I REALIZED something. Winning that award is NOT the big deal I was thinking it was!

What's REALLY important is living a life that pleases God. I don't think HE'S impressed if I am rich or famous OR have an Academy Award. I think—no, I KNOW—that He's more INTERESTED in how I live my LIFE as a Christian. THAT may never win me a little gold statue—but the ETERNAL REWARD of heaven will last a WHOLE lot longer! I'm out of here—to pursue some ETERNAL AWARDS! *(Exits.)*

Leader invites a student to read 1 Timothy 6:18-19 from the Key Verse Card. **Unlike many actresses, our guest tonight was brief and to the point: There are awards to be handed out in heaven that have nothing to do with how people view us here. God is the audience. He picks US as His award-winners when we live lives that show our love and obedience to Him!**

Close in prayer, thanking God for His love and asking His help for students to remember that their lives are gaining awards and rewards that will last forever.

And the Award Goes to . . .

DISCUSSION SHEET

Here's an easy question: We have an earthly life and an eternal life. Which life lasts longer? Now here's a harder question: Which one is "truly life"?
Find Psalm 39:4-5 and 1 Timothy 6:18-19.

Should we focus more on earthly awards or heavenly awards? Why?
Find Colossians 3:2.

What kind of rewards can we receive in heaven?
Find 2 Timothy 4:7-8.

For what reasons will we get those rewards?
Find Micah 6:8.

Who will give us our rewards?
Find Matthew 16:27.

Of all those we might want to impress, who should we most want to impress with our lives?
Find Galatians 1:10.

KEY VERSE CARD

1 Timothy 6:18-19
"Command them to do good, to be rich in good deeds, and to be generous and willing to share. In this way they will lay up treasure for themselves as a firm foundation for the coming age, so that they may take hold of the life that is truly life."

The Pilgrimage

TOPIC
History of Thanksgiving

CHARACTER
A Pilgrim from the Mayflower

SUMMARY
This Pilgrim tells of the crossing of the Mayflower and how God protects His people.

KEY VERSE
Psalm 91:14-16
"'Because he loves me,' says the LORD, 'I will rescue him; I will protect him, for he acknowledges my name. He will call upon me, and I will answer him; I will be with him in trouble, I will deliver him and honor him. With long life will I satisfy him and show him my salvation.'"

PROPS
Pilgrim costume, large wooden bowl covered with a towel or filled with an appropriate Pilgrim-style snack

OPTIONAL PROPS
Cooking utensils, cooking tripod and cast-iron pot

PREP POINTERS
Consider sharing a snack of popcorn, corn nuts, cranberries or other Pilgrim-style snack; include comments about that food in the presentation.

SCHEDULE
Small-Group Warm-up (5-10 minutes)
Large-Group Presentation (5-10 minutes)
Small-Group Discussion (10-20 minutes)
Grand Finale (5-10 minutes)

SMALL-GROUP WARM-UP
Meet, greet and discuss the following questions in your small group:
• **When have you had to do something scary?**
• **What made it scary? What happened?**
• **What goal is so important that you would do something scary to accomplish it?**

THE PILGRIMAGE

LARGE-GROUP PRESENTATION

(PILGRIM *enters, carrying large wooden bowl.*)
Good eve! Have you all come for the feast? I daresay we'll need a might bit more FOOD than we'd originally thought. No matter! We're quite happy to have you. Please, sit! You are our honored guests!

TOUGH TIMES

It's been a long, hard winter. I don't mind telling you, it has been frightening, as well. I never thought when I was a child back in England that I would someday end up in a land with no civilization! Then again, MANY things I've seen and experienced were unexpected!

When I lived in England, King James declared that there was only one way to worship God—HIS way. This was nothing new: Every recent ruler of England made rules for how everyone worshiped. But my parents and many in our congregation had copies of the Bible and had been reading it for themselves. This made them realize that some things King James insisted we must do contradicted the Word of God.

The members of our church decided that they would not change what they believed to please a human king. Of course, this brought King James's magistrates out to PUNISH those who disagreed! Many were put in prison. Some had their homes and property taken away. Some were even STONED to death! Others were condemned to die in other ways. It was a very frightening time.

NEW FREEDOM

We were called Separatists. Our pastor, John Robinson, decided to move to Holland where he would be free to worship the way the Bible says. About 300 people followed him, including my family. We worshiped God without persecution in Holland for 11 years. I grew up and was married there. But we didn't like some things about living in Dutch society. We longed to raise our children away from this influence and began speaking of settling in the New World. The idea caught on quickly—the thought that we could establish a colony where everyone would be free to worship without persecution was exciting! Our young family was determined to be a part of this bold pilgrimage.

NEW DIFFICULTIES

The sea voyage was filled with difficulties. Our first ship, the *Speedwell*, sprang a leak—twice! The second time it returned to the harbor, some of us joined those aboard the *Mayflower*. We set sail on September 6, 1620. I was quite seasick for the first few days. After 66 days—more than two MONTHS—we found harbor, but even then we had to stay on the ship until December 21st. By that time, two babies had been born! That made 37 Pilgrims altogether!

NEW LAND

Life was so very hard that winter. Everything was unfamiliar. The sounds, the plants and trees, the strange animals, the native people—I wished on several occasions that I had never left England! Many people died. It was heartbreaking.

But we begged God for help. And God answered our prayers! He sent the natives to help us and show us how to successfully plant crops and hunt food. Our gardens have now produced a great crop of a grain called corn. It is sweet and delicious and makes many kinds of food. One native named Squanto has been especially helpful to us—he even speaks English!

Our governor, Mr. Bradford, has declared this three-day feast as a celebration of Thanksgiving to God for His protection and goodness to us. Our native friends will come to share in the bounty God has provided. I am very grateful that our new home now has plentiful food. But I am even more thankful for the freedom to worship God without fear of being persecuted—that is even more wonderful!

NEW QUESTIONS

I'm sure that years from now, this land will be quite populated. I wonder if people will still be free to worship in the way they believe the Bible teaches. *(To herself.)* I wonder if they will be glad for such freedom. Will they be punished as we were in England? I have heard that persecution in England has not eased for fellow believers there. And the Bible tells us that in the Early Church, many were thrown in prison or even killed for their beliefs. I wonder—will folk in latter days still follow Christ if they're likely to be harmed?

(To audience.) What would you do? Would you still be a Christian? Many questions for you to talk about—don't let me keep you from it! I'll finish the cornmeal mush and set the eel pie in the oven. *(Exits.)*

SMALL-GROUP DISCUSSION TIME

Provide one "The Pilgrimage" Discussion Sheet (p. 92) to each student. Invite students to find verses and discuss answers to questions on the sheet. Invite interested students to talk more with you about joining God's family (see "Leading a Child to Christ" on p. 11).

GRAND FINALE

(PILGRIM returns.)

Thanksgiving is part of history. But more important, it is a celebration of God's care and goodness. That means far more than just being thankful for food and other good things in our lives. It's ALSO about thanking God that even when things seem very hard or difficult to us, He is always with us, loving us and protecting us. We all have more to be thankful for than we can imagine. My prayer is that none of us will take our blessings for granted this Thanksgiving but will take time to truly thank God for His mercy and salvation. You all have a wonderful Thanksgiving! *(Exits.)*

Leader invites a student to read Psalm 91:14-16 from the Key Verse Card. **There are great promises in those verses. Let's start off the Thanksgiving season by thanking God for these promises He gives us.**

Close in prayer, thanking God for His promises and for freedom to worship Him.

The Pilgrimage

DISCUSSION SHEET

What are ways God shows His love and care for us?
Find Psalm 91:14-16 and Psalm 103:1-5.

What does the Bible say about getting in trouble for following Jesus?
Find James 1:2-4.

What can we do when we're in trouble and don't know what to do?
Find James 1:5 and 2 Peter 1:3.

What does God promise to people who don't give up when trouble comes?
Find Romans 8:28-29,31-32 and James 1:12.

KEY VERSE CARD

Psalm 91:14-16
" 'Because he loves me,' says the LORD, 'I will rescue him;
I will protect him, for he acknowledges my name. He will
call upon me, and I will answer him; I will be with him in
trouble, I will deliver him and honor him. With long life
will I satisfy him and show him my salvation.' "

Jealousy Is a Vacuum

TOPIC
Jealousy

CHARACTER
Door-to-door vacuum cleaner salesman

SUMMARY
The salesman discovers how the powerful suction of jealousy can clean every smidgen of joy from life.

KEY VERSE
Psalm 37:1-6
"Do not fret because of evil men or be envious of those who do wrong; for like the grass they will soon wither, like green plants they will soon die away. Trust in the LORD and do good; dwell in the land and enjoy safe pasture. Delight yourself in the LORD and he will give you the desires of your heart. Commit your way to the LORD; trust in him and he will do this: He will make your righteousness shine like the dawn, the justice of your cause like the noonday sun."

PROPS
Suit and tie or sport coat, canister-type vacuum cleaner

OPTIONAL PROPS
Brochures for vacation destinations; magazine ads for an expensive car, a house with a pool

PREP POINTERS
Practice sighing between every few sentences to add to characterization!

SCHEDULE
Small-Group Warm-up (5-10 minutes)
Large-Group Presentation (5-10 minutes)
Small-Group Discussion (10-20 minutes)
Grand Finale (5-10 minutes)

SMALL-GROUP WARM-UP
Meet, greet and discuss the following questions in your small group:
- **When have you seen someone get something another person really wanted? How did that seem to make the other person feel?**
- **Has this ever happened to you? How did you feel?**
- **Why do you think you felt that way?**

Jealousy is a Vacuum

LARGE-GROUP PRESENTATION

(VACUUM CLEANER SALESMAN enters, walking dejectedly and yanking on the hose of the canister vacuum to drag it along with him.)
Hi. I don't suppose any of you want to buy a VACUUM cleaner, would you? Look here. This is our top model—the SuctionMaster 6000. It can clean ANYTHING off ANY carpet. Dirt, play dough, a herd of miniature cows, fish heads—ANYTHING! But you probably don't WANT one, right? No, I didn't THINK so. *(Sighs.)*

That makes . . . let's see . . . exactly ZERO vacuum cleaners I've sold today. I've only sold TWO this week. Doesn't ANYBODY care about CLEAN CARPETS anymore? *(Sighs.)* You know, PART of the problem is the PRICE of these things. You can go to Appliances 'R' Us and get them for at least $50 less.

NOTHING BUT SUCCESS

Of course, NOTHING stops good old SAM KIRBY from selling vacuum cleaners. SAM sold 28 last month alone! He's the ALL-TIME leading salesman for our company, Suction Production. *(Sighs.)* The company gives incentive awards to the person who sells the most vacuums each month. And Sam? Oh, our buddy SAM has WON for 17 months STRAIGHT!

You should see the CAR he drives. It's so classy—leather seats, V-8 engine, shiny silver hood ornament. *(Sighs.)* I would LOVE to have that car. And the VACATIONS he's been on—he went to Aruba, Cancun, Kauai, Cozumel, and three countries in Europe! *(Sighs.)* And those are only the ones I can REMEMBER. *(Sighs, shakes his head.)*

NOTHING BUT JEALOUSY

Every time they announce at the monthly meeting that SAM KIRBY is the top producer, I just feel like going CRAZY! *(Sighs.)* I think about him packing his bags and climbing on an airplane, heading off to some tropical location. It makes me NUTS!

He makes enough money to buy expensive suits. So he ALWAYS looks real sharp. *(Sighs.)* He's got a motorcycle and a ski boat and a huge house with a swimming pool. Sometimes I can't SLEEP at night just THINKING about how LUCKY Sam is.

And to top it off, he still has ALL HIS HAIR! *(Sighs.)* This guy's got EVERYTHING. And it's NOT FAIR! I work JUST as hard. I sell the SAME product. So why do I drive a beat-up old car, buy my suits at Cheap Clothes Emporium and consider a trip to the ice cream store a VACATION?

I DESERVE what Sam has. It isn't FAIR that he's got so much and I don't. *(Sighs.)* They've probably posted everyone's sales totals on the bulletin board by now. I'm going to go check to see who tops the list. I just KNOW it's going to be SAM again. Maybe I'll do what I did last month and draw a huge nose and crossed eyes on his picture. Anybody got a marker? *(Sighs; begins to walk away.)* Yeah, that will make me feel better. I'll be back in a few minutes. *(Over shoulder.)* Think about buying a vacuum, OK? *(Exits.)*

SMALL-GROUP DISCUSSION TIME

Provide one "Jealousy Is a Vacuum" Discussion Sheet (p. 96) to each student. Invite students to find verses and discuss answers to questions on the sheet. Invite interested students to talk more with you about joining God's family (see "Leading a Child to Christ" on p. 11).

GRAND FINALE

(VACUUM CLEANER SALESMAN returns.)

You know how LONG I've been selling vacuum cleaners? Nine years. For NINE YEARS I've been going from house to house, demonstrating the powerful suction of our vacuums. Nine years. And it just now OCCURRED to me that OTHER things besides the SuctionMaster 6000 have some powerful SUCTION, too. *(Sighs.)*

The thing that's been sucking all the JOY from my life is—JEALOUSY. *(Sighs.)* I've been so obsessed with Sam and all his money and possessions that I haven't been able to enjoy ANYTHING. I've been so wrapped up in my JEALOUSY that I don't even remember TASTING my ice cream the last time I had some. I haven't enjoyed driving MY car through the countryside because I've been so jealous of SAM'S car. Look at me. I've become so envious and bitter that I drew on Sam's picture like a little kid would do! How stupid is THAT?!

(Sighs; shakes head.) What a fool I've been. It's not like it wouldn't be NICE to have some of the things that Sam has, but I've got to stop ENVYING him and start ENJOYING what I DO have—like GOD, who LOVES me. God has blessed me with everything I need. I was so busy being JEALOUS that I completely forgot to THANK God for my health and my home and my job—and even for my old beat up car that gets me wherever I need to go!

(Sighs.) Jealousy has spoiled ENOUGH of my life. I want my JOY back! So I've asked God for forgiveness. And I've asked Him for help to let go of my envious feelings. *(Stops and thinks.)* Suddenly, I feel better than I have in a LONG time. I feel as GOOD as a dirt-free CARPET! Only GOD has enough SUCTION POWER to REMOVE sin like that! Thanks for listening! Oh—and CALL me when you need a vacuum cleaner! *(Exits, dragging vacuum cleaner and whistling.)*

Leader invites a student to read Psalm 37:1-6 from the Key Verse Card. **Like our salesman friend, we can live in bitterness and defeat—or in thankfulness and joy. It all depends on what we do with jealousy. Let's take a moment to think about situations where we might be holding on to envy or jealousy. Take time to pray silently and then I will close in prayer.**

Close in prayer, thanking God for His love and asking His help to release and forgive others instead of envying them or being jealous.

Jealousy Is a Vacuum

DISCUSSION SHEET

The word "jealousy" has two very different definitions:
1. Resentful or painful desire for another's advantages; to covet or envy
2. Close vigilance

Let's talk about the first definition.
Does God want us to be jealous of others?
Find 1 Peter 2:1.

Should we be jealous of the things other people have?
Find 1 John 2:15-17.

Why should stuff we want not matter very much to us?
Find 2 Corinthians 4:18.

Where do feelings of jealousy come from?
Find James 3:14-16.

Is being jealous good for us?
Find Proverbs 14:30.

If it is wrong to be jealous, why does the Bible call God a "jealous God"?
Find Exodus 34:14.

(Look again at the second definition for jealousy: God watches over us with close vigilance because He loves us and wants us to love Him above all others!)

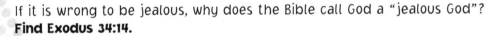

KEY VERSE CARD

Psalm 37:1-6
"Do not fret because of evil men or be envious of those who do wrong; for like the grass they will soon wither, like green plants they will soon die away. Trust in the Lord and do good; dwell in the land and enjoy safe pasture. Delight yourself in the Lord and he will give you the desires of your heart. Commit your way to the Lord; trust in him and he will do this: He will make your righteousness shine like the dawn, the justice of your cause like the noonday sun."

Christmas Lamb

TOPIC
Jesus, Lamb of God

CHARACTER
A lamb

SUMMARY
A little lamb tells why Jesus was born at Christmas—to be God's Lamb.

KEY VERSE
1 John 4:9-10
"This is how God showed his love among us: He sent his one and only Son into the world that we might live through him. This is love: not that we loved God, but that he loved us and sent his Son as an atoning sacrifice for our sins."

PROPS
White sweatpants and hooded sweatshirt, animal-ear headband, black gloves and shoes, black greasepaint for nose

OPTIONAL PROPS
Lamb costume (instead of items listed above) or lamb puppet, nativity set

PREP POINTERS
The lamb character should be portrayed as sweet and innocent, but not silly.

SCHEDULE
Small-Group Warm-up (5-10 minutes)
Large-Group Presentation (5-10 minutes)
Small-Group Discussion (10-20 minutes)
Grand Finale (5-10 minutes)

SMALL-GROUP WARM-UP
Meet, greet and discuss the following questions in your small group:
- **What do you like best about Christmas? How does your family celebrate?**
- **What do you think is the most important reason to celebrate Christmas?**
- **When have you seen a lamb? What can you tell us about lambs?**

CHRISTMAS LaMB

LARGE-GROUP PRESENTATION

(LAMB *enters bouncing and baaing, turns to face audience.*)
Hi! I'm a little lamb! What are you? *(Waits for audience's response.)* My ewey and rammy love me. Do you know what a ewey and a rammy are? *(Waits for audience's response.)* That's right. They're my mommy and daddy. They call me their Christmas lamb because I was born last year on Christmas Day!

You know what ELSE my ewey and rammy told me? They said that if I'd been born a long time ago, back in Bible times, I probably would have gotten SAC-RIFICED. Do you know what "sacrificed" means? *(Waits for audience's response.)*

SACRIFICED

That's right. "Sacrificed" means I'd be KILLED! Lambs who lived a long, long time ago had to take the punishment for PEOPLE'S sins. *(Looks around.)* I'm NOT kidding!

Have you ever heard the story of when the Israelites were slaves in Egypt? Way b-a-a-a-ck in the time of Moses, the Israelites asked God to please get them OUT of slavery. The Pharaoh, the king of Egypt, wasn't ABOUT to let them leave Egypt! So God had to send all kinds of punishments. But Pharaoh STILL would not listen! God prepared to send one LAST punishment: All firstborn males in Egypt would DIE. But to keep the Israelites safe, God instructed each family to kill a perfect young lamb and smear the blood of that perfect lamb on the doorposts of their homes. This would be a sign so that death would pass by them. In every home where blood was on the doorposts, the people were safe. Every year since then, the Israelites have celebrated Passover to remember how God kept them safe and then delivered them from slavery.

But did you HEAR that? A little LAMB—perfect, with no blemishes or defects—THAT'S who had to give BLOOD! If I'd BEEN there, I might have been KILLED!

THE LAST SACRIFICE

But here's ANOTHER story from long ago. About 2,000 years ago, the VERY LAST Lamb EVER was sacrificed. But this lamb was DIFFERENT. This story was passed down from my great, great-, great-, great-, great-, great-, great-, (and ma-a-a-aybe a few more "greats") great-RAMpa! And my Rampa MET this VERY LAST Lamb who was ever sacrificed for sin.

One night, Rampa was out in the fields with the rest of his flock. They snuggled close to their shepherds, who always protected them and weren't afraid of ANYTHING! But suddenly, the DARKNESS became BRIGHT! Rampa saw that his shepherds were TERRIFIED! Then an ANGEL told them that a Savior had been born in Bethlehem.

Then the sky FILLED with angels, all SINGING! When the angels disappeared, it was quiet. The shepherds did something they had NEVER done before: They LEFT the sheep! But my Rampa followed them. They all went to a STABLE where a baby was lying asleep in a MANGER! Rampa had never seen a baby in a manger—because THAT'S where sheep usually eat their FOOD! The shepherds knelt down to worship this baby. On the way back, the shepherds told everyone that the SAVIOR had been born!

It's quite a story! My Rampa said that this BABY was the VERY LAST Lamb ever to be sacrificed. But the baby was HUMAN. He wasn't even a LAMB! What do YOU think HIS story means? I'd be glad to know what you find out! *(Exits.)*

SMALL-GROUP DISCUSSION TIME

Provide a "Christmas Lamb" Discussion Sheet (p. 100) to each student. Invite students to find verses and discuss answers to questions on the sheet. Invite interested students to talk more with you about joining God's family (see "Leading a Child to Christ" on p. 11).

GRAND FINALE

(Person who played the LAMB *returns without costume items.)*
Now you know! Now no lamb has to WORRY about becoming a SACRIFICE! No more sacrifices! The baby who came was JESUS. God sent Him to be born here on Earth. He was called the Lamb of God. He came to offer Himself as the VERY LAST sacrifice for sin—ever! No lamb ever sacrificed could take away the guilt of sin forever. No other lamb was completely perfect. No other lamb could give eternal life—only Jesus! Because of Jesus, no animal ever needs to be sacrificed—Jesus sacrificed Himself and gave His life for you. Now YOU can live with God forever if you ask Jesus to be YOUR Savior. At Christmas, you can give your LIFE to Him! THAT'S the REAL reason we can say, "MERRY CHRISTMAS!" *(Exits.)*

Leader invites a student to read 1 John 4:9-10 from the Key Verse Card. **Jesus is God's perfect Lamb. He loved each of us so much that He came to Earth to be born as a baby. Then He died on the cross to take the punishment for our sins. He died as the last sacrifice. But because He did not STAY dead, He can give US eternal life, too, when we join His family! It's the BEST family to belong to at Christmas—or anytime!**

Close in prayer, thanking God for sending Jesus to be the last sacrifice for sin and asking God to help students accept His sacrifice for them and join God's family.

Christmas Lamb

DISCUSSION SHEET

Why did the Israelites have to sacrifice innocent animals, like lambs? **Find Hebrews 9:22.**

Who do you think the prophets are talking about in the following verses?
Find Isaiah 7:14, Micah 5:2 and Zechariah 9:9.

BONUS QUESTION:

How long before Jesus was born did God give these prophecies to the prophets? (Take a guess!)

Isaiah a. about 10 years b. about 700 years c. about 25 years

Micah a. about 700 years b. about 40 years c. about 18 years

Zechariah a. about 20 years b. about 35 years c. about 500 years

Where do you think prophets gained such detailed information so long before it happened?

Why do you think God wanted the Israelites to know the prophecies about Jesus? What did John the Baptist call Jesus? **Find John 1:29.**

Was Jesus good enough to be the final sacrifice for our sins? **Find 1 Peter 1:18-19.**

Why do we no longer need to sacrifice lambs to pay for our sins? **Find Hebrews 10:8-10.**

Answers: Isaiah: b. Micah: a. Zechariah: b.

KEY VERSE CARD

1 John 4:9-10
"This is how God showed his love among us: He sent his one and only Son into the world that we might live through him. This is love: not that we loved God, but that he loved us and sent his Son as an atoning sacrifice for our sins."

For Goodness' Sake!

TOPIC
Jesus, our example

CHARACTER
Quality-control inspector

SUMMARY
The QC inspector makes clear to us what good is and how we can do good and be good—with Jesus as our pattern of perfection.

KEY VERSE
Matthew 5:16
"Let your light shine before men, that they may see your good deeds and praise your Father in heaven."

PROPS
Factory worker-type clothing (like Rosie the Riveter), various kinds and styles of (new) underwear (especially in white), box marked "BAD"

OPTIONAL PROPS
Pair of new, perfect underwear pressed in a picture frame, dot stickers

PREP POINTERS
The character can inspect garments (and add stickers, if desired) during the entire presentation.

SCHEDULE
Small-Group Warm-up (5-10 minutes)
Large-Group Presentation (5-10 minutes)
Small-Group Discussion (10-20 minutes)
Grand Finale (5-10 minutes)

SMALL-GROUP WARM-UP
Meet, greet and discuss the following questions in your small group:
- **When have you had a perfect homework paper?**
- **How did you feel about it?**
- **What is something you do well? Have you ever felt that you had done it perfectly?**

FOR GOODNESS' SAKE!

LARGE-GROUP PRESENTATION

(QC INSPECTOR stands behind a table holding piles of underwear and a box labeled "BAD." Speaks wearily.)
Good evening. Sorry if I seem a little tired. It's the end of my 8-hour shift here at the Fine Fanny Fashions Factory. We make fine fanny fashions here—otherwise known as underwear. I've been working in this place, 8 hours a day, 5 days a week, for 12 years now.

SERIOUS WORK

I started off as an elastic tester, but I've worked my way up to inspector. That's right, I'm Inspector #27. Have you ever purchased a package of underwear and when you opened them, you found a sticker that said "Inspected by . . ." and then a number? Well, I put my number, #27, on every piece of underwear that PASSES my inspection.

SERIOUS INSPECTOR

I take my job seriously. *(With more energy.)* How would you like to buy a pair of underwear only to discover that there's ONE LEG HOLE? That sort of thing does happen! About five years ago an inspector WAS fired because she let a pair of underwear through that had NO ELASTIC in the waistband. Imagine putting on underwear that falls around your ANKLES every time you move! NOT a pretty picture!

THAT'S why I take my job seriously. I pick up each pair and check to see that they are good. If they are, I put one of my "Inspected by #27" stickers on them. Then they are sent down to the packaging room. If the pair is NOT good, I remove it and drop it in this box labeled "BAD." *(Gestures at box.)* THIS underwear ends up as rags that are eventually burned in the trash incinerator.

BAD UNDERWEAR

Usually the bad underwear is bad because of holes in the fabric or oil stains from the machinery. Oil drips are EASY to spot on WHITE underpants. Even the tiniest little drop shows up. And even if that's the ONLY thing wrong with the underwear, that pair has to go in the "BAD" box. Only the GOOD underwear gets one of my "Inspected by #27" stickers.

GOOD UNDERWEAR

There is a pair of underwear that hangs in a frame in front of me. The sign above it reads, "The Perfect Underwear." ALL of the inspectors are supposed to look at that PERFECT underwear whenever they need to decide if the pair they are inspecting is good enough. If the underwear doesn't meet the standard, it goes in the "BAD" box. ONLY good underwear is useful for its intended purpose.

You know, God is an inspector, too. No, NOT at Fine Fanny Fashions, but at creation. After He created something, He inspected it. And do you know what He said after He inspected each thing He created? He said it was "GOOD." Even GOD checks His work! I think WE should, too. *(Holds up pair of underwear.)* Just like I check the underwear.

"Goodness" is a fruit of the Holy Spirit. It is listed in Galatians 5:22. So if we are Christians, then other people should see GOODNESS in our lives. But how do you KNOW goodness when you SEE it? Why don't you all find out what "good" means to God—while I get this work done! *(Goes on working during small group time.)*

SMALL-GROUP DISCUSSION TIME

Provide one "For Goodness' Sake!" Discussion Sheet (p. 104) to each student. Invite students to find verses and discuss answers to questions on the sheet. Invite interested students to talk more with you about joining God's family (see "Leading a Child to Christ" on p. 11).

GRAND FINALE

(QC INSPECTOR resumes speaking after audience is assembled.)
Now, if GOD says something is good, does that mean that it's just OK? Just mediocre? That it barely passes inspection? I don't THINK so. I think it's like that PERFECT pair of underwear that hangs on the wall. I think that to God, "good" means complete, mature and free of pollution. So THAT'S what we should make our goal. God's FAMILY should try to LOOK LIKE Him—by being good like GOD is good. THAT'S a tall order. BUT hey, you read it right there in God's Word—it CAN be done!

Well, I should head home. I've got another long day inspecting underwear tomorrow. You know, after our talk today, I think I'll be more AWARE of ways I can show goodness to the people I work with so that they know GOD puts HIS sticker on Inspector #27 and that Inspector #27 loves God and wants to please Him! *(Exits.)*

Leader invites a student to read Matthew 5:16 from the Key Verse Card. **God knows we are not perfect. But He wants us to grow up in Him and make it our goal to look more like Him in what we do every day. As we look at who Jesus is and follow His example, we can become more complete, mature and uncontaminated. That's the way we can strive for goodness!**

Close in prayer, asking God to help students find ways to express goodness and follow Jesus' example of goodness as a way to show love to Him.

For Goodness' Sake!

DISCUSSION SHEET

Who is good? Are you good?
Find Luke 18:18-19.

How much good can we do on our own?
Find John 15:5.

If we do good deeds without God's love as our reason, how do those good things look to God?
Find Isaiah 64:6.

How can we get help to do what is good?
Find Philippians 4:13.

What does God already have planned for us to do?
Find Ephesians 2:10.

Christians will someday be with God in heaven. Will God know if we have tried to do good?
Find Matthew 25:23.

KEY VERSE CARD

Matthew 5:16
"Let your light shine before men, that they may see your good deeds and praise your Father in heaven."

The Case of the Missing Savior

TOPIC
Jesus' resurrection

CHARACTER
Detective Tuesday

SUMMARY
It's a cold trail, but our faithful detective ferrets out the truth about Jesus' resurrection.

KEY VERSE
1 Corinthians 15:17
"And if Christ has not been raised, your faith is futile; you are still in your sins."

PROPS
Bible, magnifying glass, suit coat or trench coat, hat, notebook, pen, piece of paper (new assignment)

OPTIONAL PROPS
Coffee cup, magazine picture of a swimming pool

PREP POINTERS
This character is a take-off on Joe Friday of the old TV series *Dragnet*. Practice your best crusty old detective!

SCHEDULE
Small-Group Warm-up (5-10 minutes)
Large-Group Presentation (5-10 minutes)
Small-Group Discussion (10-20 minutes)
Grand Finale (5-10 minutes)

SMALL-GROUP WARM-UP
Meet, greet and discuss the following questions in your small group:
- **What are some things your family does at Easter?**
- **Why do you think your family has these Easter traditions?**
- **How do you think these traditions got started?**

THE CaSE OF THE MISSING SaVIOR

LARGE-GROUP PRESENTATION

(DETECTIVE TUESDAY enters, frowning at notes in his notebook, looking through magnifying glass as if looking for clues.)
Evening. I'm Detective Tuesday. I've been a detective with the Cold Case Division for 30 years now. I'm close to retirement—I'm looking FORWARD to it, too. I have PLANS.

I'm gonna buy a HUGE swimming pool for my backyard. And you know those floating lounge chairs? I'm gonna get me one of those, too. Then I'm gonna grab a HUGE glass of iced tea, gather up ALL the detective novels I've EVER wanted to read and lie there in my lounge chair in the pool until I've read EVERY SINGLE NOVEL. Now THERE'S something to look forward to!

NOT YET RETIRED

In the meantime, I've got a REALLY difficult cold case to solve. You'd think since I'm so close to retirement, they'd give me something EASY. But not MY boss! He's some young kid, only 15 years out of college. Says he needs my EXPERTISE on this case.

So I ask him, "How cold IS the case? Did it happen 5 years ago? 10? 20?" He just keeps shaking his head.

"So how old IS it?" I asked. Guess what he tells me—he says he's assigning me a case that's nearly 2,000 years old. You gotta be KIDDING!

"All right," I said to him, "give me the details. What's the crime?"

"You ever read the Bible?" he asks.

"Yeah, sure, I know about the Bible. What ABOUT it?" So he proceeds to tell me that I'm supposed to solve the MYSTERY of Jesus' DISAPPEARANCE from the tomb on what we NOW call Easter Sunday! I thought he was pulling my leg. We got some real cut-ups on the force, guys who are always trying to put over a practical joke. But he was SERIOUS—serious as a toothache!

NOT A BIG DEAL?

So I'm supposed to figure out how Jesus went missing from the tomb where He was put—after being CRUCIFIED. This case was so LONG ago. Does is even matter if it's TRUE or not that Jesus was raised from the dead? What's the big DEAL?

(To himself.) Oh, WAIT a minute. I guess that WOULD be a big deal. If Jesus didn't really RISE from the dead, then all of Christianity is based on a LIE! If Jesus didn't really DIE, then I guess you can't say He died for our sins. And if He didn't DIE to pay the price for our sins, then we're still IN our sins. We can NEVER go to heaven! If He died and didn't rise up from the grave, that means He wasn't REALLY the Savior He claimed to be.

(To audience.) I guess this case is more IMPORTANT than I thought. The consequences could be LIFE-CHANGING! I've got to SOLVE this case!

NO NEW EVIDENCE

OK, OK. I know how to do this. It's like any OTHER case: I start by going through the evidence. Even though this happened a long time ago, eyewitness reports WERE taken—(Holds up Bible.) they're all here in the Bible! The way I see it, there are only four possible explanations to the fact that Jesus' body was missing:

(Opens notebook; starts to write.)
1. The disciples stole His body.

2. The disciples were hallucinating—they saw something that wasn't there.

3. Jesus only fainted; He didn't really die.

4. Jesus really DID die and then He really DID rise from the dead, which makes the whole story . . . TRUE.

Look, if I'm going to CONTINUE this investigation, I'm going to need a cup of coffee. Hot, strong and black— that's the way we detectives like our coffee. Get started with this investigation for me, would ya? (Exits.)

SMALL-GROUP DISCUSSION TIME

Provide one "The Case of the Missing Savior" Discussion Sheet (p. 108) to each student. Invite students to find verses and discuss answers to questions on the sheet. Invite interested students to talk more with you about joining God's family (see "Leading a Child to Christ" on p. 11).

GRAND FINALE

(DETECTIVE TUESDAY returns.)

You guys found some GREAT evidence! Good work! Here's some other stuff I uncovered. In Matthew 28:11-15, the soldiers were TOLD to lie. They were paid MONEY to say that the disciples had stolen Jesus from the tomb while they were asleep. How do THEY know what went on if they were SLEEPING?

John 20:6-7 says that the cloth that had covered Jesus' face was folded up by itself, separated from the other linens. Do thieves take time to FOLD? Come on!

I've checked all the facts, investigated all the evidence, left no stone unturned: This case is SOLVED. Jesus ROSE from the dead! He is JUST who He says He is! Case closed!

Wait a minute. (Pulls out paper.) Here's the order for my NEXT cold-case assignment: "Ever since the invention of the electric dryer, socks have gone missing. Find out WHY." NOW they're pulling my leg for SURE! Thanks for your help with the Jesus case, but you guys have to find your OWN socks! (Exits.)

Leader invites a student to read 1 Corinthians 15:17 from the Key Verse Card. **Well, that case is wrapped up tightly! Jesus is who He claimed to be. His resurrection proves that He is Lord. And if we put our faith and trust in Him, He will make us part of God's family!**

Close in prayer, asking God to help students understand the importance of Jesus' resurrection.

The Case of the Missing Savior

DISCUSSION SHEET

What happened to Jesus' body? Did He really die? Did He really rise again to life? Let's look at the evidence. Some say Jesus only fainted and didn't actually die. What did the soldiers say? **Find John 19:33-35.**

Joseph and Nicodemus both handled His body at the tomb. Wouldn't they have told everyone if He was alive? They would have been thrilled that Jesus wasn't really dead! **Find John 19:38-42.**

Some people say that the disciples stole the body of Jesus. Was that possible? Do you think the disciples were brave enough to steal a body from under the noses of Roman guards? Why or why not? **Find Matthew 26:69-75 and Mark 14:50-51.**

Was the tomb well guarded? **Find Matthew 27:62-66.**

Some say the disciples were all hallucinating. How many people would have to have been hallucinating at the same time? **Find 1 Corinthians 15:6.**

Can you touch something that isn't there? **Find Luke 24:39-40.**

Do hallucinations eat? **Find Luke 24:41-43.**

What was reported to Pilate? **Find Mark 15:43-45.**

So if Jesus' body wasn't stolen by the disciples, if the disciples weren't hallucinating, if Jesus really died and was seen alive three days later, what do the facts of this case tell us?

KEY VERSE CARD

1 Corinthians 15:17
"And if Christ has not been raised, your faith is futile; you are still in your sins."

Here Comes the Judge

TOPIC
Justice and mercy

CHARACTERS
Judge; Bailiff (optional)

SUMMARY
The judge helps us understand the difference between the world's clamor for justice and what God expects of us.

KEY VERSE
Proverbs 11:21
"Be sure of this: The wicked will not go unpunished, but those who are righteous will go free."

PROPS
Judge's robe, gavel

OPTIONAL PROPS
Table or desk where the judge may sit; costume for the person acting as bailiff (police-style shirt, etc.)

PREP POINTERS
Having a bailiff announce the judge (see script) will add realism!

SCHEDULE
Small-Group Warm-up (5-10 minutes)
Large-Group Presentation (5-10 minutes)
Small-Group Discussion (10-20 minutes)
Grand Finale (5-10 minutes)

SMALL-GROUP WARM-UP
Meet, greet and discuss the following questions in your small group:
• **Tell about a time someone did something unfair to you.**
• **How did it make you feel? How did you know it was not fair?**
• **What do people do when they think something is not fair?**

Here Comes the Judge

Large-Group Presentation

(BAILIFF *speaks as* JUDGE *enters.*)
All rise. Court is now in session. The Honorable Jess B. Guessin presiding. *(Speaks after JUDGE moves to front of audience.)* You may now be seated.

(JUDGE sits, bangs gavel and then speaks to audience.) Welcome to my courtroom. I understand that you have come today to learn about the justice system—very good! A judge must develop a good sense of fairness and an understanding of right and wrong. Sometimes, a case is very clear. The decision is easy. Other times, cases are NOT so easily decided. For instance, how would you have decided THESE cases? *(Bangs gavel several times and then reads cases below aloud.)*

Case #1
A 10-year-old boy was absent from school on a Thursday because he was ill. That day, it was announced that there would be a test on Friday. His parents' rule is that if he gets a test score lower than 80 percent, he is grounded for the weekend. He returned to school on Friday unprepared for the test and received a 77 percent on the test. Is he INNOCENT? Should he be GROUNDED?

Case #2
A family of four goes into a section of the city known for its high crime rate and gang activity. While they are serving meals to homeless people at a homeless shelter, their car is stolen. The insurance company REFUSES to pay them for the loss of their car because they INTENTIONALLY parked it in a high-crime area. Should the insurance company pay? Were the people negligent or not?

Case #3
You bought a shirt for $25. Because it doesn't fit, you decide to return it but cannot find your receipt. The store's policy is that a return without a receipt gets store credit at the current price. The shirt has now gone on sale. This means you would only get back $17.70. Should you get back what you PAID? Or should you get only the sale amount?

UNFAIR!

Is it FAIR or UNFAIR that a drug dealer drives a brand-new cherry-red Corvette while your kind, sweet aunt has to drive an old minivan that is falling apart?

Is it FAIR or UNFAIR that one man steals, beats his children, cheats on his wife, drinks and takes drugs and smokes all his life—and lives to be 92? And is it FAIR or UNFAIR that another man spends his life loving and providing for his family, exercises regularly, doesn't smoke or drink—and gets liver cancer and dies at the age of 46?

Do those things sound like JUSTICE? Is it FAIR that SOME people who do WRONG have good things happen to them and that people who do GOOD things have BAD things happen? *(Bangs gavel several times.)*

If YOU were the judge, what would YOU say? We always SAY we want what is fair. We want the good people to be rewarded for their goodness and the bad people to be punished for their badness. But that ISN'T the way it is in REAL life.

So why doesn't God do what WE think is fair? Why doesn't He reward the GOOD people and punish the BAD? Is He making a MISTAKE? It's time to find out! I'm declaring a recess while you do the research! *(Bangs gavel several times and then exits.)*

SMALL-GROUP DISCUSSION TIME

Provide one "Here Comes the Judge" Discussion Sheet (p. 112) to each student. Invite students to find verses and discuss answers to questions on the sheet. Invite interested students to talk more with you about joining God's family (see "Leading a Child to Christ" on p. 11).

GRAND FINALE

(JUDGE returns.)

So now, let's talk about JUSTICE: Is it JUST to take a sledgehammer to the beautiful car of the drug dealer? Should we punch out the kid who cheated in tetherball? Should we be snotty to the teacher who gave us a *B* on a report that we think should have gotten an *A*? *(Bangs gavel several times.)*

Ladies and gentlemen, the answer is NO. If anyone has been unfair, the Bible makes it clear that GOD is the only one we can trust to JUDGE that person. So when things don't seem FAIR, our job is to TRUST GOD—and leave ULTIMATE JUSTICE to HIM! *(Bangs gavel.)*

You know, we have ALL done wrong. We are ALL sinners who deserve PUNISHMENT for our sins. But the TRUTH about JUSTICE is that we have a great and LOVING God. Jesus was willing to take that punishment on HIMSELF so that all of us—every last GUILTY one of us—could have a chance to be with Him forever. I think that makes Him a VERY MERCIFUL judge. And the Bible says that He expects US to be merciful, too! Think about THAT kind of justice next time you think you've been treated unfairly! *(Bangs gavel several times and then exits.)*

Leader invites a student to read Proverbs 11:21 from the Key Verse Card. **Some people tell us that we should always FIGHT for our rights. But the Bible says that God expects us to be merciful because of the great mercy HE has shown to US. That is VERY different from what we hear most of the time. Let's ask God to help us start thinking and acting in ways that show His mercy!**

Close in prayer, thanking God that we don't get what we deserve and asking Him to help us act and think in ways that show His kind of mercy to others.

Here Comes the Judge

DISCUSSION SHEET

Does the Bible say that life will always be fair?
Find Matthew 5:45b.

God knows that you will sometimes be treated unfairly. How does He want you to react?
Find 1 Peter 2:19-20.

Why does God let people get away with treating others unfairly?
Find Genesis 50:20.

How should a Christian feel about people who treat him or her unfairly?
Find Luke 6:27-28.

Why shouldn't we judge or retaliate against people who treat us unfairly?
Find Luke 6:41-42.

Will those who treat us unfairly ever be judged?
Find Romans 12:19.

What if we want to get even with the person who treated us unfairly?
Find Proverbs 20:22.

KEY VERSE CARD

Proverbs 11:21
"Be sure of this: The wicked will not go unpunished, but those who are righteous will go free."

An Audience of One

TOPIC
Living for Jesus

CHARACTER
Preteen girl or boy (written for a girl)

SUMMARY
The preteen describes the frustration of trying to be cool and please everyone and is glad to learn that we need to please only God—the "audience of one."

KEY VERSE
Galatians 1:10
"Am I now trying to win the approval of men, or of God? Or am I trying to please men? If I were still trying to please men, I would not be a servant of Christ."

PROPS
Backpack, chair and table, small index card lettered as directed in Grand Finale

OPTIONAL PROPS
Orange shirt, paperback book, lunch bag with sandwich in plastic baggie, CD (place items in the backpack)

PREP POINTERS
The kid in this presentation is very like your students. Don't play the character in a sarcastic manner that might indicate you think these problems are laughable.

SCHEDULE
Small-Group Warm-up (5-10 minutes)
Large-Group Presentation (5-10 minutes)
Small-Group Discussion (10-20 minutes)
Grand Finale (5-10 minutes)

SMALL-GROUP WARM-UP
Meet, greet and discuss the following questions in your small group:
- **Tell about a time you have seen a person embarrass someone else by saying unkind words or tripping them, for example. What happened?**
- **What do you think you might have done if you had been embarrassed in that way?**
- **Why do you think someone might want to embarrass another person?**

AN AUDIENCE OF ONE

LARGE-GROUP PRESENTATION

(PRETEEN enters, carrying backpack, obviously upset. Drops backpack; plops into chair.)

I'm NEVER going to leave my room EVER again for as long as I live. It never fails. I ALWAYS do something stupid or say something WRONG in front of people. Does that ever happen to you? TODAY is a perfect example. From the minute I woke up I couldn't do ANYTHING right!

MY CLOTHES

I went to my closet to decide what to wear. Yesterday I wore my favorite orange shirt, but Dana said orange is the UGLIEST color in the world. So much for all my orange clothes! I was going to wear the blue shirt, but then I remembered that the last time I wore it my mom said, "Don't YOU look cute!"

I couldn't wear my khaki pants because they're getting a little short. The kids at school are RUTHLESS with anyone whose pants are too short. I finally decided on my black pants and a plain black T-shirt.

When I got to school, Dana said, "So where's the FUNERAL?" Man, I thought I was SAFE wearing plain black clothes!

MY IDEAS

Later, in class, we were discussing this book we had to read. It was called *Captain Richard's First Mate*. It was about this sea captain who hired a new first mate, Lou Sharp. What he doesn't know is that Lou is actually a girl, Louise. She does a great job, but when the captain finds out he's a she, he gets really mad and FIRES her. Later on, they fall in love and get married. It was such a GREAT story!

My teacher asked the class, "What did you think of the book?"

I raised my hand to tell her I thought it was awesome, but she called on Bono first. He's real popular. And Bono said, "It was such a LAME book, Mrs. Carpenter. WHY did you make us read it?"

So Mrs. Carpenter asked, "Any other opinions? How about you, (your name)? You had your hand up. What did YOU think?"

Well, there was no WAY I was going to say how GREAT it was after Bono TRASHED it. So I just said, "It was OK."

Bono says, "You've got to be joking. There was NOTHING OK about it." Then everyone starts agreeing with him. I felt like such an IDIOT!

MY LUNCH

Finally, the bell rang for lunchtime. A bunch of us always sit together at the same table. We started opening our lunches, talking about our science projects.

I'm taking a bite of my sandwich and Shana goes, "Eeuuwww! You're eating MAYONNAISE?" Well, I didn't want her to think I was STRANGE, so I said, "That's how my mom makes baloney sandwiches."

"ICK! I would NEVER eat a sandwich with mayonnaise," decreed Queen Shana. I didn't want her to think I was GROSS, so I didn't finish my sandwich. I wondered what my mom would think if she found out I wasn't eating my lunch.

MY MUSIC

After school, some of us were walking home. Rona said she had just bought the new Twirling Aardvarks CD. She was going on and on about how great it was. I don't really like the Twirling Aardvarks that much. They're okay, but I actually like to listen to Broadway musicals.

"Hey!" she said, "Are you going to buy the new Twirling Aardvarks CD?"

"No," I said. "I'm saving up to buy the soundtrack from *Cats*."

"No WAY!" she says. "You gotta get out of the DARK AGES! How UNCOOL are YOU?!" I didn't say one more word about the kind of music I like.

EVEN MY CANDY!

Could I possibly make anyone ELSE think I'm a complete dweeb? My soccer coach thought I was strange because I wore my SOCKS rolled down! Then my brother and his friend gave me a hard time for painting my FINGERNAILS different colors! Then the girl who sells candy at the mall—a TOTAL STRANGER—thought I was WEIRD because I wanted Good and Plenty!

(Imitates candy seller.) "Don't you know those are LICORICE? Licorice is GROSS." So I ended up getting Starbursts, which I DON'T like as much as Good and Plenty.

HOW ON EARTH AM I SUPPOSED TO MAKE EVERYONE HAPPY???? Look, I'd appreciate any help you could give me. I'll be over here—HIDING! *(Turns and sits with back to group.)*

SMALL-GROUP DISCUSSION TIME

Provide one "An Audience of One" Discussion Sheet (p. 116) to each student. Invite students to find verses and discuss answers to questions on the sheet. Invite interested students to talk more with you about joining God's family (see "Leading a Child to Christ" on p. 11).

GRAND FINALE

(PRETEEN holds up a small card and addresses audience.) Look. Some weird lady handed this card to me. Can you see what it says? LIVE FOR AN AUDIENCE OF ONE.

Now, wouldn't THAT be nice—to worry ONLY about what ONE person thinks! I wonder who the "one" is? There's a Bible verse on the other side. Here, let me read it. See if it makes any sense to you guys. *(Reads Key Verse Card aloud.)*

Oh, WOW! Do you realize what this SAYS? I should live to please God and not worry about what ANYBODY else thinks! Boy, do I feel like a JERK. Here I am, a Christian, worrying about what everybody EXCEPT God thinks of me! I worry about my friends, my parents, my teacher, my coach, my dumb brother, even the candy seller—but not ONCE did I stop to worry what GOD thought!

All right. Let me see if I have this straight: If I only have to think about what GOD thinks, that SURE makes things a whole lot easier! I can wear ORANGE if it's OK with God—and I'm sure it is. He CREATED orange! And if I like a good book, God will be OK with the fact that I enjoyed it! And if I LIKE mayonnaise, that is NO BIG DEAL! Does God prefer me to listen to the Twirling Aardvarks? I doubt it! So it's OK if I DON'T buy their CD! God CERTAINLY doesn't care if my socks are rolled down or which candy I like! How about colorful fingernails? I don't think He'd mind. Hey, this having to just please GOD is GREAT! YOU ought to give it a try! *(Picks up backpack and walks off, whistling.)*

Leader invites a student to read Galatians 1:10 from the Key Verse Card. **We all want for others to like us. But it's easy to drive ourselves crazy worrying about what PEOPLE will think of what we say or do. According to this verse, we need only to be God-pleasers! God is the one whose approval really matters. And the best part is, He loves us and will help us please Him—if we will ask!**

Close in prayer, thanking God for helping students remember that He is the one whose opinion really matters and asking Him to help students put Him first this week.

An Audience of One

DISCUSSION SHEET

It's impossible to please everyone! What makes it possible to please God?
Find Hebrews 11:6.

What is a good way to please God?
Find Romans 12:1-2.

How does God respond when we do something to please Him, like walk away from a person telling a dirty joke? What are some of the blessings that come from pleasing God?
Find Psalm 128:1-2.
Find Proverbs 16:7.
Find 1 John 2:28-29.

What should you do if you have gone along with something you knew would not please God?
Find 1 John 1:9.

What words and actions are pleasing to God?
Find Hebrews 13:15-16.

KEY VERSE CARD

Galatians 1:10
"Am I now trying to win the approval of men, or of God? Or am I trying to please men? If I were still trying to please men, I would not be a servant of Christ."

Thanksliving

TOPIC
Living thankfully

CHARACTER
A turkey

SUMMARY
A turkey tells us why Thanksgiving shouldn't be limited to one day of the year.

KEY VERSE
James 1:17-18
"Every good and perfect gift is from above, coming down from the Father of the heavenly lights, who does not change like shifting shadows. He chose to give us birth through the word of truth, that we might be a kind of firstfruits of all he created."

PROPS
Bird costume, or bird beak and feathers for "tail"; large handkerchief

OPTIONAL PROPS
Turkey platter (wave it when talking about being eaten)

PREP POINTERS
Use the large handkerchief to mop brow while talking about Thanksgiving dinner and for dramatic crying at the end!

SCHEDULE
Small-Group Warm-up (5-10 minutes)
Large-Group Presentation (5-10 minutes)
Small-Group Discussion (10-20 minutes)
Grand Finale (5-10 minutes)

SMALL-GROUP WARM-UP
Meet, greet and discuss the following questions in your small group:
- **How does your family celebrate Thanksgiving?**
- **What parts of Thanksgiving do you like best?**
- **What is the best gift you have ever received? Why is it the best?**

THANKSLIVING

LARGE-GROUP PRESENTATION

(TURKEY enters, gobbling. Stops with back to audience; flaps wings and then turns to audience.)
What's the matter? Haven't you ever seen a turkey before? Oh, I get it. I KNOW what you're thinking. You're thinking I'd look mighty GOOD sitting on your grandma's silver platter! Stop looking at my DRUM-STICKS like that! You're making me nervous. *(Pulls out handkerchief; mops brow.)*

WHAT'S THANKSGIVING?

Look, maybe I wouldn't feel so—AWKWARD if I knew a little bit more about this Thanksgiving Day you're all getting ready to celebrate! So, I hear it's a day of thanks, RIGHT? I GET that part. But thanks for WHAT? And thanks to WHO?

See, the farmer who owns me, he's got this kid, Hank. The kid takes me to SCHOOL yesterday for Show and Tell! And the teacher, she starts asking all the kids what they are THANKFUL for. The kids start saying things like, their homes, their families, their friends, their video games—well, that's just peachy. But who are they thankful TO? I mean, you say THANK YOU to someone when they do something NICE for you, right? So WHO are they THANKING? I don't GET it!

THANK WHO?

So I came home yesterday afternoon. I'm hanging out in the barn, telling the cow about the whole deal. She says maybe we should be thankful to the FARMER. You know, because he gives us a home and food to eat. All right, she had a point there.

But you know something? Those kids at the SCHOOL thought I was something special. I'm a pretty good-looking bird, if I DO say so myself. Maybe the FARMER should be thankful that he owns such a FINE feathered fowl! I mean, he DOES feed me, but he just scatters the feed all over the ground. I have to hunt around and peck it out of the DIRT! But the cows' and horses' feed goes in a big TROUGH! And in the house, people eat off PLATES with pretty little flowers all around the edges. That's not FAIR!

After all, a top-notch turkey like me should get treated JUST as well. And I think I should get to eat FIRST, too. What's a farm without a TURKEY? What could be MORE important on this farm than making ME well fed and happy?

OK, this whole day of Thanksgiving is coming up. But I want to know what's the POINT! I want to know exactly WHO you're thankful to and WHY. I'll be back, and I expect some ANSWERS! *(Exits.)*

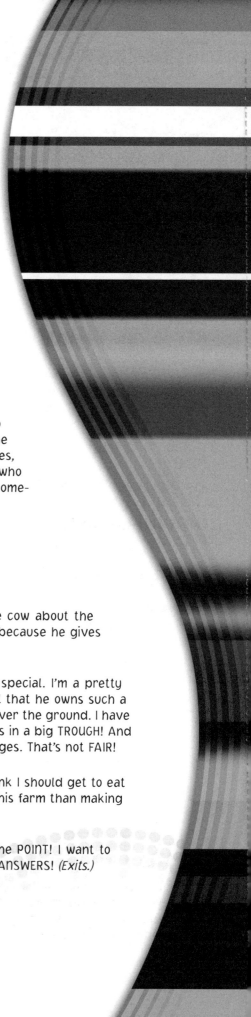

SMALL-GROUP DISCUSSION TIME

Provide one "Thanksliving" Discussion Sheet (p. 120) to each student. Invite students to find verses and discuss answers to questions on the sheet. Invite interested students to talk more with you about joining God's family (see "Leading a Child to Christ" on p. 11).

GRAND FINALE

(TURKEY returns.)

So—I think I get it now. Thanksgiving is WAY more than this one-day holiday! It's not about ME, ME, ME and what I have—OR what I think I DESERVE. I guess I need to be THANKFUL, instead of whining about what I think I DESERVE! After all—YOU ALL think I deserve to be on your grandma's PLATTER!

It sounds to THIS turkey like giving thanks to God should be an EVERYDAY thing! Hey, you shouldn't call this Thanksgiving—you should call it THANKSLIVING! Which would mean living EVERY day in thankfulness to God for His blessings! *(Begins to weep and wipes eyes.)* It's a beautiful thing—you being thankful to God and Him being PLEASED that you're thankful—Him blessing you and then you THANKING Him and Him blessing you MORE. It's TOUCHING! *(Sniffs.)* Oh, my. I must have feather dust in my eye.

Happy THANKSLIVING, everyone! Oh—and think about having TOFU turkey for your big dinner. I've HEARD it tastes JUST like CHICKEN! *(Exits.)*

Leader invites a student to read James 1:17-18 from the Key Verse Card. **Any turkey can COMPLAIN. But what are some ways we can really LIVE with thankfulness and show God we are grateful to Him?** (Read and obey His Word, not complain, spend time with Him in prayer, serve others, tell others about Him, tithe, etc.)

Close in prayer, thanking God for His gifts and blessings and asking God to help us be truly thankful every day so that we learn thanksLIVING.

Thanksliving

DISCUSSION SHEET

Who can we be thankful to?
Find Psalm 107:1.

What can keep us from being thankful to God?
Find Psalm 10:4, Philippians 2:3-4 and Philippians 2:14.

Why does God want us to thank Him?
Find Luke 17:11-19.

When should we be thankful to God?
Find 1 Thessalonians 5:18.

How can you show God you are thankful?
Find Psalm 107:21-22 and Hebrews 13:15-16.

What are other ways to show our thanks to God?

KEY VERSE CARD

1 Timothy 6:18-19
"Command them to do good, to be rich in good deeds, and to be generous and willing to share. In this way they will lay up treasure for themselves as a firm foundation for the coming age, so that they may take hold of the life that is truly life."

Superfriend!

TOPIC
Loving our siblings

CHARACTER
Superfriend

SUMMARY
Superfriend finds out that even superheroes can treat siblings not as evil enemies, but as valued allies, using God's supernatural strength.

KEY VERSE
1 John 3:10
"This is how we know who the children of God are and who the children of the devil are: Anyone who does not do what is right is not a child of God; nor is anyone who does not love his brother."

PROPS
Bible, superhero costume or cape (a large bath towel will do nicely)

OPTIONAL PROPS
Superhero T-shirt or a superhero logo drawn on paper and pinned to the front of a T-shirt

PREP POINTERS
This character is really a kid in a superhero costume. Play up the dramatic "superhero" language as a contrast for both humor and reality!

SCHEDULE
Small-Group Warm-up (5-10 minutes)
Large-Group Presentation (5-10 minutes)
Small-Group Discussion (10-20 minutes)
Grand Finale (5-10 minutes)

SMALL-GROUP WARM-UP
Meet, greet and discuss the following questions in your small group:
- **If you could change one thing about your family, what would you change?**
- **How many brothers or sisters do you have?**
- **When has a brother or sister really annoyed you? What happened?**

SUPERFRIEND!

LARGE-GROUP PRESENTATION

(SUPERFRIEND *enters, pausing to pose in superhero-type postures while speaking.*)

FASTER than a speeding TURTLE . . . more POWERFUL than a toy LOCOMO-TIVE . . . able to leap tall CHIHUAHUAS in a single bound! Never fear—SUPERFRIEND is here!

As far as superheroes go, my powers are pretty nonexistent. But when it comes to FRIENDSHIP, look no further! I AM—SUPERFRIEND!! Want someone to hang around with? Need someone to help with your homework? Want someone to share your secrets with? Need someone to talk to or play with or pray with? Call on ME—SUPERFRIEND!

A GOOD FRIEND

(*Relaxing from superhero pose.*) I used to wonder what it meant to be a good friend, so I went on a QUEST to find out. After asking a lot of people, praying and reading the Bible, I learned that a good friend is kind and compassionate and helpful and caring. Once I was able to put these SUPER behaviors into effect, I became—SUPERFRIEND!

Why, just the other day I helped a new kid at school who needed help getting around the school grounds. Later, I helped a friend with his homework. Actually . . . that didn't GO too well. I have this little brother who kept INTERRUPTING us.

(*Imitates little brother.*) "What are you doing? Can I draw on your paper? Will you make me some peanut butter toast?" That little brat can be SO pesky. I told him to go away and leave us alone. When he kept bothering us, I yelled at him. When he STILL wouldn't go away, I threatened him: "I'm telling MOM!"

He's such a DISTRACTION when I'm trying to utilize my superpowers of kindness and compassion toward my friends! But he's not the ONLY problem I have. I ALSO have an older SISTER who tries to keep me from my Superfriend duties. Just yesterday I was on the phone, talking a friend through her grief over a bad haircut. My sister had the NERVE to come up to me and say, "Hang up. I have to make a phone call." As if HER phone call would be more important than MINE.

She also just LOVES to make fun of my Superfriend suit. She says things like, "Oh look! There goes the caped SUPERGEEK!" How am I supposed to perform my Superfriend duties to the best of my ability when I have a brother and sister who try to THWART my efforts at every TURN? (*Strikes a superhero pose.*) Am I, SUPERFRIEND, a match for their powers of ANNOYANCE? Will GOOD FRIENDSHIP triumph over SIBLING RIVALRY? See what you can find out! Right now, I have to fly to my next SUPERFRIEND assignment! Up, up and AWAY! (*Exits in superhero pose.*)

SMALL-GROUP DISCUSSION TIME

Provide one "Superfriend!" Discussion Sheet (p. 124) to each student. Invite students to find verses and discuss answers to questions on the sheet. Invite interested students to talk more with you about joining God's family (see "Leading a Child to Christ" on p. 11).

GRAND FINALE

(SUPERFRIEND returns.)

Well, your research was certainly, uh, CLARIFYING. Talking about annoying siblings, I guess I've been one myself! I've been trying to be a good friend to everyone EXCEPT the people in my own HOME. Sometimes the people you LIVE with are the hardest people to get along with because they know you BEST.

But if I'm going to TRULY be Superfriend, I guess I need to show that kind of FRIENDSHIP even to my SIBLINGS, instead of only to my friends. *(Sighs.)* I'm not sure I'm worthy to wear my cape anymore. Being kind, compassionate, helpful and caring toward my little brother and big sister is NOT going to be EASY. They may not choose to be kind back, no matter what I do! But that doesn't give me an excuse NOT to love them and treat them kindly the way Jesus commands me to do. If I say that I love GOD, then I need to love EVEN my family members. I need to follow ALL His commands, not just the ones that are EASY for me. How I treat my brother and sister actually shows how much I love God.

(Strikes a superhero pose.) Loving my siblings is going to take SUPERHUMAN strength! Where will I get THAT superpower? Wait a minute, look! It's here in the Superhero Manual! *(Opens Bible.)* Philippians 4:13 says that I can do EVERYTHING through Christ who gives me strength! The strength to be a SUPERSIBLING comes from Jesus! HE'LL give me the strength—SUPERNATURAL POWER!

(Strikes a different superhero pose, speaking to the air.) Ahhh . . . With the power of GOD on my side, I'm beginning to feel SUPER again! I CAN be a Superfriend to my siblings— with God's SUPERNATURAL help! Look! Up in the sky! It's a bird! It's a plane! It's . . . nothing but a dirty ceiling tile! *(To audience.)* You didn't actually think I could FLY, did you? But I CAN do something AMAZING. I can be a Superfriend to my siblings because Christ gives me the strength! Up, up, and AWAY! *(Exits in superhero pose.)*

Leader invites a student to read 1 John 3:10 from the Key Verse Card. **Superfriend is right. It takes SUPERNATURAL strength to be able to really show love to our siblings. But it CAN be done! Let's ask God for His SUPERNATURAL help right now!**

Close in prayer, asking God to help students rely on His supernatural power to love the people in their homes.

Superfriend!

DISCUSSION SHEET

Did Jesus have siblings?
Find Luke 8:19-20.

Did Jesus' siblings always get along with Him?
Find John 7:4-5.

How does Jesus say we should treat others—including our siblings?
Find John 13:34-35.

What if your siblings are a real pain?
Find Matthew 7:3-5.

Are we commanded to love our siblings?
Find 1 John 4:20-21.

How do we show God that we love Him?
Find John 14:15.

Who are Jesus' siblings?
Find Mark 3:31-34.

KEY VERSE CARD

1 John 3:10
"This is how we know who the children of God are
and who the children of the devil are: Anyone who
does not do what is right is not a child of God; nor
is anyone who does not love his brother."

Take a Tip

TOPIC
Money and possessions

CHARACTER
Diner waitress

SUMMARY
The diner waitress learns that riches may not be found in money.

KEY VERSE
Proverbs 30:8-9
"Keep falsehood and lies far from me; give me neither poverty nor riches, but give me only my daily bread. Otherwise, I may have too much and disown you and say, 'Who is the LORD?' Or I may become poor and steal, and so dishonor the name of my God."

PROPS
Waitress uniform, receipt pad, pen, pennies

OPTIONAL PROPS
Magazine pictures of sports car, clothes, jewels, mansion, etc.

PREP POINTERS
To point out the waitress's money-focused character, toss pennies on the floor in random fashion ahead of time. Whenever she sees a penny, the waitress is compelled to pick it up and put it in her pocket.

SCHEDULE
Small-Group Warm-up (5-10 minutes)
Large-Group Presentation (5-10 minutes)
Small-Group Discussion (10-20 minutes)
Grand Finale (5-10 minutes)

SMALL-GROUP WARM-UP
Meet, greet and discuss the following questions in your small group:
- **Why do you think people need money?**
- **When have you earned money? For doing what?**
- **How did it make you feel to have money? What did you do with the money?**

Take a TIP

LARGE-GROUP PRESENTATION

(WAITRESS *enters; slaps a receipt on a table in front of audience member.*)
That'll be $22.63. You can pay the cashier up front. But don't forget to leave a TIP. I'm reminding you because you might FORGET like some of the OTHER customers that have been in today. Feel free to leave a BIG tip. I wouldn't REFUSE a $20 bill! HA! Don't look so shocked!

MONEY, MONEY

I really DID have a guy in here that tipped me $50 once. He was pretty OLD. I don't think he could SEE too well, so there's a chance he thought he was leaving me a FIVE, but hey—who am I to deprive the man of the JOY of making me so HAPPY?

And if there's ONE thing that makes me happy, it's MONEY. Beautiful, cold, hard cash. Bills of BLISS. Delightful dollars embossed with the pleasing portraits of past presidents. I wish I had MILLIONS of 'em!

Why, if I had LOTS of money, I'd go shopping every DAY. I'd climb into my brand-new, elegant, EXPENSIVE purple sports car. I'd drive to the CLASSIEST stores and buy the BEST clothes money could buy. Twenty-four new outfits, one for every HOUR of the DAY—WITH matching shoes and handbags, of course! Then I'd go to the JEWELRY store and I wouldn't come out until I was absolutely DRIPPING with diamonds and gems. I'd even get a TIARA!

TIME, TIME

Then I would drive to the airport to board my private JET for a quick trip to HAWAII for lunch. While there, I would see how things looked on my HUGE YACHT. Then I'd fly back home to my 15,000-square-foot MANSION. My staff of servants would prepare my bath in my Olympic pool-sized bathtub where I would soak for an entire HOUR in pure spring water sprinkled with ROSE petals. My chef would prepare a gourmet meal for me to enjoy as I sat surrounded by the elegant furnishings and fine art in my dining room.

My day would end as I'd crawl between pure satin sheets on a bed so soft, it would be like sleeping on a CLOUD. You can't tell ME life wouldn't be absolutely PERFECT if I had the money to have THAT kind of lifestyle.

NOW, NOW

Who am I kidding? I'm NEVER going to get rich working at THIS dinky diner. I need to think of what ELSE I can do to get wealthy. I've spent about $900 on LOTTERY tickets so far, but I don't think that's a good way to go. I wish I could become a ROCK STAR. THEY'RE rich! The only PROBLEM with that is, I don't play an instrument—and people have told me that my singing sounds like a CAT in PAIN. (*Demonstrates awful singing.*) What do you think?

I've thought about going on that *Survival* reality show, but I would like to retain SOME of my dignity. It's EVEN crossed my mind to rob a bank, but when I was a kid in church, I DID learn that stealing is wrong.

Wait! Maybe that's it! ANOTHER thing I learned in church was that God answers PRAYERS! Maybe all I have to do is PRAY and GOD will make me rich! Hey, you've all got those books, uh, whadda-ya-call-'ems? Bibles, yeah! Look in there for me to find out what it says about God and money, will ya? I'm going to go start praying for my FORTUNE right now! (*Exits.*)

SMALL-GROUP DISCUSSION TIME

Provide one "Take a Tip" Discussion Sheet (p. 128) to each student. Invite students to find verses and discuss answers to questions on the sheet. Invite interested students to talk more with you about joining God's family (see "Leading a Child to Christ" on p. 11).

GRAND FINALE

(WAITRESS returns.)

Guess what happened when I was praying for money? I was praying, BEGGING, "God, PLEASE make me rich! I promise to always be good and never miss church and to always help old ladies cross the street!"

When I OPENED my eyes, I looked down and saw a PENNY on the ground. I said to myself, "God has a SICK sense of HUMOR!" But then I noticed what the penny SAYS.

It says, "In God We Trust." Do ya think GOD is trying to TELL me something?!

I've been thinking that being RICH would make me happy and give me a good life. BUT maybe GOD is telling me that if I TRUST in Him, THEN I'll be happy and have a good life—even if I ONLY have THIS penny to my name—and I DO have LOTS more pennies! *(Pats pocket happily.)*

You guys found out that God has a treasure in mind for ALL of us if we trust Him. But it's not like an expensive purple sports car! Jesus told His disciples that in His Father's house are MANY mansions. He said He was going there to prepare a PLACE for people who put their trust in Him. And He paid a VERY HIGH PRICE in order to do that for us. He paid with His LIFE. SO I guess that means I'm pretty VALUABLE—a treasure to God! So I guess that ALSO means it's high time to start living like the valuable person I AM—not rich with money or POSSESSIONS, but rich with LOVE and KINDNESS and JOY and PEACE and all those other things that God wants to GIVE me!

Oh, I'm not saying that there's not still a part of me that would love to have a million bucks and buy anything I wanted—but I don't need that to make my life WORTHWHILE. What I really NEED is a close relationship with Jesus. Because SOMEDAY, when I'm in heaven—where gold is used as STREET pavement—I'll THANK God for making me RICH by giving me this PENNY. It's the BIGGEST tip I ever got! *(Exits.)*

Leader invites a student to read Proverbs 30:8-9 from the Key Verse Card. **TV and movies tell us that if we have more money, we will be happy. But God's Word makes it clear that the GREATEST riches in life are to know HIM—and that is ABSOLUTELY FREE to us, though it cost Jesus everything. Let's thank Him.**

Close in prayer, thanking God for His riches of grace in saving us and drawing us close to Him.

Take a Tip

DISCUSSION SHEET

If we pray to God, will He make us rich?
Find James 4:3.

According to God's Word, does wealth bring us contentment?
Find Philippians 4:12-13 and 1 Timothy 6:8-10.

When can money be a BAD thing?
Find Matthew 19:21-24.

If God gives you financial wealth, how does He want you to use it?
Find 1 Timothy 6:17-19.

How rich was Jesus?
Find Luke 9:58.

How does God want to benefit and care for His children?
Find Psalm 145:17-19.

Why should a Christian value relationship with God more than money?
Find 1 John 2:15-17 and Matthew 6:19-21.

Can't we love money AND God?
Find Matthew 6:24.

KEY VERSE CARD

Proverbs 30:8-9
"Keep falsehood and lies far from me; give me neither poverty nor riches, but give me only my daily bread. Otherwise, I may have too much and disown you and say, 'Who is the Lord?' Or I may become poor and steal, and so dishonor the name of my God."

Mission Control

TOPIC
Obeying parents

CHARACTER
Astronaut

SUMMARY
The astronaut helps us remember why we want to listen to those who have more information than we do.

KEY VERSE
Ephesians 6:1-3
"Children, obey your parents in the Lord, for this is right. 'Honor your father and mother'—which is the first commandment with a promise—'that it may go well with you and that you may enjoy long life on the earth.'"

PROPS
Astronaut costume or T-shirt with an astronaut logo, light blue face paint

OPTIONAL PROPS
Cage containing white mice, earpiece to wear and remove

PREP POINTERS
A blue face is an important part of the story; face paint will be easiest to remove.

SCHEDULE
Small-Group Warm-up (5-10 minutes)
Large-Group Presentation (5-10 minutes)
Small-Group Discussion (10-20 minutes)
Grand Finale (5-10 minutes)

SMALL-GROUP WARM-UP
Meet, greet and discuss the following questions in your small group:
- **When have you followed directions to do something you'd never done?**
- **What happened? Was it easy or hard to do?**
- **If you described your experience following directions in one word, what would it be?**

MISSION CONTROL

LARGE-GROUP PRESENTATION

(ASTRONAUT *enters, shaking hands with random individuals and waving.*)
Good evening. It's a pleasure to be here. My name is Annie (or Arnie) and I'm an astronaut for NASA. I just got back from my first space shuttle mission. It was a thrill!

IN MY EAR

I've wanted to travel in space ALL MY LIFE. I wanted to float weightlessly about and look down from up high at our amazing planet, Earth. Oh, the FREEDOM! My trip into space was everything I thought it would be!

Well, ALMOST. You see, I wasn't COMPLETELY free. I had an EARPIECE in my ear at all times and I was CONSTANTLY receiving orders from Mission Control—CONSTANTLY! Mission Control told me when to EAT, when to WORK, when to EXERCISE, when to SLEEP. When my body temperature was down, they told me to turn up the heat in my SPACE suit. When my heart rate was elevated, they told me to sit down and REST.

NO MORE NOISE

EVERY MINUTE, they were there in my head, telling me what to DO. Well, one day, I'd just had ENOUGH. All I wanted was a little QUIET while I looked out the window at the planets and stars.

(Sighs.) So I did a NASA no-no: I took out my earpiece for the radio from Mission Control and floated unstrapped from my seat. At first, it was absolutely thrilling—NO one to BUG me! I floated in pure peace and quiet as I gazed out the window into the vastness of space.

But suddenly, something SLAMMED INTO the shuttle! Since I wasn't strapped in, I began spinning! As I tumbled about, my foot accidentally kicked the TOILET flush mechanism. This released BRIGHT BLUE water globules that floated around inside the shuttle. THEN I banged my elbow against a table where one of the science experiments was being conducted. Suddenly, 40 WHITE MICE were now ALSO floating around!

But the WORST part was when my head banged into the CONTROL console. I hit the GRAVITY button and INSTANTLY—me, 40 white mice and a GALLON of BRIGHT BLUE TOILET WATER all came CRASHING down!

I lay there on the floor with a bruised foot, a sore elbow, a goose egg on my head—and a BLUE face. Forty BLUE MICE were running chaotically around the cabin! My fellow astronauts—who had KEPT their connection to Mission Control—had received the message to BUCKLE UP. THEY were NOT AMUSED. I thought they might throw me out the CARGO BAY doors!

NO BETTER CONTROL

Let me tell you, I was REAL sorry I had tuned out Mission Control! If I had been LISTENING, I would have known to buckle up. We were entering an ASTEROID shower!

You know, Mission Control is a LOT like having parents. Always there, telling you what to do and when to do it. I KNOW they can be annoying sometimes. But they are even MORE important than Mission Control. What does the Bible tell us about parents? Take a look at that for me, would you, Space Cadets? I really have GOT to try to get this blue TOILET BOWL dye off my face! (Exits.)

SMALL-GROUP DISCUSSION TIME

Provide one "Mission Control" Discussion Sheet (p. 132) to each student. Invite students to find verses and discuss answers to questions on the sheet. Invite interested students to talk more with you about joining God's family (see "Leading a Child to Christ" on p. 11).

GRAND FINALE

(ASTRONAUT returns.)

You know, Space Cadets, one BIG way God shows His care for us is by giving us parents or guardians who give us direction and guidance. They have lived LONGER than us. They have experienced MORE of life. That means, like it or not, they have SUPERIOR INFORMATION!

Any astronaut who tries to spacewalk without being tethered to the shuttle will just float aimlessly away into space FOREVER. That's a LOT like listening to our parents, too. If we don't stay in the guidance of our parents, we can end up drifting away aimlessly, getting into who knows WHAT kind of trouble and heartache!

I guess you could say that parents and guardians have a MISSION from God: to see that their children are brought up to be healthy, happy people who love God. God has given us a command to honor and obey them. I know, I KNOW. They're not PERFECT. But then again, are WE? Just like my experience with Mission Control, we should think twice before we forget or ignore their guidance. Remember, the command to honor our parents comes with a promise: that we'll LIVE LONG and PROSPER! *(Smiles, gives a salute and exits.)*

Leader invites a student to read Ephesians 6:1-3 from the Key Verse Card. **Often, we think we know best for our lives. That is because we don't realize how much we DON'T know. Like it or not, it's true that understanding comes only with age and experience! So next time your parents tell you to do something, remember Mission Control. You don't want to be covered in blue toilet water like our friend!**

Close in prayer, thanking God for our parents and guardians and asking Him to help students appreciate and listen to their guidance.

Mission Control

DISCUSSION SHEET

How does God want you to treat your parents?
Find Exodus 20:12.

What happens if you honor your father and mother?
Find Deuteronomy 5:16.

How does the way you act affect your parents?
Find Proverbs 10:1 and Proverbs 11:29.

Why does God WANT your parents to discipline (teach) you?
Find Proverbs 29:17.

What's a reason to honor your father and mother?
Find James 1:22.

KEY VERSE CARD

Ephesians 6:1-3
"Children, obey your parents in the Lord, for this is right. 'Honor your father and mother'—which is the first commandment with a promise—'that it may go well with you and that you may enjoy long life on the earth.'"

Turkey Talk

TOPIC
One way of salvation

CHARACTER
Turkey rancher

SUMMARY
The turkey rancher helps us understand why Jesus did what He did to save us.

KEY VERSE
Romans 5:8
"But God demonstrates his own love for us in this: While we were still sinners, Christ died for us."

PROPS
Ranch clothing, piece of hay for chewing

OPTIONAL PROPS
Offstage lightning and thunder production (flick light switches for lightning and twist a thin metal cookie sheet for thunder)

PREP POINTERS
This character can be a corny or a serious rancher of turkeys.

SCHEDULE
Small-Group Warm-up (5-10 minutes)
Large-Group Presentation (5-10 minutes)
Small-Group Discussion (10-20 minutes)
Grand Finale (5-10 minutes)

SMALL-GROUP WARM-UP
Meet, greet and discuss the following questions in your small group:
- **What's an animal you think is funny? Why?**
- **What's an animal you think is unusual? Why?**
- **What is something an animal does that you think is a smart idea?**

TURKEY TALK

LARGE-GROUP PRESENTATION

(TURKEY RANCHER *enters, chewing on a long piece of hay.*)
Howdy, y'all! My name is Bobbie Sue. I'm a rancher—but I betcha can't GUESS what I raise. *(Responds to audience's guesses.)* I raise TURKEYS! I live on a TURKEY ranch!

I LOVE turkeys! They're pretty funny. Turkeys always do things that make me laugh! They can act real dumb sometimes. When it rains, if they are not under a shelter, my turkeys will look up at the rain to see what popped them on the head. They'll stand out in the rain until the rain soaks 'em to the skin. Then they get sick and DIE! They aren't the brightest critters, but I love 'em.

Anyway, what I wanted tell you was what my turkeys taught ME about JESUS. That's right! Now, my parents have been takin' me to church since before I had my first tooth. I've listened to Miss Mertie, my Sunday School teacher, teach about Jesus all my LIFE. But I never understood WHY Jesus had to DIE for our sins.

WHY did He have to do it the way He did? Couldn't Jesus have just yelled out so the whole WORLD could hear, "Believe that I'm the Savior and you'll go to heaven!" Or couldn't He have sent a bunch of angels to tell everybody about Him? I just didn't understand why Jesus had to come to Earth and DIE so that we could go to heaven!

WANT TO KNOW

Well, one time in Sunday School, I asked Miss Mertie, "So, tell me. Why did Jesus have to DIE for my sins? Why didn't He save us some OTHER way?"

Now Miss Mertie's just the sweetest lady. She bakes the best oatmeal cookies you ever ate. She looked at me and said, "I'll be praying for you, Bobbie Sue, that God shows you why Jesus DID what He did in the WAY He did it."

I thanked her, grabbed another oatmeal cookie and headed home.

EASTER DRESSED

Well, I kept WAITING for God to answer her prayer. But I went back to Sunday School for WEEKS and told her nothing had happened.

Easter Sunday was soon upon us. (Note: If presenter is male, adjust clothing descriptions as needed.) My mom had sewed me a frilly new dress with ruffles and lace and pearly buttons. She curled my hair and pinned it back in pink barrettes. I had new white shoes and a bright-white pair of gloves. When I looked at myself in the mirror, I hardly KNEW me, I looked so pretty!

But as I stood there, a flash of lightning exploded outdoors. It was followed by a loud boom of thunder. Oh, NO! I looked out the window. It was raining BUCKETS! But that wasn't ALL I saw: ALL my turkeys were out wandering!

NO WAY

I threw open the window and started yelling, "Get in the SHED, you TURKEYS! You're going to get SOAKED and KILL yourselves!" They looked up, confused. They heard me, but no matter how LOUD I yelled, they kept standing in the rain! They didn't have the sense to go inside where they'd be safe.

Then I saw our farmhand, Hank, out by the shed. I hollered, "Hank! Help! Get my turkeys inside before they get soaked!"

Hank said, "I'll try!" He tried to chase the birds toward the shed. But since they didn't KNOW him, they wouldn't GO—because they were SCARED of him! They gobbled and scattered, but since they didn't know him, they just PECKED him in the backside and ran away!

ONLY WAY

Well, there was only ONE THING left to do! I'd have to save my turkeys MYSELF! I RAN outside and called them. I CHASED them and CAUGHT them and FINALLY I got them all SAFELY into the shed. What a JOB!

Of course, I got soaking wet. My beautiful new dress was muddy and sopping wet. It hung like a rag. My hair was dripping and flat. My shoes were a muddy mess and my gloves were not white any longer! But I had no time to change. We had to leave right THEN for church. But at least ALL my turkeys were now SAFE. I was glad of that!

TURKEY TRUTH!

Anyway, when I got to Sunday School, Miss Mertie took one look at me and said, "Bobbie Sue, what HAPPENED to you?"

Well, I told her the whole story, how I tried to yell from the window, how Hank had tried to get the turkeys out of the rain but they didn't follow him, and how I finally had to do it myself.

And you know what Miss Mertie did? She laughed and laughed! I asked her, "What's so funny?"

She said, "Oh, Bobbie Sue, God ANSWERED my prayer for you! I asked God to show you WHY Jesus did what He did the way He did it. And He DID!"

Now I was a little befuddled by that. So would you help me? See if YOU can figure out what she meant! *(Exits.)*

SMALL-GROUP DISCUSSION TIME

Provide one "Turkey Talk" Discussion Sheet (p. 136) to each student. Invite students to find verses and discuss answers to questions on the sheet. Invite interested students to talk more with you about joining God's family (see "Leading a Child to Christ" on p. 11).

GRAND FINALE

(TURKEY RANCHER returns.)

Okey dokey, so now I understand. We're just like those turkeys of mine. There was only ONE WAY to save them from themselves! And God loves us too much to just let us go out and kill ourselves!

So THAT'S why Jesus HAD TO come to live among us—He showed us what God is like. And Jesus was the ONLY one who ever could live a PERFECT life—He was God's PERFECT sacrifice to pay for our sins. He was the ONLY ONE who could take the punishment for our sins and He DID it. I guess He COULD have yelled from heaven or sent angels. But THEN we'd have died in our sins—separated from God forever!

When I remember that Jesus died for my sins, now I understand WHY He did WHAT He did the WAY He did it—thanks to my TURKEYS! There was NO OTHER WAY to save us! THAT'S the best news ever! See you later! *(Exits.)*

Leader invites a student to read Romans 5:8 from the Key Verse Card. **There's often more than one way to do a thing. But in the case of paying the price and taking the punishment for our sins, Jesus took the ONLY way. And He is the ONLY one who could do that! Let's thank Him for loving us that much!**

Close in prayer, thanking God for His great love and for Jesus' willingness to take the punishment for our sins.

Turkey Talk

DISCUSSION SHEET

Who are sinners that need to be saved?
Find Romans 3:10-11.

What do we need to be saved from?
Find Romans 3:23 and 2 Thessalonians 1:8-9.

Do people always know they need to be saved?
Find Proverbs 14:12.

Why did Jesus come down to Earth and die on a cross to save us
instead of another way?
Find Romans 5:6-8, Hebrews 9:22 and 1 John 4:10.

Why was Jesus willing to die for you?
Find John 3:16

What can you do to earn your way to heaven?
Find Ephesians 2:8-9.

Is there another way to heaven than to accept Jesus as your Savior?
Find Acts 4:12.

Have you asked Jesus to be your Savior? Do you know you are going to heaven?

KEY VERSE CARD

Romans 5:8
"But God demonstrates his own love for us in this:
While we were still sinners, Christ died for us."

Superstar

TOPIC
Our value in Christ

CHARACTER
Superstar (rock or pop music singing star)

SUMMARY
The "superstar" learns about the value we have in God's eyes—with or without superstar status in this world.

KEY VERSE
1 John 2:15-17
"Do not love the world or anything in the world. If anyone loves the world, the love of the Father is not in him. For everything in the world—the cravings of sinful man, the lust of his eyes and the boasting of what he has and does—comes not from the Father but from the world. The world and its desires pass away, but the man who does the will of God lives forever."

PROPS
Guitar, pen, fashionable clothes

OPTIONAL PROPS
Wig, sunglasses, gloves, fancy jacket

PREP POINTERS
The superstar character can be as over-the-top as you'd like it to be. Consider wearing a wig, sunglasses and other disguising items that you remove one at a time as you confess to being an ordinary person.

SCHEDULE
Small-Group Warm-up (5-10 minutes)
Large-Group Presentation (5-10 minutes)
Small-Group Discussion (10-20 minutes)
Grand Finale (5-10 minutes)

SMALL-GROUP WARM-UP
Meet, greet and discuss the following questions in your small group:
- **What famous person would you like to meet?**
- **What would you like about this person? What might you not like?**
- **How do you think a famous person feels about him- or herself? Why?**

SUPERSTAR

LARGE-GROUP PRESENTATION

(SUPERSTAR enters, waving as if to a huge crowd.)
Thank you! Thank you! I LOVE you ALL! Of COURSE I'd be happy to give an autograph. It's a pleasure to be here tonight. When my agent asked me to come and give an interview, I was HAPPY to say yes. After all, I was once just a plain, ordinary person like YOU.

GOT IT ALL

But NOW I have a very successful recording career. THREE of my CDs have just gone DOUBLE PLATINUM. And did you hear about my FILM? I have a new movie coming out, which I'm sure is just the START of a very successful film career. It was SUCH fun. My house? Oh, I have a 36-room mansion in the Hollywood Hills. Then there's the Malibu place. That's just a cottage, really. Car? I drive a custom-built Mercedes—it's one of a kind.

Would you like for me to sing my latest Number One Hit for you? *(Waits for audience's response.)*

I said, "Do you want to HEAR it?" *(Waits for audience's response.)* Let me hear some NOISE! *(Waits for audience's response.)* OK—put your HANDS together like this. Here we go!

JUST THE TRUTH

(Begins singing, hits bad notes, stops, looks at audience.) Oh, who am I KIDDING? I'm NOT a famous singer. I just thought you would all LIKE me better if you thought I was rich and famous. EVERYBODY loves FAMOUS people, right? They have the BEST lives, don't they? All the movie stars and rock stars are rich, talented and famous. People SCREAM their names and try to dress like them and BE like them! I just wanted you all to think I was—well, SPECIAL.

(Removes disguising items while talking.) After all, what's SPECIAL about a plain, ordinary person like me? NOBODY screams my name when I walk into a room. I don't get fan letters. My picture is NEVER on the covers of magazines. I live in an ordinary house in an ordinary neighborhood. I go to an ordinary school where I get ordinary grades. I'm NOT special. The votes are all in—and guess what? I'm ORDINARY!

ORDINARY ME

Do YOU ever feel that way? I mean, what's life going to be LIKE if you never become FAMOUS? What if you end up with the SAME lives as your PARENTS? What if you're never FAMOUS or POPULAR or ADORED by MILLIONS? Who would think you were WONDERFUL, even if you weren't rich and famous? What would make you SPECIAL? Unique? You guys see if you can figure it out, will ya? I'm going to sit over here and practice being ORDINARY. *(Exits.)*

SMALL-GROUP DISCUSSION TIME

Provide one "Superstar" Discussion Sheet (p. 140) to each student. Invite students to find verses and discuss answers to questions on the sheet. Invite interested students to talk more with you about joining God's family (see "Leading a Child to Christ" on p. 11).

GRAND FINALE

(SUPERSTAR returns.)

Well, imagine that! I've been a "Superstar" all along and I didn't even KNOW it! What could be more AMAZING than being GOD'S own kid, part of His royal FAMILY? That's pretty SPECIAL, even for an ordinary person!

OK, so I'll never have hordes of fans screaming out my name. But I think I'd rather be known for being a faithful follower of Christ than for being some superficial person who's IMPORTANT today and FORGOTTEN tomorrow. Besides, my friends and family love me, too—even if I CAN'T sing a NOTE! *(Tries singing again, stops singing and then exits.)*

Leader invites a student to read 1 John 2:15-17 from the Key Verse Card. **It's easy to think that what the world has to offer us will make us feel special, loved and important. But God wants us to understand that it won't—and that HE thinks we are special, loved and important RIGHT NOW. We don't have to become famous! Let's thank God for that.**

Close in prayer, thanking God for His amazing love and for making us important, loved and special because we are part of His family.

Superstar

DISCUSSION SHEET

What does God want to do for us?
Find Psalm 37:4.

According to the Bible, will we find happiness in being rich?
Find 1 Timothy 6:9-10.

Will we find happiness in being famous or popular?
Find Proverbs 18:24.

How well does God know us?
Find Psalm 139:1-4.

How much does God really love us?
Find Romans 5:6-8.

What kinds of plans does God have for our lives?
Find Jeremiah 29:11-13.

How can we be superstars for Christ?
Find Philippians 2:14-16.

Who will always make us feel like superstars?
Find Zephaniah 3:17.

KEY VERSE CARD

1 John 2:15-17
"Do not love the world or anything in the world. If anyone loves the world, the love of the Father is not in him. For everything in the world—the cravings of sinful man, the lust of his eyes and the boasting of what he has and does—comes not from the Father but from the world. The world and its desires pass away, but the man who does the will of God lives forever."

Jaws

TOPIC
Power of words

CHARACTER
Surfer dude or dudette (written for a male)

SUMMARY
The surfer encounters the jaws of a land shark and learns how words can shred—and not in a good way!

KEY VERSE
Ephesians 4:29
"Do not let any unwholesome talk come out of your mouths, but only what is helpful for building others up according to their needs, that it may benefit those who listen."

PROPS
Surfer clothes, surfboard

OPTIONAL PROPS
Sunglasses, wild hair wig (to look like salty, sandy hair)

PREP POINTERS
Practice your "Yo, dude!" slack-jawed speech and attitude to be more convincing!

SCHEDULE
Small-Group Warm-up (5-10 minutes)
Large-Group Presentation (5-10 minutes)
Small-Group Discussion (10-20 minutes)
Grand Finale (5-10 minutes)

SMALL-GROUP WARM-UP

Meet, greet and discuss the following questions in your small group:
- **When have you heard someone say mean words to another person?**
- **What happened as a result?**
- **What is the kindest thing anyone has ever said to you?**
- **How did those words make you feel?**

JAWS

LARGE-GROUP PRESENTATION

(SURFER enters, carrying surfboard, nearly hitting a few people; looks around and greets audience members.)
Yo, dudes! 'Sup?! *(Turns, nearly hits another person with surfboard.)*
Oh, yeah, sorry about the gear. I've been out surfin'! The conditions were RAD today! The sets were awesome. The waves were glassy and peelin' off in perfect lefts. And the tubes were GNARLY!

TUBING

I love riding in the tubes. That's how I got my nickname—Tubemonster. I just LOVE to drop in on a five-footer, carve down the face and then slip into the tube. Barrels, curls, call them what you want, there's no other feeling like ridin' in one!

SHARKING

Actually, today was my first time back to my favorite beach after an encounter with JAWS. If you think I mean a great white shark, you're totally wrong.

Dude, here's the story. About six months ago, I grabbed my board and headed out to catch some waves. The surf was dumping, which was a bummer, but sometimes I just like being out there even if the conditions are not the best. Anyway, I dropped in on this one wave and got totally POUNDED. I did an endo and wiped out to the highest order. Dude, I was so dizzy and waterlogged, I just sort of crawled up to shore for some chill time.

So I'm sittin' in the sand, just chillin' and tryin' to recover. This guy comes up to me and starts RIPPIN' into me.

He says, "You're the worst surfer I've ever SEEN! You couldn't catch a wave in a KIDDIE POOL. Your STANCE stinks, you've got no moves and you LOOK like a BOZO out there. And your board shorts are so UGLY that they remind me of PUKE."

Then he walked away. Dudes, forget the WAVE that had pounded me. That was NOTHING compared to this! I had just been SHREDDED by the most DANGEROUS of land sharks, Jaws. After he said all those things, I kept thinking about it. Every time I thought about going out to catch some more waves, ALL of his words came back to me. I KNEW it was BOGUS, but it TOTALLY affected me. For days, I would sit on the shore and his words would replay in my head: "You're the WORST surfer ever. Your board shorts look like puke." It was like a mental WIPE OUT!

SHREDDING

That land shark used his OVERSIZED JAWS to shred my confidence to PIECES! The thing is, I'm actually a pretty good surfer! I've won a few local competitions. Nothing major, but dude, I don't STINK. I'm tellin' ya, I always thought WAVES were powerful, but WORDS are like, WAY heavy. They have the power to affect how people feel and think and act—or NOT act, in my case.

And the DEAL is, we ALL possess that power. But it's like the waves, dude. You have to learn how to USE the power, CONTROL the power. So why don't you dive into the BIG Word and find out more about OUR words. 'Cause I'm TOTALLY starvin'! So I'm gonna, like, go don the apron. Later! *(Exits, carrying board, nearly hitting several audience members.)*

Provide one "Jaws" Discussion Sheet (p. 144) to each student. Invite students to find verses and discuss answers to questions on the sheet. Invite interested students to talk more with you about joining God's family (see "Leading a Child to Christ" on p. 11).

GRAND FINALE

(SURFER returns, carrying board.)

Dude, I've got to admit that I haven't always been COOL with the way I talk. I totally used to call my little brother names. And even while I was DOIN' it, I knew it hurt him. But I've been thinking about how JAWS's words felt to ME. Now I see how wrong those kinds of words can be.

Dude, I'm going to take the little guppy out for some ice cream and ask for his forgiveness. I don't want to hurt him. I even LOVE that little grem! Besides, God wants me to care about him.

And if I ever run into any land sharks again, I'll remember that it's not what THEY think about me that matters; it's what GOD thinks that matters. I don't even have to argue with them because God knows the truth—and that's all that matters. Dude, doing things God's way is RADICAL! He totally wants us to say good stuff and be kind. He wants us to use words that build each other up, not SHRED each other! That's just awesome. Dude, I am so stoked about Jesus. He's totally righteous. And He promises to HELP us say good stuff! Later! *(Exits.)*

Leader invites a student to read Ephesians 4:29 from the Key Verse Card. **Whoa, dudes. This is radical truth. Now your job is to think of one person to whom you've said some really shredding words. You know who that person is. What could you say to that person tomorrow? Let's take a tip from the surfer and ask God to help us say those words and not use our JAWS to shred anyone anymore!**

Close in prayer, asking God's help in keeping our words from hurting others.

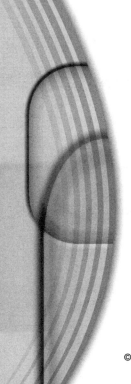

Jaws

DISCUSSION SHEET

What will people know about us by the way we use our words?
Find Proverbs 17:27-28 and Proverbs 18:2.

What's the problem with swearing?
Find Matthew 5:33-37.

What's wrong with arguing and complaining?
Find 2 Timothy 2:23-24 and Proverbs 17:14.

How does God feel about saying cusswords or telling dirty jokes?
Find Ephesians 5:4 and Colossians 3:8.

Why should we not mock people or call them names?
Find Psalm 15:1-3.

What's a way kind words can affect us?
Find Proverbs 16:24.

KEY VERSE CARD

Ephesians 4:29
"Do not let any unwholesome talk come out of your mouths,
but only what is helpful for building others up according to
their needs, that it may benefit those who listen."

An Appointment with God

TOPIC
Prayer

CHARACTER
Secretary

SUMMARY
A secretary (male or female) considers ways to help God answer prayer efficiently—or not!

KEY VERSE
Philippians 4:6-7
"Do not be anxious about anything, but in everything, by prayer and petition, with thanksgiving, present your requests to God. And the peace of God, which transcends all understanding, will guard your hearts and your minds in Christ Jesus."

PROPS
Desk or table, chair, Bible, appointment calendar, clock or watch, telephone, computer

OPTIONAL PROPS
Sign for wall or desktop that reads "ALL TIED UP, INC."

PREP POINTERS
Place prop items on the desk or table to look like a secretary's desk.

SCHEDULE
Small-Group Warm-up (5-10 minutes)
Large-Group Presentation (5-10 minutes)
Small-Group Discussion (10-20 minutes)
Grand Finale (5-10 minutes)

SMALL-GROUP WARM-UP
Meet, greet and discuss the following questions in your small group:
- **Tell about a time a person you know has prayed for something.**
- **What was the result of that prayer?**
- **Was the answer fast or slow? Surprising or expected?**
- **What do you think is the best time to pray? Why?**

AN APPOINTMENT WITH GOD

LARGE-GROUP PRESENTATION

(SECRETARY *sits behind desk and begins checking computer, opening appointment calendar, etc. Looks up, realizing there are visitors in the room.)*

EFFICIENT WORK

Hello! Welcome to ALL TIED UP, INCORPORATED! We're always glad to have visitors. I'm the executive secretary (your name).

All Tied Up is the PREMIERE shoelace manufacturer in the region! We make high-quality shoelaces of all kinds, styles and colors. We began as a small company that made only short shoelaces for men's dress shoes. But through good ORGANIZATION, we increased our efficiency. That made us able to expand into other kinds of laces.

On Monday, we make short, black laces. On Tuesday, we make colored bootlaces. On Wednesday, we make white sneaker laces, and so on. Because we are SO well organized, we've become VERY SUCCESSFUL!

Now as executive secretary, ORGANIZATION is VITAL to my job. When I was young, I took the "All B. Timely Correspondence Course." This was an IMPORTANT step in increasing my efficiency. I learned how to keep everything on schedule! Then I went on to take classes in organization. Now I have an ADVANCED degree in SCHEDULING and MEMO POSTING!

PERFECT ORGANIZATION

My abilities in organization and efficiency have served me well both professionally AND personally. My boss, Mr. Longlace, attributes HIS success to the fact that I keep him ORGANIZED. He never misses a phone call or a scheduled meeting. He can ALWAYS find the forms and contracts he needs because of my impeccable filing system.

As for me, my personal life is COMPLETELY efficient. I NEVER send late birthday cards, I NEVER forget to pick up my dry cleaning and I am NEVER late for church. I LOVE efficiency!

In fact, here's my daily schedule—it's SO efficient! I'm up at 6. From 6-6:15, I have an appointment with God for prayer. Promptly at 6:15, my coffee is ready. I read my Bible while I drink my coffee. I eat breakfast at 6:45, shower at 7. Then I dress, read the paper and leave for work at precisely 7:30, using the most efficient route my computer recommends. I work from exactly 8 until noon, when I eat lunch. From 12:30-12:45, I take a brisk walk. Precisely at 12:45, I have prayer time until 1:00 . . .

HEAVENLY HELP

Did you notice that I SCHEDULE my prayer times? Without making and keeping an appointment with God, time slips away and I don't pray. You know what they say: "Fail to plan, plan to fail"!

(Stops; thinks.) Speaking of prayer, have you ever prayed for something and it seemed that the answer wasn't EFFICIENT? That nothing HAPPENED? Or the answer was DIFFFERENT from what you expected? It seems to happen quite often. Now, I KNOW God loves us and listens to our prayers, so I think that giving such IRREGULAR answers must be because He gets BEHIND in PRAYER ANSWERING! He must get MILLIONS of requests every day. Maybe He needs help with ORGANIZATION. If THAT'S the case, I DO have several helpful ideas! For instance:

INBOX ANGELS

God could appoint a team of angels who organize His "In Box." THEY would listen to prayers to categorize the requests: you know, Health Requests, Material Requests, Political Requests . . . I suppose they'd need a category for "other" requests, too.

Now, as the requests are organized into categories, God would have certain days to WORK ON each category—JUST the way we do it here at ALL TIED UP, INCORPORATED! He could answer Health Requests on Monday, Material Requests on Tuesday, Political Requests on Wednesday . . . that would give Him SEVERAL days free to handle requests from the "other" category. My system should have God answering prayer efficiently in NO time!

GUIDELINES

Of course, in OUR business, we have guidelines we follow. For instance, a shoelace salesperson must remember to call a SHOE salesperson in the MORNINGS—before SHOE salespersons get finger fatigue from tying so many shoelaces! Finger fatigue makes shoe salespersons quite cranky about shoelaces in general and therefore UNRECEPTIVE to shoelace business altogether!

I wonder what guidelines GOD might have for His PRAYER business? Oh, I know! The BIBLE is FULL of God's guidelines. *(Opens Bible.)* Let's just take a look in here to find out what God's guidelines are! *(Begins reading Bible; ignores audience.)*

SMALL-GROUP DISCUSSION TIME

Provide one "An Appointment with God" Discussion Sheet (p. 148) to each student. Invite students to find verses and discuss answers to questions on the sheet. Invite interested students to talk more with you about joining God's family (see "Leading a Child to Christ" on p. 11).

GRAND FINALE

(SECRETARY looks up from reading; speaks to audience.)

Well! This was quite revealing. Now I see that God's answers are NOT a matter of organization and efficiency! God is NOT a cosmic vending machine who grants our every wish! Instead, it seems that the goal of prayer is to help US understand what HE wants—so that OUR desires come from what HE desires. Certainly, if God created this whole WORLD and us, too, then He really DOES know what He's doing!

Perhaps I should view prayer as a PRIVILEGE. God's Word invites me to take my needs to my Creator who loves me and wants what is BEST for me. That is FAR MORE important than simply ASKING for something and then thinking, *God should answer me now. I asked Him for a CAR—and hey, it's Tuesday, the day for Material requests!* God has BIGGER plans for me than that, good plans full of His love!

Thank you all for visiting All Tied Up, Incorporated! Feel free to take a sample shoelace as a souvenir! *(Goes back to work at desk; ignores audience.)*

Leader invites a student to read Philippians 4:6-7 from the Key Verse Card. **Prayer is not like sending a list of what you want for Christmas to your grandma. It's an appointment for taking time with God! We not only ask God but also thank Him. We not only talk, but we also listen—by reading His Word and thinking about what it says to help us understand what He wants. As our secretary said, it's a privilege! Let's pray right now.**

Close in prayer, thanking God for His love and asking Him to help each student set up and keep a daily appointment with Him this week for prayer.

An Appointment with God

DISCUSSION SHEET

What is a reason we should pray?
Find Jeremiah 33:2-3.

When is the right time to pray?
Find 1 Thessalonians 5:17.

What is a reason that some prayers are not answered?
Find James 4:2b-3.

Why should we pray for God's will?
Find Isaiah 40:28.

Does God answer all our prayers?
Find 1 John 5:14-15.

Why should we pray for God's will instead of our own will?
Find Psalm 18:30.

Did Jesus pray for God's will or for His own?
Find Matthew 26:39.

What can keep God from answering our prayers?
Find Isaiah 59:2.

KEY VERSE CARD

Philippians 4:6-7
"Do not be anxious about anything, but in everything, by prayer and petition, with thanksgiving, present your requests to God. And the peace of God, which transcends all understanding, will guard your hearts and your minds in Christ Jesus."

Holiday Heart Survey

TOPIC
Priorities and materialism

CHARACTER
Survey taker

SUMMARY
The survey taker helps us recognize the importance of wanting the best gifts at Christmas.

KEY VERSE
Psalm 119:36-37
"Turn my heart toward your statutes and not toward selfish gain. Turn my eyes away from worthless things; preserve my life according to your word."

PROPS
Business suit, notebook, pen

OPTIONAL PROPS
Laptop computer (can pretend to type in answers)

PREP POINTERS
Your perky and professional presence will help point out the irony of the world's emphasis on material things!

SCHEDULE
Small-Group Warm-up (5-10 minutes)
Large-Group Presentation (5-10 minutes)
Small-Group Discussion (10-20 minutes)
Grand Finale (5-10 minutes)

SMALL-GROUP WARM-UP
Meet, greet and discuss the following questions in your small group:
- **What would you do if you had a million dollars? Where would you shop?**
- **What is something you really, really want to have?**
- **What makes you want to have this?**

HOLIDAY HEART SURVEY

LARGE-GROUP PRESENTATION

(SURVEY TAKER *enters, moving quickly to emphasize her efficiency.*)
Hi. My name is Fran. I'm a survey taker in the marketing and research division of Spendit Corporation. I want to thank you for allowing me to come here tonight to conduct one of our IMPORTANT Spendit CUSTOM surveys: our annual Holiday Heart Survey!

Let me start off by getting to know you a little. (*Approaches a student.*)
Hi. What's your name? Age? What is your occupation? Married or single?

WHAT'S COOL

(*To audience.*) Now, in order for companies to SELL you what they make, they need to know exactly what it is that you WANT. That way, YOU'RE happy—and THEY make TONS of money. It works for EVERYONE!

OK. Let's start with shoes, shall we? Who wants to tell me their favorite brand of shoes? (*Listens and pretends to write down or input replies.*)

What is it about these shoes that you like? (*Listens and pretends to write down or input replies.*)

Favorite style? (*Listens and pretends to write down or input replies.*) Which is the most fashionable color? (*Listens and pretends to write down or input replies.*) Does someone you know already HAVE them? (*Listens and pretends to write down or input replies.*) Great. Thank you.

Our next topic is brands of CLOTHES. What logo is MOST cool to have on a T-shirt? (*Listens and pretends to write down or input replies.*) Why do you want to wear that logo? (*Listens and pretends to write down or input replies.*)

WHAT MATTERS

Let me tell you why this survey is SO VERY important. A few years back, we at the Spendit Corporation had GREAT financial success with a product called "Blabbering Shoes." With every step, the shoes said something funny like, "Don't follow me, I'm lost!" or "Watch where you're walking, buddy!" or "Inside me are some UGLY feet!"

Every kid in America wanted a pair. We sold MILLIONS of pairs. Of course, you don't see people wearing them NOW. Turns out, they were about the most ANNOYING product ever invented. It was ESPECIALLY bad when a whole CLASSROOM full of kids wore them! Teachers EVERYWHERE began taking time off for mental health reasons. But we sure made a lot of MONEY while the fad lasted!

WHAT COUNTS

That's the funny thing about fads. EVERYONE just HAS to have the item everyone ELSE has. And then, it's not long before no one even REMEMBERS that item! For instance, do you remember your favorite gift from Christmas last year? What was it? (*Listens and pretends to write down or input replies.*)

Have you ever really, really, really wanted something for Christmas and when you got it, it was EVERYTHING you thought it would be? Pets don't count—they can't be manufactured! (*Listens and pretends to write down or input replies.*)

Have any of you ever really, really, really wanted something—and then when you got it, you were DISAPPOINTED? (*Listens and pretends to write down or input replies.*)

At Christmas, what would you like to find under YOUR Christmas tree? *(Listens and pretends to write down or input replies.)* What is your reason for wanting that gift? *(Listens and pretends to write down or input replies.)*

WHAT TO WANT

Thank you so much. This is very helpful information. Did you know we've actually studied what people wanted in different periods of history? One person's wish list struck us as QUITE unusual.

A man named David really, really, really wanted something. He wrote these words: "O God, you are my God, EARNESTLY I seek you; my SOUL thirsts for you, my body LONGS for you, in a dry and weary land where there is no water." Now why would he long after GOD so much?

What I REALLY need is for you to do some of your OWN market research. Find out what it IS that David wanted so much from God, OK? Maybe there's a way for me to MARKET this! *(Exits.)*

SMALL-GROUP DISCUSSION TIME

Provide one "Holiday Heart Survey" Discussion Sheet (p. 152) to each student. Invite students to find verses and discuss answers to questions on the sheet. Invite interested students to talk more with you about joining God's family (see "Leading a Child to Christ" on p. 11).

GRAND FINALE

(SURVEY TAKER returns, checking her data.)

Well, my research is done here. I appreciate your help. Our survey has given ME some very IMPORTANT information. First, what comes from God is FREE. It has already been PAID for! Second, HIS gifts are ours for the asking. You can't BUY them and you can't EARN them. I don't understand why MORE people don't want GOD'S gifts!

Of ALL the things ever put on a list of things to want, putting "a closer relationship with God" at the top sounds to me like the most VALUABLE thing you could want! After all, HE is the one who started this whole gift-giving thing. Without HIM, there would be NO Christmas at ALL!

Putting God at the top of YOUR list means you'll NEVER get a gift that will DISAPPOINT you! Well, see you all at the mall! *(Exits, checking statistics.)*

Leader invites a student to read Psalm 119:36-37 from the Key Verse Card. **It's easy to focus on what we WANT for Christmas—or any other time. But to long for a closer relationship with God is a life-changing gift! He is always willing to give that gift! Let's thank Him.**

Close in prayer, thanking God for His gift of Jesus and His gifts of salvation and a life in relationship with Him.

Holiday Heart Survey

DISCUSSION SHEET

Make a gift list! Find these verses to help you complete a list of gifts only God can give: **Psalm 103:1-5.** (You can't get THOSE gifts at the mall!)

Find John 14:27 and John 15:11. (Better than anything you can buy to fill your stocking!)

Find 2 Corinthians 1:3-4 and James 1:5. (Could you put anything better on this list?!)

Why do we sometimes value God's gifts less than an item we hope to find under the Christmas tree? **Find Galatians 1:10.**

KEY VERSE CARD

Psalm 119:36-37
"Turn my heart toward your statutes and not toward selfish gain. Turn my eyes away from worthless things; preserve my life according to your word."

Fear No Evil

TOPIC
Proper fear

CHARACTER
A cowardly lion

SUMMARY
The cowardly lion learns that for God's family, there is less to fear than we imagine.

KEY VERSE
Philippians 4:8
"Finally, brothers, whatever is true, whatever is noble, whatever is right, whatever is pure, whatever is lovely, whatever is admirable—if anything is excellent or praiseworthy—think about such things."

PROPS
Lion costume or mask, table

OPTIONAL PROPS
Security blanket

PREP POINTERS
Practice jumping at the slightest noise!

SCHEDULE
Small-Group Warm-up (5-10 minutes)
Large-Group Presentation (5-10 minutes)
Small-Group Discussion (10-20 minutes)
Grand Finale (5-10 minutes)

SMALL-GROUP WARM-UP
Meet, greet and discuss the following questions in your small group:
- **What are some things people really should be afraid of? Some things that people might not really need to be afraid of?**
- **Tell about a time when something frightened you or someone you know. What happened to create more fear? To eliminate fear?**

Fear No Evil

Large-Group Presentation

(LION *enters cautiously, as if in a dark forest, jumping fearfully at everything.*)

EEEK! What's that noise? I HEARD something! This place is SCARY! I know what you're thinking—you're thinking that I'm the king of BEASTS and that I shouldn't be AFRAID of anything. But have you ever SEEN a wicked witch, or even worse, a yappy little DOG? I tell you, YOU would tremble in fear, too, if you were being chased by a WITCH—or a YORKIE!

SCARY STUFF

But those aren't the ONLY frightening things in this forest. When NIGHT comes, it's as DARK as dark can be. NOISES come out of the darkness—(*Jumps.*) YAAH! Horrible sounds like—oh I don't know, maybe flying monkeys. And then there are the TREES. They begin to YELL at you, and throw ACORNS! You just can't begin to imagine the TERROR I feel. My heart starts to pound like a million DRUMS—and THAT scares me, too! Will I have a HEART ATTACK!?

(*Jumps; looks around.*) Ahhh! What was that?! Who's SNEAKING UP on me and pulling my tail?! Oh. I pulled my own tail. You SEE? I'm in a TERRIBLE state! I'm MISERABLE from always being so TERRIFIED!

SCARY PEOPLE

I've heard of OTHER frightening things, too. One time, a girl named Dorothy came through here. She brought that AWFUL little mutt with her. That was scary enough. But then she told me about all the SCARY things she had ever heard about—like GHOSTS!

She told me about people who went to a gathering called a SEANCE to try to get DEAD people to talk to them! She ALSO told me about a fortune-teller she met. She said he looked into his crystal ball and KNEW things about her. She said people go to fortune-tellers to find out what will HAPPEN to them in the future. And she had RUN AWAY from a wicked witch! She told me all about the SPELLS the witch could cast on people to bring them harm.

(*Jumps.*) YAAH! All this stuff gives me the CREEPS! I'm just SO SCARED. I have so many QUESTIONS! Is all this scary stuff for REAL? Is it OK for people to try to talk to DEAD PEOPLE or go to fortune-tellers? Will GHOSTS come to HAUNT me? Is there ANY way to STOP feeling so AFRAID? You look like smart, BRAVE people. Maybe YOU can find the answers for me. If you need me, I'll just be under this table—COWERING! (*Crawls under table and lies down.*)

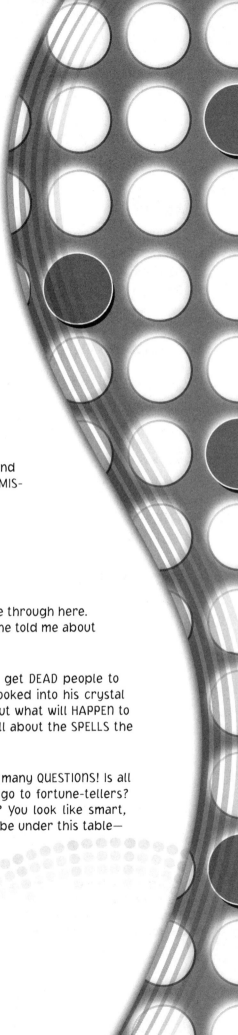

SMALL-GROUP DISCUSSION TIME

Provide one "Fear No Evil" Discussion Sheet (p. 156) to each student. Invite students to find verses and discuss answers to questions on the sheet. Invite interested students to talk more with you about joining God's family (see "Leading a Child to Christ" on p. 11).

GRAND FINALE

(LION comes out from under the table, moving confidently.)
Why, this is wonderful news! YOU all have discovered that there is someone GREATER than ALL the EVIL in the world! Imagine THAT! There is someone who can overcome ALL the dark, scary things, whether they are real—or in my IMAGINATION! I'm so TIRED of living in fear. I'm READY to have some peace and COURAGE!

THANK YOU for telling me that Jesus is stronger and more powerful than anything or anyone! He'll always be there for me, so I have nothing to fear! Of course, you're RIGHT. For MY part, I DO have to keep my thoughts on HIM instead of letting myself think about *(Shudders.)* OTHER stuff.

You just don't know how free this makes me feel! I feel almost COURAGEOUS. I feel like I could . . . ROAR!! *(Exits, roaring.)*

Leader invites a student to read Philippians 4:8 from the Key Verse Card. **It's easy to be fearful when we think of all the evil, scary things in the world. That's why God's Word says to take charge of our thoughts. When we focus on God and what He can do, He helps us remember that He is stronger than anything! Let's ask Him to help us with that this week.**

Close in prayer, asking God to help students trust Him, focus on Him and take charge of their thoughts.

Fear No Evil

DISCUSSION SHEET

What are you afraid of?

• There are some fears—like a fear of burning ourselves on a hot stove or of jumping off a cliff—that we SHOULD have. Those fears come from God to help us stay alive!

• There are some OTHER fears—like a fear of ghosts or witches, of graveyards or the dark—which we might have for many reasons. Are those the same kinds of fear as a fear of touching a hot iron? What are ways to overcome those fears?

Why did God's people choose not to practice witchcraft in Old Testament times?
Find Deuteronomy 18:10-12.

What do we need to remember at the end of the day?
Find Psalm 4:8.

What did David learn about protection?
Find Psalm 27:1-3.

Who will always protect you?
Find Psalm 27:10.

Who is the light of the world?
Find John 8:12.

So should we walk in light or in darkness?
Find 1 John 1:5-7.

Who is more powerful, God or the devil?
Find 1 John 4:4.

KEY VERSE CARD

Philippians 4:8
"Finally, brothers, whatever is true, whatever is noble, whatever is right, whatever is pure, whatever is lovely, whatever is admirable—if anything is excellent or praiseworthy—think about such things."

Trash Talk

TOPIC
Purity and integrity

CHARACTER
Trash collector

SUMMARY
The trash collector talks about what we should NOT throw away.

KEY VERSE
Matthew 7:6
"Do not give dogs what is sacred; do not throw your pearls to pigs. If you do, they may trample them under their feet, and then turn and tear you to pieces."

PROPS
Coveralls, garbage can(s)

OPTIONAL PROPS
Trash items mentioned in script (empty paper cup, wad of gum, etc.)

PREP POINTERS
A Jersey accent seems to be the perfect complement for this character!

SCHEDULE
Small-Group Warm-up (5-10 minutes)
Large-Group Presentation (5-10 minutes)
Small-Group Discussion (10-20 minutes)
Grand Finale (5-10 minutes)

SMALL-GROUP WARM-UP

Meet, greet and discuss the following questions in your small group:
- **When have you heard someone say a really mean thing?**
- **Why do you think the person said what he or she said?**
- **What are some things a kid your age might not think are important?**

TRASH TALK

LARGE-GROUP PRESENTATION

(TRASH COLLECTOR enters, dragging a garbage can and wiping hand to shake hands with random individuals.)
Yo. My name is Eddie and I'm a garbage collector. You got a PROBLEM with that? I been doin' this job for 17 years. I'm here tonight because me and some of the other garbage collectors want to EDUCATE you people about TRASH DISPOSAL. You got a PROBLEM with that?

WHICH CAN?

You got your BLUE can where all your REGULAR trash goes. Then you got your GREEN can where you put your recyclables. Don't be puttin' your GRASS CLIPPINGS in the green one—use the GRAY can for that.

And hey, how's about you dump your beverages down the SINK before you throw the cups away? Do ya know how DISGUSTING it is to have those liquids come dripping down your ARM when you're dumpin' a can into the truck?

And ANOTHER thing. How about you WRAP your gum in PAPER before you toss it? Juicy Fruit is HARD to get out of my HAIR. YUK! Wrap up your gum—it ain't ROCKET SCIENCE! You got a PROBLEM with that?

WHAT'S VALUABLE?

Lemme tell ya, people throw away the STRANGEST stuff. One time there was an entire MOOSE head—antlers and all. I've seen about 30 of those SINGING FISH plaques. Someone even tossed out about 220 pounds of Gouda cheese. Ya gotta WONDER, why did someone even HAVE 220 pounds of Gouda cheese to throw AWAY?

But then there are times when someone has thrown out something really VALUABLE. Two years ago, there was an ORIGINAL Picasso painting in someone's can. I realize not everyone APPRECIATES Picasso, but why throw a MILLION-DOLLAR painting in the trash? Just last week, a DIAMOND RING fell out of a hole in a trash bag I was liftin' into the truck! The thing was GORGEOUS. Why would someone want to throw it AWAY?

But ya know, sometimes we ALL get tempted to throw away things that are even MORE valuable. These things are precious, 'cause they're things we can never get back once they're gone. I see people do it all the time. They tell LIES and THROW AWAY their integrity. When people go out with anybody and have sex without bein' married, that's throwin' away their PURITY. Even though you can't SEE 'em, integrity and purity aren't GARBAGE. They're PRECIOUS, 'cause you can never get 'em back. They're even MORE VALUABLE than that diamond ring!

Then sometimes, people even TRY to throw away their whole LIVES—mainly 'cause they feel bad about the parts of their lives they think are TRASHED. What a shame. Hey, while I go out and find a cup of fresh coffee, why don't you all check to see if you might be throwin' away any valuables without knowin' it! *(Exits.)*

SMALL-GROUP DISCUSSION TIME

Provide one "Trash Talk" Discussion Sheet (p. 160) to each student. Invite students to find verses and discuss answers to questions on the sheet. Invite interested students to talk more with you about joining God's family (see "Leading a Child to Christ" on p. 11).

GRAND FINALE

(TRASH COLLECTOR returns.)
You know that PICASSO I found in the trash? Well, I turned it over to the art museum. They cleaned it up and hung it in the museum. NOW it's a prized possession!

That's kind of like God. Think about it. He considers YOU to be HIS prized possessions, even when you feel like trash, even if you've been throwing away some of your VALUABLES. He still loves you. And you can stop TRASHIN' anytime. Just ask God to FORGIVE you and He will clean you up and draw you close. He'll treat you like the VALUABLE person you are to Him!

And another thing: Spend time with God. THAT will help you to THINK before you TRASH any of your VALUABLES! You DON'T got a problem with THAT, do ya? *(Exits.)*

Leader invites a student to read Matthew 7:6 from the Key Verse Card. **Well, our friend Eddie has it right. The most VALUABLE things in life are NOT things that can be bought. And those valuable things can be thrown away very easily. That's what Satan loves to do—to trick us into throwing away what is truly valuable. Let's ask God to help us value and hang on to our integrity and purity.**

Close in prayer, asking God's forgiveness for taking our integrity and purity lightly, and asking His help to keep these valuables safe instead of throwing them away.

Trash Talk

DISCUSSION SHEET

What is some trash we should throw out of our lives?
Find Ephesians 4:25-31 and Ephesians 5:3-7.

What are some things that God has given us to treat as precious and valuable?

Integrity can also be defined as honesty, as being the same all the time (not two-faced), or as having no hidden motives. Personal integrity is extremely valuable.

What are ways that people throw away their integrity?

What's the problem with lying?
Find Proverbs 12:22.

What's the problem with cheating?
Find Proverbs 20:23.

Gossiping?
Find Proverbs 20:19.

Drunkenness?
Find Proverbs 20:1.

Why do you think God doesn't want us to throw away what He gives us?
Find Deuteronomy 30:15-16.

KEY VERSE CARD

Matthew 7:6
"Do not give dogs what is sacred; do not throw your pearls to pigs. If you do, they may trample them under their feet, and then turn and tear you to pieces."

The Chef's Croissants

TOPIC
Recipe for the Christian life

CHARACTER
French Chef

SUMMARY
The French Chef demonstrates how the ingredients of the Christian life are very like those of a great croissant!

KEY VERSES
2 Timothy 3:14-15
"Continue in what you have learned and have become convinced of, because you know those from whom you learned it, and how from infancy you have known the holy Scriptures, which are able to make you wise for salvation through faith in Christ Jesus."

PROPS
Mixing bowl, whisk or spoon, chef's hat or beret

OPTIONAL PROPS
White shirt or apron, listed ingredients, finished croissants (to share as a snack)

PREP POINTERS
Practice your French pronunciations and use an accent! Share croissants as a snack: Line a large bowl with croissants and then set a smaller bowl inside the larger one. Pretend to mix ingredients in the smaller bowl, and then when appropriate, toss finished croissants to students!

SCHEDULE
Small-Group Warm-up (5-10 minutes)
Large-Group Presentation (5-10 minutes)
Small-Group Discussion (10-20 minutes)
Grand Finale (5-10 minutes)

SMALL-GROUP WARM-UP
Meet, greet and discuss the following questions in your small group:
- **When have you baked (a cake)?**
- **What did you have to do to make the (cookies)? How did they turn out?**
- **What do you think would have happened if you had added sawdust instead of flour? Salt in place of sugar?**

THE CHEF'S CROISSANTS

LARGE-GROUP PRESENTATION

(CHEF *enters, stirring imaginary ingredients in a large bowl he is carrying.*) I am Chef (your name) from France. MANY wonderful things come from my great country. Can you name anything that comes from France? *(Waits for answers, calls on audience members and responds.)* Ah! Yes! Correct!

And what about the great MONUMENTS, eh? The Eiffel Tower? The Arc de Triomphe? Then there is the great ART. You know the great painters, like Monet and Cézanne?

One of the very BEST things from France is the French cuisine. That word means the cooking, the fine food. Some fine French specialties are the bouillabaisse—a fine fish soup. And what about a soufflé? Do you know what that is? *(Waits for answers, calls on audience members and responds.)* A soufflé is a wonderful, light baked pudding! Then, ah—fromage—the wonderful CHEESE for which my country is famous!

But the wonderful BAKED goods! Ah, who can resist a fresh baguette? Do you know what a baguette is? Do you know other kinds of French bread? *(Waits for answers, calls on audience members and responds.)*

MIXING IT UP

Today, we make a French SPECIALTY—the CROISSANT! But first, I must say that COOKING is a lot like the LIFE of the Christian, the one who follows Jesus! Many INGREDIENTS must BLEND together PROPERLY if you want your croissant—OR your Christian life—to turn out the BEST! Now here are the ingredients:

For a croissant, the FLOUR is the basis for everything else; without flour, you make NO croissants! For the Christian life, believing in God is like the flour, the basis. Until we believe in Him, know He made us and loves us, we cannot even BEGIN!

Then come the EGGS. In baking, egg BINDS the ingredients, holds them together. For the Christian like me, I must believe that Jesus is God's Son—God Himself in a human body. In the Bible, it even SAYS that JESUS holds EVERYTHING together—just like the egg!

Next, the BUTTER. Without the butter, it is NO croissant! Like the butter is the belief that Jesus died to take the punishment for our sins—the KEY ingredient, if we want real life in God's family. Without this, what you have is NOT a CROISSANT!

Ah, my good friend, YEAST. It is NECESSARY to make the dough RISE and be stretchy! In the same way, we must believe that Jesus not only DIED, but also that He ROSE from death! He proved that HE is stronger than anything. NOTHING kept HIM from rising!

And now, the MILK. It is like FAITH. When we BELIEVE that Jesus is God's Son, that He died to take our punishment on the cross, that He rose from the dead and that He can FORGIVE our sins if we ask, it is like the milk that helps us MIX TOGETHER the ingredients we need for making the croissant—OR the Christian life!

SALT may not seem important. But did you know? The salt CONTROLS other ingredients so that the dough is JUST RIGHT! This is like having the Holy Spirit of God living in us. When we join God's family, He comes to help us, even if we don't always notice Him. He helps us grow in love, peace, patience, and even—self-CONTROL! Such good things happen ONLY when the Holy Spirit is in us, to make us JUST RIGHT!

Ah! And then, the final ingredient to make a croissant PERFECT—the SUGAR. To make a croissant COMPLETE, you MUST add sugar. And in LIFE, if you want life to be really SWEET and complete, you MUST put Jesus FIRST in your life. Daily, you talk with Him and read His Word, ask Him to guide you in what you do—whether cooking, schoolwork, playing sports or doing chores. If He is in EVERYTHING, life is COMPLETE.

And now, my CROISSANT dough is COMPLETE, also! Time for me to BAKE while you chefs make sure you include EVERY ingredient for the recipe of SPIRITUAL life! Au revoir! *(Exits.)*

SMALL-GROUP DISCUSSION TIME

Provide one "The Chef's Croissants" Discussion Sheet (p. 164) to each student. Invite students to find verses and discuss answers to questions on the sheet. Invite interested students to talk more with you about joining God's family (see "Leading a Child to Christ" on p. 11).

GRAND FINALE

(CHEF returns.)
Putting Jesus FIRST in our lives is ALSO much like following a recipe: We cannot PRETEND to follow it or do it in ANY old way. No matter if we stir and stir so that we LOOK like we follow the recipe. That is SILLINESS! We fool only ourselves if we think we can do it any way we WANT. We WILL have something, but NOT croissants—probably just a MESS!

BUT when we follow the WHOLE recipe, when we put Jesus first, we can wake up in the morning and ask, "Jesus, what do YOU want me to do today?" When we read His Word, think about what HE says and trust HIM, we follow HIS recipe EXACTLY. Like our croissants, our spiritual lives are the same in this way—we must COMPLETELY follow the recipe. That means we must put Jesus FIRST in all we do!

(Shows finished croissants.) Who wants to taste a finished croissant? They contain two very special French ingredients—escargot and caviar. Do you know these—the snails and the fish eggs? Ha, ha! No! I joke. Bon appétit! *(Exits.)*

Leader invites a student to read 2 Timothy 3:14-15 from the Key Verse Card. **Our chef has certainly shown us why we need to be sure we have ALL of the right ingredients and FULLY follow Jesus and put HIM first so that our lives turn out to be all they can be! Let's ask God to help us fully obey and put Jesus first every day.**

Close in prayer, thanking God for His love and asking Him to help students put Jesus Christ first in their lives and decisions.

The Chef's Croissants

DISCUSSION SHEET

THE RECIPE FOR THE CHRISTIAN LIFE

What must you believe about God that is like the flour? **Find Hebrews 11:6.**

What must you believe about Jesus that is like the eggs? **Find Mark 1:9-11 and Colossians 1:16-17.**

What must you believe about Jesus' death that is like the butter? **Find Romans 4:25.**

What must you believe about Jesus' resurrection that is like the yeast? **Find 1 Corinthians 15:3-4.**

What must you believe about Jesus' forgiveness that is like the milk? **Find Mark 2:3-12.**

What must you believe about the Holy Spirit of God that is like the salt? **Find Romans 8:9 and Galatians 5:22-23.**

What must you do about putting Jesus first in everything? **Find 2 Corinthians 5:15-17 and Romans 12:1-2.**

Place life completely in God's hands so that He can mix it, shape it and make it the very best it can be!

KEY VERSE CARD

2 Timothy 3:14-15
"Continue in what you have learned and have become
convinced of, because you know those from whom
you learned it, and how from infancy you have known
the holy Scriptures, which are able to make you wise
for salvation through faith in Christ Jesus."

Prospecting for the Truth

TOPIC
Religion and Christianity

CHARACTER
Hank the Prospector

SUMMARY
Hank the prospector tells how using God's Word helps us understand God's truth.

KEY VERSE
Proverbs 2:3-5
"If you call out for insight and cry aloud for understanding, and if you look for it as for silver and search for it as for hidden treasure, then you will understand the fear of the LORD and find the knowledge of God."

PROPS
Bible, gold nugget (rock painted gold), old clothes and hat, prospector's gold pan (pie tin)

OPTIONAL PROPS
Pick, coil of rope (carry it across your chest)

PREP POINTERS
Practice swishing imaginary sand in your gold pan!

SCHEDULE
Small-Group Warm-up (5-10 minutes)
Large-Group Presentation (5-10 minutes)
Small-Group Discussion (10-20 minutes)
Grand Finale (5-10 minutes)

SMALL-GROUP WARM-UP
Meet, greet and discuss the following questions in your small group:
- **When have you ever panned for gold or seen a picture of someone panning for gold? How is looking for gold like looking for truth?**
- **What is something you know is true?**
- **Tell something you used to think was true but that now you're pretty sure is not true.**

PROSPECTING FOR THE TRUTH

LARGE-GROUP PRESENTATION

(PROSPECTOR enters; removes hat before speaking.)
I'm Henry. My friends call me Hank. Course, the only friend I've BEEN around fer a LONG while is my faithful pack mule, Aloysious [say, "al-oh-WISH-us"]. I been mining fer gold in these here parts fer nigh on 18 years now! And ya know WHAT? I finally struck COLOR! *(Pats pocket.)* That means I found me some GOLD.

RELIGIOUS TOWN

(Pulls gold nugget from pocket and displays it.) I headed into town to sell off my nugget—and to thank God fer my newfound riches! I thought I should find a church where I could say thanks, sort of official-like. But as I walked up and down the sidewalks, I noticed there were MANY different places of WORSHIP around.

There was one for the Mormons and another one for Jehovah's Witnesses. There was a temple for the Hindus and another one for the Buddhists. There was even a mosque for the Muslims! It got me kinda confused.

I said to myself, "Shoot! How do I know which bunch teaches the TRUTH?" If I was gonna offer my thanks to the ONE TRUE GOD, I needed to figure out where to GO! Who was really worshipin' HIM and tellin' the TRUTH about Him?

GRANDPAPPY SAID

Well, I remembered something my grandpappy told me when I headed out to the gold mines. *(Holds up gold pan.)* He said, "Henry, my boy, you see that gold pan in yer hand? You'll be puttin' a lot of SAND into that pan. But when you get to swishin' and swirlin' it around, the SAND will wash away and you'll be left with pure GOLD."

Then my grandpappy said, "The BIBLE is like that, too. It's yer REAL gold pan. Anything you come up against, why, you just pour it into the Bible. Swish it around by readin' and prayin' on it and thinkin' on it. If it don't agree with what the Bible says, just let it wash right on out, like sand. Yessir, the Bible's the way you kin sift out all the confusion. It's like the finest gold pan there is!"

So, I come to talk to you all. I hear you're mighty handy with a Bible! Thought maybe you could sort through the Bible for some NUGGETS of truth, while I do the same! *(Picks up Bible and exits.)*

SMALL-GROUP DISCUSSION TIME

Provide one "Prospecting for the Truth" Discussion Sheet (p. 168) to each student. Invite students to find verses and discuss answers to questions on the sheet. Invite interested students to talk more with you about joining God's family (see "Leading a Child to Christ" on p. 11).

GRAND FINALE

(PROSPECTOR returns, nugget and Bible in hand.)

Well, lemme tell you how my trip to town turned out! After I looked around and listened to some of these folks, I took a little time off. I went down by the mill race and read my Bible. I swished them ideas around in my head with the words I'd read in the Bible. I prayed on it. I thought about those ideas. I swished 'em around with the truth of God's Word! And you know what? Some of those ideas that sounded so GOOD at first just kind of washed out of my BRAIN pan just like my grandpappy said! He was RIGHT! It's the BEST way to figure out what is true and what isn't!

In fact, I'm gonna take the money from this big ole gold nugget and buy Bibles fer anybody who WANTS one! They'll hafta read for themselves, but they can know the TRUTH, too. Just like my grandpappy said, you gotta LOOK for gold to FIND it!

After all, if folks believe things that aren't true, there's no point in hatin' 'em or tellin' 'em they're wrong! Silly to run from 'em or ARGUE with 'em. After all, GOD loves 'em—they're just confused, is all! Grandpappy was right. Even though that big gold nugget shore looked purty in the bottom of my gold pan, I tell ya, there is NOTHIN' more beautiful than findin' the TRUTH by usin' God's Word. It's better than gold! *(Exits.)*

Leader invites a student to read Proverbs 2:3-5 from the Key Verse Card. **Hank the prospector is right. God's Word is what helps us compare and think and understand what is really true. And God wants us to share His truth in a gentle way, not acting like we're smarter or better than anyone else. Think of a person you know who might not know the truth of God's Word. Take time to pray for that person right now.**

Close in prayer, thanking God for the truth found in the Bible and asking Him to help each student pray for and share the truth with a person he or she knows.

Prospecting for the Truth

DISCUSSION SHEET

Here are some ideas that people who follow some other religions might have. Read each Bible verse to find out the truth about each idea.

According to Mormons, men in good standing in the Mormon church can become gods of their own planets after they die. **Find Isaiah 43:10b.**

According to Mormons, the Father, the Son and the Holy Spirit are three separate gods. **Find Deuteronomy 6:4.**

According to the Jehovah's Witnesses, Jesus returned to Earth in 1914. **Find Acts 1:10-11 and 1 Thessalonians 4:16.**

According to the Jehovah's Witnesses, only 144,000 people will go to heaven. The rest of the Jehovah's Witnesses will live on Earth forever. **Find Philippians 3:20-21.**

According to Hindus, you are born over and over again, each time into a different body, until you have paid for all your past sins. If you accomplish this, you have union with Brahman (the chief god). **Find Hebrews 9:27.**

According to Hinduism, chanting and meditating in certain positions will help to release you from having to pay for some of your sins. **Find Matthew 6:7.**

According to Buddhists, you reach Nirvana (a state of happy oblivion) when you no longer desire anything. **Find Psalm 103:2-5.**

According to Buddhists, there is no heaven or hell. **Find Matthew 10:28,32-33.**

According to Muslims, Jesus was just one of many prophets (like Abraham, Moses and others). **Find Hebrews 3:3.**

According to Muslims, Jesus was not crucified; He ascended to heaven without dying. **Find Mark 15:44-45.**

KEY VERSE CARD

Proverbs 2:3-5
"If you call out for insight and cry aloud for understanding, and if you look for it as for silver and search for it as for hidden treasure, then you will understand the fear of the Lord and find the knowledge of God."

Lighten the Load

TOPIC
Removing our burdens

CHARACTER
Hiker

SUMMARY
A hiker demonstrates how it helps us to eliminate unnecessary weight—both in hiking and in life.

KEY VERSE
Matthew 11:28-30
"Come to me, all you who are weary and burdened, and I will give you rest. Take my yoke upon you and learn from me, for I am gentle and humble in heart, and you will find rest for your souls. For my yoke is easy and my burden is light."

PROPS
Bible; large backpack or frame pack; 12 bulky items placed in backpack, each labeled with one of the words ("fear," "guilt," etc.) mentioned in script

OPTIONAL PROPS
Hiking boots, walking stick, hat, sunglasses

PREP POINTERS
Label backpack items ahead of time. Items representing unneeded attitudes (guilt, worry, etc.) could be large labeled rocks or heavy canned goods. Use sunglasses for a running gag (push them onto forehead so that they fall each time you look down) for extra humor!

SCHEDULE
Small-Group Warm-up (5-10 minutes)
Large-Group Presentation (5-10 minutes)
Small-Group Discussion (10-20 minutes)
Grand Finale (5-10 minutes)

SMALL-GROUP WARM-UP
Meet, greet and discuss the following questions in your small group:
- **When have you gone on a hike? Where did you go?**
- **What did you like about carrying a pack? What did you not like?**
- **What did you take along? What did you find you needed?**
- **What did you wish you had taken?**

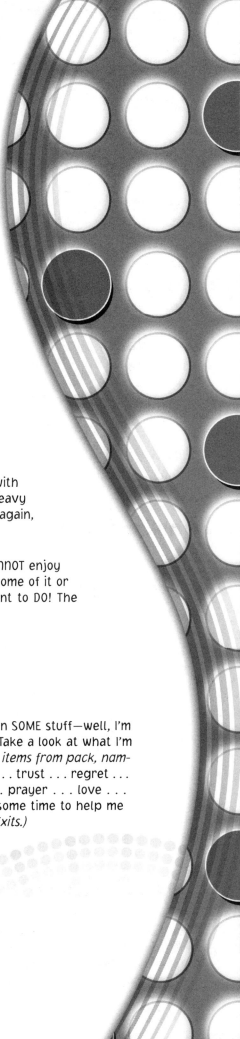

Lighten the Load

Large-Group Presentation

(HIKER enters, huffing and puffing; removes backpack and looks around.)

Oh! A REST STOP! What a sight for sore eyes! Just look at all these wonderful CHAIRS with comfortable SEATS! I have GOT to sit down and take my load off. My feet are KILLING me. It feels like I have three new blisters. My legs ache. My knees do, too.

TOO HEAVY

(Sits.) But I tell you what hurts the most—my BACK. And I know WHY! It's from carrying all this STUFF I packed for my hike of life. Do you ever feel like that? Like you've just got WAY too much to carry on YOUR hike of life?

Now, I LOVE life—just yesterday I saw a waterfall, a baby raccoon and an amazing tree. My hike has given me some incredible friends, too. But even on the days when I've met some real bozos or seen some ugly things, I still love life. But on the hike of life, SOME days are worse than others!

This was one of those WORSE days. It felt like I was hiking UPHILL all day long—with a PEBBLE in my shoe! It just hurt and hurt, but I didn't want to set down this heavy backpack, not EVEN to remove a painful pebble. I wasn't sure I could PICK IT UP again, even though my FOOT wouldn't be hurting anymore.

That's when I realized that there is altogether TOO MUCH STUFF in my pack! I CANNOT enjoy the hike of my life while I'm carrying such a heavy load. I've got to get RID of some of it or I'll NEVER be able to GO all the places I want to go and DO all the things I want to DO! The problem is, how do I KNOW what I NEED most? What can I do without?

TOO IMPORTANT?

I thought most of the stuff in here was VITALLY important when I packed it! Then SOME stuff—well, I'm not even sure HOW it got IN here! Tell you what. Would you do me a big favor? Take a look at what I'm carrying and help me decide what to keep and what to dump! *(Removes labeled items from pack, naming each one.)* Here are the things in my pack: Let's see, there's disobedience . . . trust . . . regret . . . a Bible . . . disrespect . . . forgiveness . . . guilt, that's a really heavy one . . . prayer . . . love . . . shame . . . worry . . . faith . . . salvation . . . So, how about it? Would you take some time to help me sort through this load? Thanks! I'm going to find some water and a footrest! *(Exits.)*

SMALL-GROUP DISCUSSION TIME

Provide one "Lighten the Load" Discussion Sheet (p. 172) to each student. Invite students to find verses and discuss answers to questions on the sheet. Invite interested students to talk more with you about joining God's family (see "Leading a Child to Christ" on p. 11).

GRAND FINALE

(HIKER returns and interacts with audience to replace items in backpack, leaving Bible out to pick up at conclusion.)
OK, do you have the list of what I need to eliminate? Good! I'm for SURE leaving the guilt behind! And the shame—why did I think I needed THAT? Somebody must have given me bad information on THAT one!

Man, that disobedience was way HEAVIER than I thought. I'm not sure how it got in there—but I'm not carrying it anymore! It's GONE! Dump the disrespect? OK.

And no more regret. The worry? It stays RIGHT HERE! No more carrying it around! WOW! That's a LOT of stuff I thought I HAD to carry. But God's Word says I DON'T have to! Thanks A LOT! OK—here goes! I'll try it on now.

(Puts on backpack; takes deep breath.) Oh, man! This thing is WAY lighter now! You know, I feel like I could hike for days—weeks—YEARS without that extra burden! This is amazing! I think I've finally got what I NEED in my pack instead of a bunch of heavy, useless JUNK! I feel so LIGHT!

(adjusts backpack.) Just think . . . I was MISERABLE on the hike of my life—because I was carrying around SO much UNNECESSARY stuff! You know something? This would be a good time for YOU to think about what YOU carry in YOUR pack, too. What do you REALLY need? What is it that you DON'T need to keep carrying? And what do you NEED in your pack that is missing? The hike of life can be a long, beautiful journey! But you'll enjoy it SO much more if you're PACKED RIGHT.

(Picks up Bible.) If you don't know what to pack, here's the hiker's guide. It will tell you everything you need to take and everything you need to leave behind—so that your journey gets better and BETTER—and goes on forever! *(Exits, whistling or humming.)*

Leader invites a student to read Matthew 11:28-30 from the Key Verse Card. **This is a challenge each of us needs to consider—grownups and kids. It's easy to carry a lot of junk in our packs that makes us weary and miserable! Take time this week to ask God what you need to dump from your pack and what you need to add to make YOUR journey a joy!**

Close in prayer, asking God to help students and adults to make changes in what they carry so that they are joyful and effective Christians.

Lighten the Load

DISCUSSION SHEET

What should go in YOUR pack? What should you keep, according to this verse? **Find Ephesians 6:1-3.**

How will it help you to keep what you find in **Psalm 9:10?**

Find Psalm 119:105. How will carrying this help you?

Find Romans 13:2. If you don't dump this, what kind of burden might you carry?

Find 1 John 1:9. Why should you keep this one?

Find Ephesians 2:8-10. Are these things good to carry?

Find Matthew 6:25-27,33. According to this, what should you dump? Keep? Why?

Find John 3:36. Why would you want to carry this?

KEY VERSE CARD

Matthew 11:28-30
"Come to me, all you who are weary and burdened, and I will give you rest. Take my yoke upon you and learn from me, for I am gentle and humble in heart, and you will find rest for your souls. For my yoke is easy and my burden is light."

Forward, March!

TOPIC
Resisting temptation

CHARACTER
Drill sergeant

SUMMARY
The drill sergeant helps us understand how resisting temptation makes us fit for spiritual battles we must face.

KEY VERSE
1 Peter 5:8-9
"Be self-controlled and alert. Your enemy the devil prowls around like a roaring lion looking for someone to devour. Resist him, standing firm in the faith, because you know that your brothers throughout the world are undergoing the same kind of sufferings."

PROPS
Military uniform or hat, Bible

OPTIONAL PROPS
Riding crop (to brandish when making a point)

PREP POINTERS
This will be most effective if you practice being a forceful drill sergeant!

SCHEDULE
Small-Group Warm-up (5-10 minutes)
Large-Group Presentation (5-10 minutes)
Small-Group Discussion (10-20 minutes)
Grand Finale (5-10 minutes)

SMALL-GROUP WARM-UP
Meet, greet and discuss the following questions in your small group:
- **Which of your relatives or friends are in the armed forces? Is the person in the Army, Navy, Air Force or Marines?**
- **What do you think would be the best thing about being in the armed forces?**
- **If you were in the armed forces, everything from your bed to your shoes would be inspected. When a parent inspects your room, how do you feel? Why?**

FORWARD, MARCH!

LARGE-GROUP PRESENTATION

(DRILL SERGEANT enters, looking closely and frowning at various people as if to inspect them. Shouts.) A-ten-HUT!!! On your FEET, soldiers! My name is Major Pain. I was ASSIGNED to these barracks to see what shape the troops are in.

(Points to a student who likes being the center of attention.) You there! Front and center. Atten-SHUN! Chin up! Eyes forward! Shoulders back! Stomach in! Not bad, not bad. *(Walks around student, inspecting.)* BUT I want to see those shoes SPIT-SHINED by zero six hundred hours. Do you UNDERSTAND? I can't HEAR you! Salute! Return to your platoon, soldier.

(Looks around at group before speaking; paces as he speaks.) I can SEE that I have my WORK cut OUT for me. It's time to whip you soldiers into battle-ready status! This war is NOT to be taken LIGHTLY! It is a matter of eternal LIFE or DEATH!

KNOW THE SIDE

Now, the FIRST thing we must do in ANY battle is to know which side we're FIGHTING on! THIS is the ULTIMATE WAR: GOD versus the devil. The world is under ATTACK, filled with pain and anger and meanness because the ENEMY has convinced people NOT to OBEY the COMMANDER—God!

Have you CHOSEN whose side you're on? You MAY think you can get out of the war by not choosing sides. But think again! If you have not asked Jesus Christ to be the Commanding Officer and the Lord of your LIFE—you are CHOOSING to fight on the ENEMY'S side! I STRONGLY suggest that you know for SURE which side of this war you are fighting on!

KNOW THE ENEMY

(Stops pacing; gestures with hand or riding crop.) The NEXT thing we need to know is WHO our ENEMY is. It's not the bad guy down the street. It's not even the terrorist across the world. No, PEOPLE are not the enemy. People have been TRICKED by the enemy. ALL people are under his attack!

What is the enemy LIKE? Troops, we are at war with the most low-down, no-good, mean, nasty, rotten, lying, conniving, stop-at-nothing-to-see-you-die enemy in all of HISTORY. He will stoop to ANYTHING to get you to do his bidding. He will deceive you and then laugh in your face as you SUFFER. He will TEMPT you and when you give in, he will SPIT on you and SNEER at you.

This enemy is DEADLY. He's a LIAR. He'll try to trick you into believing that he wants what is GOOD for you. Do you want to serve a commander who wants to DESTROY you? He's AFTER every ONE of us! So we must learn to FIGHT this enemy EFFECTIVELY!

THE REAL ARMY OF ONE

If we have chosen to fight in the Army of God, we can be CONFIDENT that our Commander does not leave us defenseless. First, our COMMUNICATION CHANNELS are wide-open at all times. We NEVER have to wonder what to do—we can ask Our Commander. He wants us to understand His battle plan and to DO what He says so that we fulfill the plan. Unlike the enemy, He LOVES His soldiers and wants them with Him forever after this war is over.

(Holds up and waves Bible.) Second, we have the Operations Manual. IT tells us how to be productive soldiers in God's Army. So to COMPLETE our Basic Training, we need to DIG IN TO the Manual. Get in there and READ THAT MANUAL! Let's go! MOVE it! On the double! *(Exits.)*

SMALL-GROUP DISCUSSION TIME

Provide one "Forward, March!" Discussion Sheet (p. 176) to each student. Invite students to find verses and discuss answers to questions on the sheet. Invite interested students to talk more with you about joining God's family (see "Leading a Child to Christ" on p. 11).

GRAND FINALE

(DRILL SERGEANT returns.)

Soldiers, we are IN this war every single MINUTE. The enemy wants to TRICK us, TEMPT us and TAKE US DOWN. The temptations of the enemy come at us like flaming arrows—ALL OF THE TIME!

With God's help, you can RESIST those temptations. Every time you do, you WIN A BATTLE—for yourself and for GOD'S SIDE! If you GIVE IN to temptation and commit the sin, the DEVIL gets the victory. He jumps up and down with glee that he TRICKED you! Then he plans ways to use YOU like one of his soldiers—over and over again! DON'T LET THAT HAPPEN!

Troops, we HAVE open communications with Headquarters and our Commander is ready to help us in EVERY battle. We have the Operations Manual and the better we KNOW it, the better PREPARED we are to RESIST the enemy and to WIN every BATTLE with temptation. With the WEAPONS we have, we NEVER have to let the enemy win a battle. *(Holds up and waves Bible.)*

Our Manual says right here in 1 Corinthians 10:13 that we can WIN whenever temptation attacks! With our Commanding Officer's help, we can be VICTORIOUS! When THIS war is over, it'll be a GREAT feeling to hear Him say, "Well done, good and faithful SOLDIER!"

OK, troops—ON YOUR FEET! MOVE IT! MOVE IT! GET UP AND MARCH!! REPEAT AFTER ME!!

(DRILL SERGEANT sings with a marching cadence. Troops echo each line.)

WE ARE SOLDIERS IN A WAR, *(echo)*
WE KNOW WHAT WE'RE FIGHTING FOR. *(echo)*
GOD'S ON OUR SIDE, WE WON'T FEAR, *(echo)*
WE'LL KICK SATAN IN THE REAR. *(echo)*

THIS IS WAR AND WE WILL WIN *(echo)*
RESISTING EVERY URGE TO SIN; *(echo)*
I KNOW GOD WILL STAND BY ME *(echo)*
AND HELP ME GET THE VICTORY. *(echo)*

SOUND OFF! *(echo)*
JESUS *(echo)*
DIED FOR US *(echo)*
JESUS IS THE VICTOR *(echo)*
HE WINS!!

Troops, they say the army of God marches on its KNEES. We should never go into battle without praying. So let's pray. Listen to your leader! *(Exits.)*

Leader invites a student to read 1 Peter 5:8-9 from the Key Verse Card. **The Sergeant is right! Let's pray.**

Close in prayer, asking God to help students win the battle of temptation to learn how to be good soldiers of Jesus Christ.

Forward, March!

DISCUSSION SHEET

Whose side are you on? Can you AVOID choosing sides?
Find Matthew 12:30.

What do we know about our enemy?
Find 2 Corinthians 11:14b.

How do we battle Satan? Must we fight alone?
Find James 4:7-8.

What do we need to do to be prepared?
Find Ephesians 6:10-12.

How can you be a smart soldier?
Find 2 Timothy 2:22-26.

What does God promise us about temptation?
Find 1 Corinthians 10:13.

What will finally happen to the enemy?
Find Revelation 20:10.

What will God say to a good Christian soldier?
Find Matthew 25:21.

KEY VERSE CARD

1 Peter 5:8-9
"Be self-controlled and alert. Your enemy the devil prowls around like a roaring lion looking for someone to devour. Resist him, standing firm in the faith, because you know that your brothers throughout the world are undergoing the same kind of sufferings."

On the Team?

TOPIC

Salvation

CHARACTER

Hockey player

SUMMARY

A hockey player tells what does or does not make a member of the team to help us decide if we are members of God's team.

KEY VERSES

Matthew 7:21-23

"Not everyone who says to me, 'Lord, Lord,' will enter the kingdom of heaven, but only he who does the will of my Father who is in heaven. Many will say to me on that day, 'Lord, Lord, did we not prophesy in your name, and in your name drive out demons and perform many miracles?' Then I will tell them plainly, 'I never knew you. Away from me, you evildoers!'"

PROPS

Hockey team shirt, blackened tooth

OPTIONAL PROPS

Hockey stick, helmet, pads, ice skates

PREP POINTERS

Consider blacking an eye as well to portray this character!

SCHEDULE

Small-Group Warm-up (5-10 minutes)
Large-Group Presentation (5-10 minutes)
Small-Group Discussion (10-20 minutes)
Grand Finale (5-10 minutes)

SMALL-GROUP WARM-UP

Meet, greet and discuss the following questions in your small group:

- **When have you played a team sport?**
- **When have you been part of other teams, like a drama team or a project team?**
- **What did you like about being part of a team? What did you not like?**

On the Team?

LARGE-GROUP PRESENTATION

(HOCKEY PLAYER enters, talking.)
I LOVE to play hockey. I love the ice, the body checks, the black eyes, the missing teeth. I love my teammates and I ESPECIALLY love my coach. I just LOVE being on a TEAM!

I WANNA JOIN!

I wasn't ALWAYS on the team. I WANTED to be. I even THOUGHT I was. See, it was like this: I heard about hockey and it sounded pretty cool. I wanted to learn MORE. So I went to a hockey game. It was great! I didn't understand everything that went on, but I could tell it was GREAT!

So the next day, I went to the sporting goods store and I bought this hockey shirt. *(Points to shirt.)* Pretty cool, huh?

I said to myself, "Self, NOW you can be on the team and play hockey—because you LOOK like a hockey player in this new shirt!" So I went to the ice rink.

But the guy at the desk said, "Hey, YOU'RE not on the team!"

I said, "But I'm wearing the TEAM shirt."

He said, "That DOESN'T mean you're on the team. Go talk to the COACH!"

Well, I didn't know HOW I could even talk to the coach—so I left.

I GOT THE EQUIPMENT!

But the next day I went back to the sporting goods store. I bought hockey skates, a hockey stick, some pads and a helmet.

I said to myself, "Self, now they'll HAVE to let you on the team. You have ALL the right EQUIPMENT!" I went back to the rink.

But as I passed the guy at the desk, he said, "Just because you have hockey EQUIPMENT doesn't mean you're on the TEAM. Have you talked with the COACH yet?"

Well, I wasn't SURE how to find the coach and speak to him—I didn't even know what I would SAY! So I went home to think about it.

I KNOW THE RULES!

Later that night, it CAME to me! If I knew all the rules of the game, I'd be on the team for SURE. So I got hold of a RULEBOOK and studied for three days straight! I studied while I ate breakfast. I studied while I did the dishes. I studied when I brushed my teeth. I EVEN studied in the SHOWER! Three days later, I was POSITIVE I knew ALL the rules. I went back to the rink.

"Hi. I'm back!" I said. "And I know EVERY SINGLE HOCKEY RULE!"

But the guy at the desk said, "You're STILL NOT ON THE TEAM!"

"WHY NOT?" I yelled. "I have the team SHIRT. I have all the EQUIPMENT of a hockey player. I know every single RULE a hockey player needs to know. So HOW COME I'm not on the team?!"

"Did you speak with the COACH?" he asked.

"No," I said.

"Why not?" he asked.

"Because, well . . . I . . . I don't know HOW," I finally stammered.

"Well, why didn't you just SAY so? I KNOW the coach. I can help you. Come on. We'll go talk with him RIGHT NOW!"

KNOW THE COACH!

So we did! The guy at the desk introduced me to the coach. I TALKED with the COACH! He explained what I had to do to join the team. He told me that on HIS team, members needed to listen to his instructions, do what he said and have a team player attitude. "Can you DO that?" the coach asked.

"I'd sure like to give it a try!" I told him.

REALLY ON THE TEAM!

So there you have it. I was finally ON the TEAM! And it's been GREAT! There's just no other feeling like zipping around on the ice, slapping the puck, scoring the winning goal—it's AWESOME. I LOVE THIS TEAM!

But hey, there's an even more IMPORTANT team to join. Are you really on the CHRISTIAN TEAM? Now you might LOOK like you are—you may be wearing a cross necklace or a Christian T-shirt. You might have the right EQUIPMENT—maybe you are carrying a Bible or a Christian book or CD. You might even know the RULES in God's Word—you may even have the rules memorized!

You might LOOK like a Christian. You might TALK and ACT like one. Those are all GREAT things, but they DON'T make you a Christian. How about you investigating what it takes to get onto God's team while I see if I can fix my teeth? *(Exits.)*

SMALL-GROUP DISCUSSION TIME

Provide one "On the Team?" Discussion Sheet (p. 180) to each student. Invite students to find verses and discuss answers to questions on the sheet. Invite interested students to talk more with you about joining God's family (see "Leading a Child to Christ" on p. 11).

GRAND FINALE

(HOCKEY PLAYER returns, teeth back to normal.)
GOD is the Coach of THIS team. Have you actually TALKED with the COACH? Have you prayed to God and told Him you believe He sent Jesus to take the punishment for your sins?

Remember the guy at the desk at the ice rink? When I didn't know how to talk with the coach, he helped me. He knew the coach. Your small-group leader is here to help you talk to God—the Coach of the Christian team!

Hockey is a great sport, but it WON'T get me to heaven. Being here is great, too, but IT won't get you to heaven, either. Do you want to be on the ONLY team guaranteed to win? Ask Jesus to be your Savior. Do it soon. Maybe now! I'd LOVE for all of us to be on GOD'S TEAM! *(HOCKEY PLAYER cheers and moves around room, giving high fives while exiting.)* GO, GOD'S TEAM! COME ON, GIVE IT UP FOR THE WINNING TEAM! HIGH FIVES! OH, YEAH!

Leader invites a student to read Matthew 7:21-23 from the Key Verse Card. **People may look like Christians or act like followers of Jesus, but Jesus says that those things are not enough. You must know Him. If you are interested in joining God's team, you can always talk with your small group leaders. They'd love to help you understand how to become part of God's winning team!**

Close in prayer, asking God to help students understand and respond to the verses they read about salvation.

On the Team?

DISCUSSION SHEET

TRUE OR FALSE?

You are a Christian if you attend church regularly.

You are a Christian if your parents are Christians.

You are a Christian if you memorize Bible verses.

You are a Christian if your bedroom is clean.

How can you know you're on God's team? Here are some clues to follow!

How does God feel about you? **Find 1 John 3:1.**

What keeps us from getting on God's team? **Find Romans 3:23.**

What did Jesus do to make it possible for you to get on God's team? **Find John 3:16, Romans 6:23, Hebrews 9:15 and 1 Peter 2:24.**

What should we do about sin? **Find 1 John 1:9.**

What else do we need to do to join the team? **Find Romans 10:9-10.**

What are some things God's team members do? **Find 2 Corinthians 5:15 and 1 John 2:3-6.**

KEY VERSE CARD

Matthew 7:21-23
"Not everyone who says to me, 'Lord, Lord,' will enter the kingdom of heaven, but only he who does the will of my Father who is in heaven. Many will say to me on that day, 'Lord, Lord, did we not prophesy in your name, and in your name drive out demons and perform many miracles?' Then I will tell them plainly, 'I never knew you. Away from me, you evildoers!' "

It's the Pits

TOPIC
Sharing the Good News

CHARACTER
Preteen girl or boy

SUMMARY
A preteen tells why separation from God is like being stuck in a pit and why we're smart to tell our friends the good news about Jesus.

KEY VERSE
1 Peter 3:15
"But in your hearts set apart Christ as Lord. Always be prepared to give an answer to everyone who asks you to give the reason for the hope that you have. But do this with gentleness and respect."

PROPS
Large circle cut from black paper or fabric and laid on floor to represent the hole

OPTIONAL PROPS
Megaphone

PREP POINTERS
This character can be somewhat silly, but the point is serious. Don't overplay the silliness of the situation.

SCHEDULE
Small-Group Warm-up (5-10 minutes)
Large-Group Presentation (5-10 minutes)
Small-Group Discussion (10-20 minutes)
Grand Finale (5-10 minutes)

SMALL-GROUP WARM-UP

Meet, greet and discuss the following questions in your small group:
- **When have you been stuck somewhere?**
- **What was done to help you get out of the situation?**
- **What are other ways people get "stuck"?**

IT'S THE PITS

LARGE-GROUP PRESENTATION

(PRETEEN runs in, shouting toward "hole" on floor.)
Lucy! Lucy! Can you hear me?! I just called for the fire department to come. Hang in there, Lucy! Are you okay? *(Listens into hole.)* You feel like a trout? *(Listens into hole.)* Oh, you want to get out. I know. Hang in there. *(To audience.)* I bet you're wondering what HAPPENED! It's my friend, Lucy. She fell down into this deep hole! The fire department should be here soon to rescue her. But actually, it may BE a while—because this is the THIRD call they've had for a person down a hole TODAY!

EVERYBODY'S DOING IT!

I KNOW why this is happening. See, several months ago, some kids at school decided it would be cool to start walking BACKWARD all the time. All the POPULAR kids started doing it. Many of my friends did too, like Lucy here. I even tried it a couple of times, but my parents told me not to. They said that if we were MEANT to walk backward, our eyes would be in the back of our HEAD.

When Lucy asked me why I wasn't walking backward like everyone ELSE, I told her what my parents said. She LAUGHED! You know what HER parents told HER? They said it was important for her to find her own way! That she needed to experiment with what was true for HER! Walking backward was an expression of her INDIVIDUALITY. They said it was HER decision to do so if she CHOSE.

SURPRISE!

Well, as it turns out, my parents were RIGHT. The walking-backward kids started dropping like flies! First, Frank was in P.E., playing football BACKWARD. When someone threw the ball to him, it hit him in the BACK of the head. That wasn't as bad as Lilly, though! She walked BACKWARD into chemistry class. Her ponytail dipped into some acid when she backed into an EXPERIMENT! Now her ponytail looks like a dead, blue WEASEL. But NOTHING compares with what's happened to poor Lucy!

(Calls into hole.) How are you doing, Lucy? *(Listens into hole.)* You smell like MOLD? *(Listens into hole.)* Oh, you're feeling COLD. Well, I imagine you WOULD!

(To audience.) You know, I ASKED Lucy if she ever worried that something like this would happen. You know what she said? She said I should just worry about MYSELF. So I didn't mention it again. But I bet she's wishing she had LISTENED to me now! And maybe I should have KEPT ON telling her that walking backward isn't smart—even though she told me to mind my own business! Then maybe she wouldn't be in that hole.

(Calls into hole.) I'm still HERE, Lucy. You what? You can't see? Well of course not. That's a deep hole. *(Listens into hole.)* Oh. You didn't say "SEE." You have to WHAT? Oh! Bummer! Well, try to hold it.

MINDING MY BUSINESS

You know, Lucy told me to leave her alone about something else BESIDES her backward walking! Every time I've tried to tell her about Jesus, she just tells me to mind my own business. Well, if she thinks sitting in that HOLE is bad, separated from her friends and family, imagine what being separated from God FOREVER could be like! Lucy IS my good friend. I want to RESPECT her and not BUG her about why she needs Jesus, but is that REALLY being a good friend? Should I just keep quiet? How important IS it for us Christians to help our friends get out of the hole and join God's family? I need your help. You figure it out while I go see if I can get a can of soda and a long string to drop Lucy a drink! *(Exits.)*

SMALL-GROUP DISCUSSION TIME

Provide one "It's the Pits" Discussion Sheet (p. 184) to each student. Invite students to find verses and discuss answers to questions on the sheet. Invite interested students to talk more with you about joining God's family (see "Leading a Child to Christ" on p. 11).

GRAND FINALE

(PRETEEN returns.)
I have GOOD NEWS! While you were busy working together, the firemen RESCUED Lucy. She had a few cuts and bruises and she was REALLY dirty! But with some soap and water and a few bandages, she'll be as good as new—on the OUTSIDE, anyway. Without Jesus, it's like her heart is still in that mucky hole. You know, she's my good friend. I like her so much that I'm going to tell her the good news about Jesus AGAIN! It's like being a spiritual PARAMEDIC—I'm helping God to do SEARCH AND RESCUE!

(Calls toward door.) Lucy, how are you doing? I've got some good news for you. What? Did you just call me KING KONG? OH!! You said, "Bring it on!" You bet I will! *(Exits.)*

Leader invites a student to read 1 Peter 5:13 from the Key Verse Card. **Being separated from God forever is MUCH worse than being stuck in a cold, dark pit! Let's take some time to think about people we know. Which of your friends or family members might need to know about Jesus? Decide now to pray for one of those people this week. Ask God to give you a chance to tell that person what you know about joining God's family!**

Close in prayer, asking God's help for each student to pray for one person this week and to ask God to give them courage to tell what they know about joining God's family as He gives them opportunity.

It's the Pits

DISCUSSION SHEET

Describe a person who is part of God's family. What is a follower of Jesus like? What did Jesus tell us to do about His good news?
Find Mark 16:15-16.

What can you remember if you are fearful about sharing your faith?
Find 2 Timothy 1:7.

What do you think it means to "give the reason for the hope that you have"?
Find 1 Peter 3:15. (Why do you think Peter reminds us to do this with gentleness and respect?)

Why do some people reject the good news of salvation through Jesus?
Find Proverbs 14:12.

Why do we never have to be ashamed of God's good news? **Find Romans 1:16.**

How can you show others what you know about Jesus without using words? **Find 1 Peter 2:12 and 1 Thessalonians 4:11-12.**

KEY VERSE CARD

1 Peter 3:15
"But in your hearts set apart Christ as Lord. Always be prepared to give an answer to everyone who asks you to give the reason for the hope that you have. But do this with gentleness and respect."

Safety First

TOPIC
Spiritual safety

CHARACTER
Safety officer

SUMMARY
The safety officer tries to help us understand what will really keep us safe.

KEY VERSE
John 11:25-26
"Jesus said to her, 'I am the resurrection and the life. He who believes in me will live, even though he dies; and whoever lives and believes in me will never die. Do you believe this?'"

PROPS
Crossing guard or security guard uniform, Bible

OPTIONAL PROPS
Stop sign (hold up randomly as a running gag)

PREP POINTERS
This character is very "by the rules." Develop a couple of quirks that emphasize that point and play up the "You could DIE!" repeated line.

SCHEDULE
Small-Group Warm-up (5-10 minutes)
Large-Group Presentation (5-10 minutes)
Small-Group Discussion (10-20 minutes)
Grand Finale (5-10 minutes)

SMALL-GROUP WARM-UP
Meet, greet and discuss the following questions in your small group:
- **What is a safety rule you know? Where did you learn that rule?**
- **What might happen if you did not follow that rule?**
- **What is the most important safety rule you can think of? Why?**

SAFETY FIRST

LARGE-GROUP PRESENTATION

(SAFETY OFFICER enters, saluting various people and saluting group on arrival at front.)
Good evening. My name is Officer Stickler. I am Captain of the (name of your church) Safety Patrol. It is not SURPRISING that I have been chosen to fill such an important office. I have a PRODIGIOUS background in the area of safety enforcement.

SAFE START

I began my career as a member of my school's safety personnel in fifth grade. I ALONE was selected from the ENTIRE grade to act as the Hall Monitor. I was ENTIRELY successful in my task of ensuring a safe and crime-free atmosphere in the hallowed halls of Main Street Elementary.

In my sixth-grade year I was given the CHALLENGING task of seeing the kindergarteners safely across the street on their way to and from school. I am humbly honored to report that NO kindergarteners were injured or killed on MY watch.

SAFE STILL

With such an impressive resumé, it is not surprising that I eventually was given this post as Safety Officer. I carry out my duties with YOUR safety in mind at all times. Today I am here to make sure you ALL are aware of ALL the safety rules we have here, which we want to see implemented at ALL times.

First of all: Although you've heard it before, it cannot be stressed ENOUGH—look BOTH ways before crossing the street or the parking lot! Do you know WHY? *(Waits for responses; regardless of response, responds.)* YOU COULD DIE!

You must always remember to keep your shoelaces tied. DO you know WHY? *(Waits for responses; regardless of response, responds.)* YOU COULD DIE! Never, never, never run with scissors. DO you know the reason? *(Waits for responses; regardless of response, responds.)* YOU COULD DIE! Always buckle your seat belt or else . . . *(Waits for responses; expects audience to respond, "You could DIE!")*

So, you can see the IMPORTANCE of following these very important rules. I feel that my job is that of a LIFESAVER: I help YOU to remember the rules so that you can save your LIFE. It is very IMPORTANT to stay alive. How many of you here are alive? *(Waits for responses.)* SAFETY is important because PEOPLE want to stay ALIVE!

But why? WHY do you want to stay alive? I mean, people spend a LOT of time and money so that they will have health and long life and not die soon. They go to the gym to get exercise—good for your heart, keeps you alive. What else do people do? *(Waits for responses, such as eat healthy, take vitamins, quit smoking, etc.)* WHY? *(Waits for audience to repeat with him.)* All together, now: "You could DIE!" But . . . truth is, you WILL die!

SAFE FOREVER

Now here's ANOTHER safety factor we were instructed to cover. Let's see, it's John 11:25-26. *(Reads verses aloud.)* Well, THIS is mighty confusing. You live if you DIE? Huh? OK, I need CLARIFICATION! But don't worry. I KNOW what to do. I'm a PROFESSIONAL. *(Holds up Bible.)* Let's check out more of the SAFETY manual. But be CAREFUL . . . you don't want any PAPER CUTS—you could DIE! *(Exits, looking carefully through Bible.)*

SMALL-GROUP DISCUSSION TIME

Provide one "Safety First" Discussion Sheet (p. 188) to each student. Invite students to find verses and discuss answers to questions on the sheet. Invite interested students to talk more with you about joining God's family (see "Leading a Child to Christ" on p. 11).

GRAND FINALE

(SAFETY OFFICER returns, carrying Bible.)
Hm . . . It seems that I've been focusing ENTIRELY too much on helping people save their PHYSICAL lives, when they need even MORE help in saving their SPIRITUAL lives! SPIRITUAL death is FAR more significant!

After all, our spirits are ETERNAL! That means we live SOMEWHERE forever! We can believe that Jesus is God's Son, invite Him to be our Savior and join God's family. We'll spend eternity in heaven. Or, we can REJECT the Son of God and spend eternity SEPARATED from God's wonderful love—FOREVER. That is more AWFUL than we can even BEGIN to imagine!

OK, let's talk about spiritual health. What are some factors we need for optimal spiritual health? *(Waits for responses such as salvation, God's Word, prayer, fellowship, etc.)* Well, I am IMPRESSED. There's a lot more to this Safety Officer job than I ever thought! It's one thing to be safe physically, but how concerned are we about our SPIRITUAL lives? Will you listen to me about SPIRITUAL safety? I hope so!

Let's read those verses in John one more time . . . I think I get it now! *(Reads verses aloud, snaps Bible shut, salutes and exits.)*

Leader invites a student to read John 11:25-26 from the Key Verse Card. **Safety is a good thing. But our officer friend has helped us to see that keeping our bodies safe is only a small part of true safety. Let's thank God for the genuine safety and security that comes from a relationship with Jesus Christ!**

Close in prayer, thanking God for His provision of salvation that keeps us safe forever!

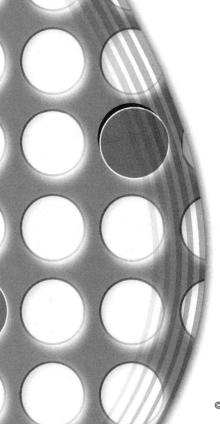

Safety First

DISCUSSION SHEET

Besides not swimming in shark-infested waters, what might people do to help them live as long as possible? These things are meant to prolong life in our physical bodies. But there is more to each of us than just a body. We each have a soul, too—the part of us that thinks and feels.

What happens to our souls when we trust Christ as Savior? **Find 2 Corinthians 5:17.**

What do we have to do to make sure that our spirit or soul isn't dead? **Read John 3:3-6.**

How do we know for sure that our souls will have eternal life?
Read John 3:16 and Romans 10:9.

If we are alive spiritually, what are some exercises that keep our spiritual selves healthy?
Find Romans 12:2; 2 Timothy 3:16-17 and 2 Peter 3:18.

KEY VERSE CARD

John 11:25-26
"Jesus said to her, 'I am the resurrection and the life. He who believes in me will live, even though he dies; and whoever lives and believes in me will never die. Do you believe this?'"

Play Ball!

TOPIC

Teamwork in God's family

CHARACTER

Baseball coach

SUMMARY

Coach helps us understand how living in God's family is like being on a baseball team.

KEY VERSE

Colossians 3:23-24

"Whatever you do, work at it with all your heart, as working for the Lord, not for men, since you know that you will receive an inheritance from the Lord as a reward. It is the Lord Christ you are serving."

PROPS

Coach's T-shirt or jacket, sports clothing, clipboard, Bible, baseball and glove

OPTIONAL PROPS

Flip-chart page with baseball diamond and positions marked on it

PREP POINTERS

Feel free to use volunteers to lead the jumping jacks if you are not so inclined!

SCHEDULE

Small-Group Warm-up (5-10 minutes)
Large-Group Presentation (5-10 minutes)
Small-Group Discussion (10-20 minutes)
Grand Finale (5-10 minutes)

SMALL-GROUP WARM-UP

Meet, greet and discuss the following questions in your small group:
- **When have you played on a sports team? What did you like about it?**
- **What is another team or group activity you like to do?**
- **What is easy about being part of a team? What is difficult?**

Play Ball!

Large-Group Presentation

(COACH enters, carrying clipboard, looking at it to check stats.)
Hello, team. My name is Coach Fred. I'll be your baseball coach this season. Now, I want you to know that I'm tough but fair. I expect you to give your BEST effort at all times and I promise to ALWAYS help you out.

BASICS

Now, it's important in baseball that we are all familiar with the FUNDAMENTALS of the game. Have you all read the rulebook? We can make some costly errors if we don't know the rules, so let's make sure we've got the fundamentals down. Who can explain the Infield Fly Rule? *(Listens to answers from audience.)* Well, maybe we'll deal with that next week.

POSITIONS

OK. Next, we're going to assign PLAYING positions. Some of you who can throw fast and hard will be pitchers. Some of you who can throw the ball a long way will be in the outfield. Some of you will play in the infield because you're quick. Somebody will be playing catcher who's got strong legs and a quick eye. We'll even need bat boys and water boys and sunflower-seed providers. We've ALL got a part to play in this—and EACH ONE of you is VITAL to the success of this team.

IN TRAINING

Now, about conditioning. We've got to be in good physical condition, team. We'll be going up against some very strong, talented teams. If we want to beat those teams, we've got to stay in tip-top shape. So, everyone! Get up and let's do some jumping jacks. *(Leads audience in several jumping jacks.)* Well, I see we have a LONG way to go with our physical conditioning, but we'll keep working on it.

KNOW THE SIGNS

Now let's talk about signs. When you are at bat and you see me do THIS *(Demonstrates.)*, it means to swing away. When I do this *(Demonstrates.)*, it means to bunt. I'll do this *(Demonstrates.)* when I want you to hit a grounder. And this *(Demonstrates.)* is the sign to get the coach another HOT DOG!

GIVE SUPPORT

All right, last but not least, it's VERY important that we support each other and cheer each other on. Baseball doesn't HAVE cheerleaders, you know. We've got to CHEER for each OTHER. Knowing that your teammates are behind you 100 percent is an IMPORTANT part of a winning attitude! So BE there for each other. Cheer for each other. Get your fellow teammates FIRED UP through your enthusiasm! That reminds me . . . baseball is like something else, something that's a LOT more important than balls and strikes and hits and runs. It's like, well . . . it's like . . . it'll come to me. Hang on. *(Shakes head.)* OK, team. You all stay here in the clubhouse and review our little chat. I'll be back in a bit to see if you've figured out how baseball is like . . . it's like . . . hmm. Maybe I need a hot dog to help jog my memory. *(Exits.)*

SMALL-GROUP DISCUSSION TIME

Provide one "Play Ball!" Discussion Sheet (p. 142) to each student. Invite students to find verses and discuss answers to questions on the sheet. Invite interested students to talk more with you about joining God's family (see "Leading a Child to Christ" on p. 11).

GRAND FINALE

(COACH returns.)

You know, that hot dog really helped! It came to me that there's ANOTHER play in baseball you need to understand. It's called the SACRIFICE fly. The batter INTENTIONALLY hits a high fly ball so that the runner on third base has enough time to run home. The batter GIVES UP a chance at a run for the good of the team. He is called out so that the team can score a run. That's like what Jesus did for us! He SACRIFICED Himself so that we could go HOME to live with Him someday. That's it!

Baseball can be a challenging game. So it really HELPS to know your teammates are there for you, cheering you on. The same thing is true for our Christian lives. It's not always easy, but we should be there for each other, cheering our brothers and sisters in Christ to do their best. Our Head Coach is THRILLED when He sees us really showing TEAMWORK! So let's get out there and PLAY BALL! *(Exits.)*

Leader invites a student to read Colossians 3:23-24 from the Key Verse Card. **Coach is right! When we think of our Christian brothers and sisters as a team, all playing on the same side and all focused on the same goal, it really helps us remember why God put us here!**

Close in prayer, thanking God for His help in working together.

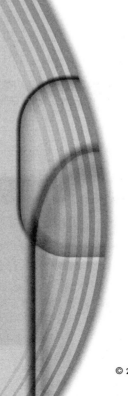

Play Ball!

DISCUSSION SHEET

Being a Christian and being part of God's family is kind of like playing baseball.
How does it help us to know the rulebook?
Find Psalm 119:9-16.

What are some of the gifts and abilities God's team might display? Why?
Find 1 Corinthians 12:7-11,27-28.

What helps us with spiritual conditioning?
Find 1 Corinthians 9:24-27 and 2 Timothy 2:1-5.

What are some ways we can cheer for and help each other?
Find Ephesians 4:29-32 and Hebrews 10:24-25.

KEY VERSE CARD

Colossians 3:23-24
"Whatever you do, work at it with all your heart, as
working for the Lord, not for men, since you know that
you will receive an inheritance from the Lord as a
reward. It is the Lord Christ you are serving."

All for the One

TOPIC
Temptation

CHARACTER
Sword-fighting Know-No-Fear (musketeer)

SUMMARY
One of the Three Know-No-Fears (like "Three Musketeers") talks about dealing with temptation.

KEY VERSE
1 Corinthians 10:13
"No temptation has seized you except what is common to man. And God is faithful; he will not let you be tempted beyond what you can bear. But when you are tempted, he will also provide a way out so that you can stand up under it."

PROPS
Plastic toy sword, tricornered hat (or other fancy hat) with feather

OPTIONAL PROPS
Velvet jacket, lace scarf, other musketeer-style clothing

PREP POINTERS
Don't focus too much on the costume; practice swashbuckling delivery!

SCHEDULE
Small-Group Warm-up (5-10 minutes)
Large-Group Presentation (5-10 minutes)
Small-Group Discussion (10-20 minutes)
Grand Finale (5-10 minutes)

SMALL-GROUP WARM-UP
Meet, greet and discuss the following questions in your small group:
- **What are wrong things a kid your age might be tempted to do?**
- **Tell about a time when you saw a kid your age (lie) to get something. What did the kid want? What happened next?**
- **What might be another reason a kid would (lie)?**

ALL FOR THE ONE

LARGE-GROUP PRESENTATION

(MUSKETEER *enters, brandishing sword and shouting.*)
"All for the ONE, for the ONE is for all!" THIS is our battle cry! Together, my two *compadres* and I are known as—the Three Know-No-Fears! (*Pauses, looks around and sees that the audience doesn't get it.*) It's like "The Three Musketeers." Get it?

Our mission is to serve our KING by going where he sends us—to do NOBLE things like rescue princesses and capture evil villains! We must always uphold the VIRTUES of our great king as we work. We are faced with many TEMPTATIONS along the way. Fighting these temptations makes our job even MORE difficult.

THE KING'S WAY

Recently, I was faced with just such a temptation. An evil king had STOLEN my king's favorite painting and I was chosen to FIND the painting and bring it back. It was a PERILOUS job! Anyone know what that word means, "perilous"? (*Waits for answer.*)

That's correct. It was a DANGEROUS job and a DANGEROUS day! In DISGUISE, I made my way into the enemy castle and discovered the painting in his own BEDCHAMBER—where the evil king was ASLEEP!

Quietly, I LIFTED the painting from the wall as the king SNORED. Now, ANOTHER painting was hanging there, too, a very BEAUTIFUL one. I thought my king would very much like to have it, TOO! I was TEMPTED to take it—after all, it was probably stolen as well!

But then I REMEMBERED my king's rule: "Take ONLY what belongs to you." I was sorry that an EVIL king possessed such a lovely work of art—but I RESISTED the temptation to STEAL it. A STOLEN painting would NOT please my king!

SWAMPS AND STABS

Another time, the QUEEN sent me to the swamp to gather cattails for her flower arrangement. Now, I HATE swamps! They are slimy and muddy and smelly—and frankly, they SCARE me a little. I did NOT want to go. I was TEMPTED to wait a week and then tell the queen that there were NO cattails growing in the swamp anymore. Or—I could tell her that 50 vicious thieves ROBBED me of the cattails, although I was able to escape with my LIFE!

There it was again! TEMPTATION! To tell the queen these things would be LYING. So even though I was fearful, I obeyed. I actually had a rather nice trip to the swamp and back! The weather was lovely. There was no danger. And although I STILL dislike swamps, I OBEYED my queen. And I spoke the TRUTH.

Sometimes, I've been tempted when I was TIRED. During one swordfight, I was SO weary that I was TEMPTED to end the fight by STABBING my enemy in the BACK as he turned. But that is EXTREMELY unfair! Instead, I prayed for strength and overcame him fairly.

FAILED

But then, there have been other times when, I must confess, I have failed. One time, I was sent to groom the king's horses—but I just didn't FEEL LIKE doing it. I thought it could wait until LATER. But the KING was about to show his beautiful steeds to a visitor! So when he entered the stables and saw his beautiful horses in less-than-perfect order, he was ANGRY! I had GIVEN IN to the temptations of LAZINESS and PROCRASTINATION. Anyone know what that word means, "procrastination"? *(Waits for answer; responds.)* That's right. Simply putting things off!

READY TO FIGHT

Even those of you who are NOT Know-No-Fears must face temptation. It is EXTREMELY important to fight temptation CONSTANTLY, for the more often we give in to it, the easier it is to give in the next time. Fighting temptation keeps us at the ready to serve our king! As you sit at your "round tables," perhaps your investigations will help us learn more about the best ways to combat temptation. *(Exits, brandishing sword.)*

SMALL-GROUP DISCUSSION TIME

Provide one "All for the One" Discussion Sheet (p. 196) to each student. Invite students to find verses and discuss answers to questions on the sheet. Invite interested students to talk more with you about joining God's family (see "Leading a Child to Christ" on p. 11).

GRAND FINALE

(MUSKETEER returns.)

One thing I have learned from being part of the Three Know-No-Fears is that to FIGHT temptation, it's important to stick TOGETHER! When we are alone, we forget the king's rules. We get frightened or tired, and we give in to temptation more easily. We NEED each other!

When we help each other, encourage each other and pray for each other, we are better able to resist every temptation. THEN we can live in ways that please the TRUE King! He is Jesus, our perfect King! He is the ONE who loved us enough to die on the cross to PAY for ALL the times that we DO give in to temptation. That's the reason for our battle cry: "All for the ONE, for the ONE is for all!"

Fight the good fight with me! With King Jesus on our side, working together and praying for each other, all for the One, we can be VICTORS in our battle against temptation! All together now: ALL FOR THE ONE, FOR THE ONE IS FOR ALL! *(Exits, shouting this battle cry.)*

Leader invites a student to read 1 Corinthians 10:13 from the Key Verse Card. **We certainly met a swashbuckling example today of how to fight temptation! We're going to take some time to pray silently. Think about one time in your life when you are often tempted to do wrong. What could you ask God to do to help you overcome that temptation?**

Close in prayer aloud after a short time of silent prayer, asking God to help each student face, fight and overcome the specific temptations prayed about.

All for the One

DISCUSSION SHEET

What are some wrong things kids your age are most tempted to do? (Fight with siblings, disobey parents, cheat, lie, steal, etc.)

Who were the first people ever to be tempted? What happened?
Find Genesis 3:6,13.

Was Jesus ever tempted?
Find Matthew 4:1.

What did Jesus do when He was tempted? What did He say?
Find Matthew 4:3-11.

Does God tempt us?
Find James 1:13-15.

Besides our own selfish desires, who else tempts us?
Find 1 Peter 5:8-9.

What is the best thing to do when we are tempted?
Find James 4:7.

What can we do about those times that we do give in to temptation?
Find 1 John 1:9.

KEY VERSE CARD

1 Corinthians 10:13
"No temptation has seized you except what is common to man. And God is faithful; he will not let you be tempted beyond what you can bear. But when you are tempted, he will also provide a way out so that you can stand up under it."

The Love Lab

TOPIC
True love

CHARACTER
Mad scientist

SUMMARY
The scientist may be a little crazy, but the love is genuine!

KEY VERSE
1 Corinthians 13:4-8a

"Love is patient, love is kind. It does not envy, it does not boast, it is not proud. It is not rude, it is not self-seeking, it is not easily angered, it keeps no record of wrongs. Love does not delight in evil but rejoices with the truth. It always protects, always trusts, always hopes, always perseveres. Love never fails."

PROPS
Lab coat, messy wig, clipboard, pizza box

OPTIONAL PROPS
Beakers containing colored water, Bunsen burner

PREP POINTERS
Practice your best Albert Einstein impression!

SCHEDULE
Small-Group Warm-up (5-10 minutes)
Large-Group Presentation (5-10 minutes)
Small-Group Discussion (10-20 minutes)
Grand Finale (5-10 minutes)

SMALL-GROUP WARM-UP
Meet, greet and discuss the following questions in your small group:
- **What is something you REALLY love?**
- **When have you seen someone fall in love? How did that person act?**
- **What are some ways parents show love to kids? Ways kids show love to brothers or sisters? To friends?**

THE LOVE LAB

LARGE-GROUP PRESENTATION

(MAD SCIENTIST enters, rubbing hands together.)
Ah. And what have we here? Children! Well, not LITTLE children. You're OLDER children, aren't you? I know this for TWO reasons: ONE, because I am a SCIENTIST and therefore I am highly OBSERVANT—and TWO, because someone outside told me!

EXPERIMENTING

Recently, I conducted an EXPERIMENT on people your age. The results were FASCINATING. I concluded from my research that people your age have an INCREDIBLE disparity in your attention spans. Do you know what that MEANS? It means that you become bored in math class less than 5 minutes after the lesson begins. But while you watch an action movie or play a video game, you are still highly alert up until the end of it! THAT experiment led me to delve DEEPER into the minds of those in your age group. What do you like to eat? What do you like to do in your spare time? What are your likes and dislikes? What do you love?

LOVING

Ah, love! We can find out SO MUCH about our species when we investigate LOVE! I have only BEGUN my research, but let's see if I'm on the right track here.

(Looks at clipboard.) Ah, yes. I have discovered that you love puppies, true? Yes. And kittens, and all manner of baby animals. You love shiny, sparkly things, correct? You love your friends and your family . . . and yes, you LOVE pizza. You love some sports. Ah, and look at this, some of you girls are starting to love BOYS! Some more than others, but yes, I see it in my evidence, definitely a love of the male human species.

Why IS that, I wonder? What makes you attracted to BOYS? It couldn't have been very long ago when most of you were of the opinion that boys are, and I quote, "GROSS." And yet, that has CHANGED. And you boys, what are your thoughts about GIRLS? *(Looks around.)* Never mind. You'll catch on in time.

THREE KINDS

Love, as you may know, comes in several forms. You certainly don't love PIZZA in the same way that you love your PARENTS. The Bible presents us with three words in Greek that we translate as "love" in English. First comes *phileo*. Say, "fill-EH-oh." *(Waits for audience to respond.)* Very good! This kind of love is what we might call friendship, brotherly or sisterly love, or loyal companionship.

Then there is *eros*. Say, "AIR-oce." *(Waits for audience to respond.)* Good job. Now THAT kind of love is sometimes talked about as romantic love or even lust. It's the kind of "love" that advertising uses so very often to get us to buy something.

And then there is my PERSONAL favorite, *agape*. Say, "ah-GAH-pay." *(Waits for audience to respond.)* Very good! You'll all be Greek scholars soon! This is the highest kind of love. It sees the loved one as infinitely valuable. It is pure and UNCONDITIONAL caring. It is willing to give, even sacrifice, for the loved one. And it never demands ANYTHING in return.

Now, God MADE all THREE kinds of love. But each is for different reasons and times. What KIND of love do you need to show in your life right now that would please your Creator? I don't need to do THAT research for you—you can do it yourself! Yes, very good. Make your observations of what God has to say about love. I'll be back. I left a frozen pizza cooking on my Bunsen burner. I'm going to go ingest a bit of nutrition. *(Exits.)*

SMALL-GROUP DISCUSSION TIME

Provide one "The Love Lab" Discussion Sheet (p. 200) to each student. Invite students to find verses and discuss answers to questions on the sheet. Invite interested students to talk more with you about joining God's family (see "Leading a Child to Christ" on p. 11).

GRAND FINALE

(MAD SCIENTIST returns, holding stomach.)
Ugh. Most uncomfortable! As a scientist, I should have KNOWN better. I ate my pizza BEFORE it was thoroughly cooked. Now I have a PAINFUL gastric inflammation—in other words, an enormous bellyache! I became impatient to have what I wanted—and now I'm sorry. I REALLY wish I had waited.

Ah. This goes back to our original topic, love! Love between a man and woman is not something to be rushed into lightly, no matter what you read in the magazines or see on TV. Impatient people who rush into what they think is love—especially without knowing WHICH kind of love they are IN—will most certainly be sorry!

If we wait for God's timing we find that it is ALWAYS perfect. In the meantime, we can ALWAYS exhibit love the way GOD loves—our friend *agape*. It's not easy all the time. After all, Jesus loved us enough to die for our sins. I could do a MILLION experiments and never discover a greater love than THAT! But if we ask Him, He will help us love like He does.

Speaking of experiments, I need to get started on my next one. I am exploring the causes for the unpleasant smells of feet. Oh, the SACRIFICES I make for science! *(Exits, sniffing feet of various people as he passes.)*

Leader invites a student to read 1 Corinthians 13:4-8a from the Key Verse Card. **We all think we know what love is and how to show love. But now we know that love is more than some of us thought! Let's ask God to help us discern WHAT kind of love we are experiencing and help us show the kind of love HE wants us to show.**

Close in prayer, asking God's help to discern what kind of love students need to understand and to help them show His love to others.

The Love Lab

DISCUSSION SHEET

Who is love? **Find 1 John 4:8.**

What is love? **Find 1 John 3:16 and 1 John 4:10.**

Why does God want us to love each other? **Find 1 John 4:11.**

Does that mean He actually wants us to love our brothers and sisters too?
Find 1 John 4:20-21.

How should we love others? **Find 1 John 3:18.**

How can we show God we love Him? **Find John 14:15.**

Why did God create men and women? **Find Genesis 2:24.**

Is it important to have boyfriends or girlfriends right now?
Find Ecclesiastes 3:1,8.

How can we trust God to show us when the time is right for marriage?
Find Psalm 25:4-5 and Matthew 6:33.

KEY VERSE CARD

1 Corinthians 13:4-8a
"Love is patient, love is kind. It does not envy, it does not boast, it is not proud. It is not rude, it is not self-seeking, it is not easily angered, it keeps no record of wrongs. Love does not delight in evil but rejoices with the truth. It always protects, always trusts, always hopes, always perseveres. Love never fails."

Man Overboard!

TOPIC
Trusting God's answers

CHARACTER
Shipwrecked person

SUMMARY
A person who falls off a cruise ship tells how he or she is cared for by God—but not as expected!

KEY VERSE
Proverbs 3:5-6
"Trust in the LORD with all your heart and lean not on your own understanding; in all your ways acknowledge him, and he will make your paths straight."

PROPS
Ragged clothes

OPTIONAL PROPS
Rock, coconut (already cracked but placed back together), inflatable palm tree

PREP POINTERS
Bring and break open a real coconut (see optional props). Use a small, sharp knife to cut samples of coconut for students to taste.

SCHEDULE
Small-Group Warm-up (5-10 minutes)
Large-Group Presentation (5-10 minutes)
Small-Group Discussion (10-20 minutes)
Grand Finale (5-10 minutes)

SMALL-GROUP WARM-UP

Meet, greet and discuss the following questions in your small group:
- **When have you been on a boat? What did you like about it? Dislike?**
- **Tell about a time you were very afraid. What happened?**
- **Did you pray? What did you ask God to do? What happened next?**

MaN OVerBoaRD!

LARGE-GROUP PRESENTATION

(SHIPWRECKED PERSON *enters, running, hugging people, shouting.*)
I'm SAVED! WOW! I've never been so happy to see people in all my LIFE!
You'll never BELIEVE what I've been through.

(*Sits down, winded.*) Let me tell you what happened. It all started when
I went on a cruise. The ship was HUGE! And there was food everywhere—
a floating BUFFET! Well, I did what ANYBODY would do: I ATE too much! I ate
SO much that I couldn't SLEEP! So I got up to take a walk. After I'd walked
awhile, I was LOST on the cruise ship! I didn't even know if I was on the right
DECK. I leaned over the railing to see if the deck below was mine—and
THAT'S when I fell OVERBOARD!

SAVE ME!

SPLASH! There I was, floating in the vast, black ocean. But I knew EXACTLY what
to do. I closed my eyes and PRAYED, "Dear God, when I open my eyes, let the
cruise ship be turning back to get me."

I opened my eyes. But the cruise ship just kept GOING! Then something bumped my
arm. I thought, Oh, NO! I'm about to become a floating BUFFET for a SHARK! But it
WASN'T a shark. It was a LOG. I grabbed that log—at least I could keep afloat!

But I NEEDED to be SAVED! I knew EXACTLY what to do. I closed my eyes and PRAYED, "Dear
God, when I open my eyes, let my log carry me right into a busy port so I'll be rescued."

I opened my eyes. I saw NO busy port. But I COULD see what looked like land on the hori-
zon. My log drifted toward that land. Soon I washed up on a deserted beach!

WATER? FOOD?

I was on land! And I was DYING of thirst. But I knew EXACTLY what to do. I closed my eyes and
prayed, "Dear God, when I open my eyes, let there be a bottle of ice-cold spring water in my hand!"

I opened my eyes. NO bottle of water appeared! But I COULD see a waterfall above some trees. I got
to my feet and headed toward the trees. I hadn't gone far when I stubbed my toe on a rock. OUCH!
My toe even BLED! I sat down and cried. Then I noticed that the rock I'd kicked was WET! I moved it.
And underneath, I found a SPRING. FRESH WATER! I drank and DRANK—it tasted SO good!

I hobbled over to sit against a palm tree and bandage my poor toe. My stomach started to rumble. I was
SO HUNGRY! But I knew EXACTLY what to do: I closed my eyes and prayed, "Dear God, when I open my
eyes, let there be an enormous steak here, ready to eat."

I opened my eyes. NO steak. But WHUMP! Something landed NEXT to me—a coconut! Coconut ISN'T my
favorite food. But when you're STARVING, it's GREAT! The problem was, I had no way to OPEN it!

CHAINSAW?

I knew EXACTLY what to do. I closed my eyes and prayed, "Dear God, when I open my eyes, let there
be a chainsaw right in front of me so I can open this coconut!"

I opened my eyes. You guessed it—NO chainsaw! But I saw a pointed stick just beyond my toe. I
picked it up. I remembered the rock I'd tripped over! With the sharp stick and the rock, I opened
the coconut! And since there were coconuts everywhere, I knew I wouldn't STARVE!

PIG PROBLEM!

I had water and food! I was eating coconut and thanking God when I heard a loud SNARL! A HUGE wild PIG with long, pointy tusks was staring at me, ready to CHARGE.

But I knew EXACTLY what to do. I closed my eyes and prayed, "Dear God, when I open my eyes, let this angry pig be GONE."

I opened my eyes. The pig was still THERE—looking even MORE ANGRY! So I RAN! And THAT'S how I got here—running from the pig! I got away—and I found YOU! I'm not LOST anymore! Hooray! *(Hugs more people.)*

ANSWERS TO PRAYER

But I CAN'T figure out why God never answered my prayers! I prayed for the ship to turn around. I prayed for a busy port. I prayed for a bottle of water. I prayed for a juicy steak. I prayed for a chain-saw. I didn't get ANY of those things! When I prayed for the pig to disappear, it didn't—but then, I DID find civilization!

Maybe there's more I need to learn about how God answers prayer! Why don't you all check it out while I go find something to eat besides coconut! *(Exits.)*

SMALL-GROUP DISCUSSION TIME

Provide one "Man Overboard!" Discussion Sheet (p. 204) to each student. Invite students to find verses and discuss answers to questions on the sheet. Invite interested students to talk more with you about joining God's family (see "Leading a Child to Christ" on p. 11).

GRAND FINALE

(SHIPWRECKED PERSON returns.)

Maybe . . . God DID answer my prayers. He just didn't answer them in the way I EXPECT-ED! Now that I've had time to think about it, I suppose GOD'S answers were even BET-TER than my ideas!

I mean, think about it: If the CRUISE SHIP had turned around or I'd drifted into a busy PORT, I probably would have been RUN OVER! If I'd gotten a BOTTLE of water or a STEAK, that's all the water and food I would have had. If God had sent me a CHAINSAW, I probably would have HURT myself—I don't know how to use a chainsaw! If the PIG had not shown up, I wouldn't have RUN here!

It's a GOOD thing God didn't answer my prayers EXACTLY as I asked or I might still be floating in the ocean—or cutting myself with a chainsaw! I guess it's really true that when I pray, I need to remember that God really DOES know best. He sees the WHOLE picture! *(Exits.)*

Leader invites a student to read Proverbs 3:5-6 from the Key Verse Card. **We're glad to see our shipwrecked friend is safe! God answers prayer—but we can trust Him to answer in His own way, which is the BEST way possible! This week, let's be sure to thank God for His answers—even if the answers surprise us. He knows best. We can trust His love and care!**

Close in prayer, thanking God for hearing our prayers, being worthy of our trust and helping students trust His answers.

Man Overboard!

DISCUSSION SHEET

What does God tell us about His plans for us?
Find Jeremiah 29:11.

Why does God want us to pray to Him?
Find Philippians 4:6.

What can keep our prayers from being answered?
Find James 4:2b-3.

When God doesn't answer prayer the way we want Him to, what can we remember?
Find Isaiah 55:9-11.

When we don't know what to pray, what can we trust God to do?
Find Romans 8:26-27.

KEY VERSE CARD

Proverbs 3:5-6
"Trust in the Lord with all your heart and lean not on
your own understanding; in all your ways acknowledge
him, and he will make your paths straight."

Here's the Scoop!

TOPIC
Trusting in God

CHARACTER
Junior newspaper reporter

SUMMARY
The reporter gives the "who, what, where, when and why" about trusting God.

KEY VERSE
Jeremiah 17:7-8

"Blessed is the man who trusts in the LORD, whose confidence is in him. He will be like a tree planted by the water that sends out its roots by the stream. It does not fear when heat comes; its leaves are always green. It has no worries in a year of drought and never fails to bear fruit."

PROPS
Bible with references bookmarked, clipboard, pencil, hat or cap

OPTIONAL PROPS
Photocopies of the script on the clipboard, if desired

PREP POINTERS
The reporter is like "Jimmy" from the Superman stories. Play it up!

SCHEDULE
Small-Group Warm-up (5-10 minutes)
Large-Group Presentation (5-10 minutes)
Small-Group Discussion (10-20 minutes)
Grand Finale (5-10 minutes)

SMALL-GROUP WARM-UP
Meet, greet and discuss the following questions in your small group:
- **When have you written a news article or a report?**
- **What did you like about writing it? What did you not like?**
- **What questions would you ask to get complete information?**

HERE'S THE SCOOP!

LARGE-GROUP PRESENTATION

(REPORTER races in, looking all around as if to find something.)
Hi! I'm Scoop. I'm a new reporter for the Daily WANNA KNOW News. I'm a little NERVOUS—this is my first BIG ASSIGNMENT! If I do a good job, the editor says I'll get my own byline and MAYBE even be promoted to "regular reporter"! Golly gee, I've always WANTED to be a reporter. Look here, I'd be real grateful if you'd HELP me with this assignment. Will ya HELP me? *(Waits for audience response.)* Gee, you're SWELL! THANKS! Okey-dokey, here's my assignment!

You know how our money says "In God We Trust"? Well, here's what I'm supposed to find out: "Can you REALLY trust God?" I got a SWELL lead from one of the senior reporters. He said the BIBLE has a lot of SUPER-DUPER stuff about God!

GET THE SCOOP

As any good reporter knows, there are basic questions that have to be answered in a well-written article! They are WHO, WHAT, WHEN, WHERE, WHY and HOW. Well, the WHO is easy. We're talking about GOD. *(Writes on clipboard.)* And WHAT are we reporting about? TRUSTING in God. Now for the WHY . . . Jeepers, why SHOULD we trust God? Is He TRUSTWORTHY? What's His TRACK RECORD on trustworthiness? Is it better to trust your life to YOURSELF—or to God?

(Picks up Bible; thumbs through it.) Hey! Looky here! Here's a story about a guy named Elijah. Leapin' lizards! Look at what HE went through! *(Summarizes the following passages in a few sentences: 1 Kings 17:1-16; 18:22-45; 2 Kings 2:11—Elijah predicted a drought, was kept fed by ravens by a brook, challenged the prophets of the false god Baal to a contest, was taken to heaven in a fiery chariot.)*

INVESTIGATIVE REPORTING

WOW! This stuff is FANTASTIC! That Elijah REALLY trusted God. Do you think God would have HELPED Elijah so much if Elijah didn't really TRUST Him? Hm . . . I wonder. Elijah really OBEYED God, too. Do ya think he would have OBEYED if he didn't think GOD knew what He was doing? You know, I think it's time for you to do some investigative reporting of your own—about trusting GOD! *(Exits.)*

SMALL-GROUP DISCUSSION TIME

Provide one "Here's the Scoop!" Discussion Sheet (p. 208) to each student. Invite students to find verses and discuss answers to questions on the sheet. Invite interested students to talk more with you about joining God's family (see "Leading a Child to Christ" on p. 11).

GRAND FINALE

(REPORTER returns, waving clipboard.)

All RIGHT! I've been putting this story together and I think I've got all my facts! Let's go through our list of questions. *(Reads off list.)* Let's see. The WHO is GOD. The WHAT is TRUST . . . the WHEN? Well, it looks like it should be ALWAYS, to me!

The WHERE has to be—EVERYWHERE! And the WHY must be, BECAUSE GOD LOVES US AND WANTS WHAT'S BEST FOR US! That's GREAT!

Oh. There's one more? HOW? That's right. It's BY FAITH! And HOW do you get faith? It's a gift from God—so all you need to do is ASK for it!

Well, gang, I need to get my article to the editor. This story is big—HUGE! I bet it makes the FRONT PAGE! I can see it now: "EXTRA! EXTRA! Read all about it! GOD IS TRUSTWORTHY! He wants what's best for us!"

Thanks a LOT for your help! See you in the funny papers! *(Exits.)*

Leader invites a student to read Jeremiah 17:7-8 from the Key Verse Card. **Well, our reporter sure gave us the scoop on trusting God. Let's each take a minute to think about a situation in our lives that worries us or makes us want to take control. Whatever it is, let's pray and ask God to help us trust Him to give us the best answers. He is trustworthy!**

Close in prayer, thanking God for being worthy of our trust and asking Him to help us trust Him to give us good answers in hard situations.

Here's the Scoop!

DISCUSSION SHEET

What are good reasons to trust God? **Find Jeremiah 29:11 and Psalm 33:11.**

We often want to be in charge of our own lives. Why should we trust God to direct our lives? **Find Proverbs 3:5-6.**

Letting go of control can be hard. What are reasons to trust God completely? **Find Hebrews 11:6 and Romans 8:28,32.**

When is a time it is hard to trust God? What would you tell a worried friend? **Find Psalm 37:3-6 and John 14:1-2.**

KEY VERSE CARD

Jeremiah 17:7-8
"Blessed is the man who trusts in the Lord, whose confidence is in him. He will be like a tree planted by the water that sends out its roots by the stream. It does not fear when heat comes; its leaves are always green. It has no worries in a year of drought and never fails to bear fruit."

Bad News, Good News

TOPIC
When bad things happen

CHARACTER
Newscaster

SUMMARY
The newscaster helps us remember what God is doing when we are faced with "bad news" times in our lives.

KEY VERSE
1 Peter 5:10-11
"And the God of all grace, who called you to his eternal glory in Christ, after you have suffered a little while, will himself restore you and make you strong, firm and steadfast. To him be the power for ever and ever. Amen."

PROPS
Business suit, table, chair, papers (news bulletins)

OPTIONAL PROPS
A notebook or laptop computer on the table from which to read the news instead of papers

PREP POINTERS
The on-air and off-air voices and personalities should be markedly different.

SCHEDULE
Small-Group Warm-up (5-10 minutes)
Large-Group Presentation (5-10 minutes)
Small-Group Discussion (10-20 minutes)
Grand Finale (5-10 minutes)

SMALL-GROUP WARM-UP
Meet, greet and discuss the following questions in your small group:
- **What is the worst thing you have ever seen happen to someone in real life?**
- **Why do you think this happened to that person?**
- **What did other people say about this person's situation? Did you agree? Why or why not?**

Bad News, Good News

LARGE-GROUP PRESENTATION

(NEWSCASTER sits at table, holding papers from which to read the news.)

ON THE AIR

(Speaking in an "on air" voice.) Good evening and welcome to the 7 o'clock news. I'm Sam Lee. At the top of the hour, we have breaking news concerning a flash flood that has just hit Elk Snout. Three homes have already been swept downriver. While there have been no reports of human deaths, one of the homes swept away was a haven for abandoned dogs. It would seem almost certain that all 14 dogs have drowned.

In more local news, a three-year-old was struck by a hit-and-run driver at around 3 this afternoon. The accident occurred at the corner of Pine and Cedar. The child is listed in critical condition at Memorial Hospital. We will attempt to keep you posted on further developments.

In world news tonight, another explosion occurred at the Central Bus Terminal in Milan, Italy. While the incident is still under investigation, it is believed to be the work of terrorists. We'll be back with the weather—right after these messages.

OFF THE RECORD

(Speaking in an "off air" voice.) Oh, man, could the news get any WORSE? Violent crime, tragic accidents, natural catastrophes—things are just plain HORRIBLE. You know, it would be ONE thing if all this bad stuff happened ONLY to the mean, rotten, bad people of the world, but it DOESN'T.

That family who lost their house in the flood? THEY were just trying to be kind to all those abandoned dogs! Oh, and the little boy hit by the car? His father is the PASTOR of Elk Snout Church. Why doesn't God take BETTER CARE of Christians? We love Him and try to do what's right. So why does BAD stuff still HAPPEN to us?

IN THE RECORD

You don't BELIEVE me? Just look at what happened to God's faithful servants in the Bible! David was hunted by King Saul because Saul wanted to KILL him—and THAT is the SAME David whom God said was a man after His own HEART!

And Elijah? HE was hunted down to be murdered, too! Job lost EVERYTHING—his children, his wealth and his health. Daniel was KIDNAPPED, Peter was IMPRISONED, Paul was AFFLICTED, Stephen was STONED to DEATH and John was EXILED! They ALL loved God. And LOOK at what God let HAPPEN to them!

Come to think of it, this would make a great news story: "Why does God let bad things happen to Christians?" We're almost back from commercial break, so would you do some research on that topic for me? I'll see you after the sports report! *(Exits.)*

SMALL-GROUP DISCUSSION TIME

Provide one "Bad News, Good News" Discussion Sheet (p. 212) to each student. Invite students to find verses and discuss answers to questions on the sheet. Invite interested students to talk more with you about joining God's family (see "Leading a Child to Christ" on p. 11).

GRAND FINALE

(NEWSCASTER returns, picking up newscast in mid-sentence. Speaking in an "on air" voice.)
So it LOOKS as if the Elk Snout Snorters will yet AGAIN fail to make the play-offs. We'll be back with entertainment news after a word from our sponsors.

(Speaking in an "off air" voice, to audience.) I've been thinking about the question I asked: "Why does God let bad things happen to Christians?" I heard the verses you read. And I guess it's pretty clear that it's because we live in this fallen world, Christians are JUST as likely as non-Christians to have to deal with the rotten things that can happen in life. Calamity, cancer, even cavities—Christians are not exempt. When it rains, we get wet just like everyone else!

But for a Christian, the DIFFERENCE is that God is there WITH His child every MINUTE of the difficulty. He hears all the prayers. He gives His children peace and comfort even through the most difficult of circumstances.

It's all a matter of trust. Even in the worst times, God gives us PEACE when we trust HIM to do what is best in a bad situation.

Imagine that! Even in the middle of being AFRAID, we can trust God to do what is BEST. God loves to make good happen, no matter HOW bad things seem. So God doesn't KEEP bad things from HAPPENING to Christians—He understands how they feel. He's there WITH them through it all. THAT'S God's love and care for His people!

(Speaking in an "on air" voice.) This just in to our studio: God will be there for you ALWAYS, whether times are good or bad. And THAT, folks, is the BEST news we've heard in a LONG time! *(Ends broadcast, collects papers and exits.)*

Leader invites a student to read 1 Peter 5:10-11 from the Key Verse Card. **Our lives won't always be free of trouble. God never promises to take trouble away from us, but He does promise to take us *through* trouble in a way that will be for His glory and for our good. Let's thank Him for that!**

Close in prayer, thanking God for His love and care and asking Him to help students trust Him when times are difficult.

Bad News, Good News

DISCUSSION SHEET

What does God say about Christians who face difficulties and tragedies?
Find Job 2:10b and Matthew 5:45b.

How are things different for Christians during times of trouble?
Find Deuteronomy 31:8, John 14:27 and 2 Corinthians 1:3-4.

How do we benefit from trusting in God during hard times?
Find James 4:8a.

What should we do when times are hard?
Find 1 Peter 4:19 and Proverbs 3:5.

What should we remember?
Find Romans 8:28.

Do we always understand why God does things the way He does them?
Find Isaiah 55:8-9.

KEY VERSE CARD

1 Peter 5:10-11
"And the God of all grace, who called you to his eternal glory in Christ, after you have suffered a little while, will himself restore you and make you strong, firm and steadfast. To him be the power for ever and ever. Amen."

God is #1!

TOPIC
Wholehearted worship

CHARACTER
Sports fan

SUMMARY
The sports fan shares some thoughts on worshiping God wholeheartedly.

KEY VERSE
Psalm 100
"Shout for joy to the LORD, all the earth. Worship the LORD with gladness; come before him with joyful songs. Know that the LORD is God. It is he who made us, and we are his; we are his people, the sheep of his pasture. Enter his gates with thanksgiving and his courts with praise; give thanks to him and praise his name. For the LORD is good and his love endures forever; his faithfulness continues through all generations."

PROPS
Any ridiculous sports fan prop (pennant, helmet, pompom, team foam finger, etc.)

OPTIONAL PROPS
Face paint in two colors

PREP POINTERS
Practice your best crazy fan character; feel free to paint your face, dye your hair or whatever makes it look like you are "wholly devoted" to the Muskrat team!

SCHEDULE
Small-Group Warm-up (5-10 minutes)
Large-Group Presentation (5-10 minutes)
Small-Group Discussion (10-20 minutes)
Grand Finale (5-10 minutes)

SMALL-GROUP WARM-UP
Meet, greet and discuss the following questions in your small group:
- **What is your favorite sports team? Favorite player?**
- **What do you do to show you really like your favorite team?**
- **Why do you think some people cheer and scream at a sporting event?**

GOD IS #1!

LARGE-GROUP PRESENTATION

(SPORTS FAN *enters excitedly, face painted, waving pennant or foam finger, shouting*)
Yeah MUSKRATS!!!! Muskrats are #1! WOO HOO!!!

THE WINNERS

I just came from the BIG GAME! Did you HEAR? The Muskrats defeated the Hedgehogs by 3 POINTS! We won! We WON! WE WON!!!!!

(*Does a little victory dance.*) The fans came out in full force to cheer on their team. EVERYONE was yelling and screaming and jumping up and down! The cheerleaders led cheers and we did The Wave about 15 TIMES! I'm telling you, the crowd just went NUTS! That's because this is the BEST team of Muskrats we've had in YEARS. They could take us all the way to the National CHAMPIONSHIP!

WORTH A CHEER

There's just NOTHING I love better than cheering on the Muskrats! It is JUST THE BEST!!!
(*Pauses, thinking.*) Well, that's not ENTIRELY true. I love my family better than the Muskrats—I THINK!

And, well, I love GOD more than the Muskrats—I mean, God CREATED me; He offered Himself as a sacrifice so that I could be SAVED; He helps me and listens to my prayers . . . I guess that compared to GOD, the Muskrats aren't THAT important.

But when you think about it, that's kind of weird, you know? I mean, I don't PERSONALLY know one single PLAYER on the Muskrat team. And yet I yell myself hoarse cheering for them! And even though I know Jesus as my Savior, I NEVER yell and cheer about HIM! I mean, I sing along in church during services, sometimes I even clap along, but it's not EXCITED clapping like the kind I do when I'm at a Muskrat game!

WORTHY OF PRAISE

Why IS that? I mean, why don't we get excited about praising GOD? Shouldn't we be MORE excited about praising Him than we are about some SPORTS team? Is it because church is the ONLY time and place we praise God? Or should we praise Him other times, too? Does God even WANT our praise? Wow. All these questions are giving me INDIGESTION! Well, THAT and the four CHILI CHEESE DOGS I ate at the game. I'm going to get an antacid, OK? While I'm gone, find some answers for me about praising God, will ya? Yea! You can do it! Go TEAM! (*Exits.*)

SMALL-GROUP DISCUSSION TIME

Provide one "God is #1!" Discussion Sheet (p. 216) to each student. Invite students to find verses and discuss answers to questions on the sheet. Invite interested students to talk more with you about joining God's family (see "Leading a Child to Christ" on p. 11).

GRAND FINALE

(SPORTS FAN returns, thoughtfully waving a pennant.)

God is AMAZING. He is WAY more awesome than the Muskrats on their VERY BEST DAY! He DESERVES my praise. I love Him and I want Him to KNOW it! I want to praise Him bigger and better and LOUDER than I have EVER cheered for the Muskrats!

How about you? I know that sometimes when we are singing in church, I'm thinking more about how my VOICE sounds or how people around me THINK I sound. BUT I'm SUPPOSED to be focused on God, not thinking more about ME, ME, ME! And I should praise Him ALL the time, not just wait until church! I want to praise Him with my whole heart and mind.

OK, then. Want to give it a TRY? Let's think only about GOD and how wonderful HE is! On the count of 3 we'll shout, "Praise God!" Ready? 1, 2, 3—PRAISE GOD! *(Looks up.)* Did you LIKE that, God? We want YOU to be pleased with our praise and worship. I know. How about a CHEER? Let's do a cheer for GOD!

If you love God, let's hear you yell: "God Rocks!"

(Audience responds.) God Rocks!

Why is Jesus worth our Praise? You can yell it—"He Saves!"

(Audience responds.) He Saves!

Who is greater than our God? You can yell, "No One!"

(Audience responds.) No One!

God is glad to hear us praise Him the way He DESERVES to be praised! YEA, GOD! You're number 1! Woo Hoo! *(Exits, continuing to shout.)*

Leader invites a student to read Psalm 100 from the Key Verse Card. **Our sports fan is right: We need to praise God all the time! We don't have to be shouting cheers to worship Him, but we can praise Him and tell Him how awesome He is no matter where we are! Let's ask God to help us remember to worship Him and praise Him all the time!**

Close in prayer, asking God to help students remember that He is worthy of our praise and worship all of the time.

God is #1!

DISCUSSION SHEET

What makes God worthy of our praise?
Find Deuteronomy 32:3-4.

Who should praise Him?
Find Psalm 148:1-13.

Where should we praise Him?
Find Acts 16:23-25.

When should we praise Him?
Find Psalm 146:1-2.

How should we praise Him?
Find Psalm 47:1 and Psalm 150.

Why should we praise Him?
Find Psalm 103:1-5.

KEY VERSE CARD

Psalm 100
"Shout for joy to the Lord, all the earth. Worship the Lord with gladness; come before him with joyful songs. Know that the Lord is God. It is he who made us, and we are his; we are his people, the sheep of his pasture. Enter his gates with thanksgiving and his courts with praise; give thanks to him and praise his name. For the Lord is good and his love endures forever; his faithfulness continues through all generations."

Time for God

TOPIC

Why we study Scripture

CHARACTER

Preteen boy or girl (adjust names accordingly)

SUMMARY

A preteen helps us understand why it's important to make time for God.

KEY VERSE

Psalm 119:11,105

"I have hidden your word in my heart that I might not sin against you. Your word is a lamp to my feet and a light for my path."

PROPS

Desk or table, papers, books, cellular phone, chair

OPTIONAL PROPS

Bag of dry cat food, bag of Cheetos, trash can, toothpaste, toothbrush, sunblock, cat dish

PREP POINTERS

Write out the note from Mom to read aloud; practice the cat food/Cheetos and the sunblock/toothpaste gags ahead of time.

SCHEDULE

Small-Group Warm-up (5-10 minutes)
Large-Group Presentation (5-10 minutes)
Small-Group Discussion (10-20 minutes)
Grand Finale (5-10 minutes)

SMALL-GROUP WARM-UP

Meet, greet and discuss the following questions in your small group:
- **What do you think you spend the most time doing? The next most?**
- **What is one thing you wish you had more time to do?**
- **What time do you already have planned for (Bible study, verse memorization)?**

TIME FOR GOD

LARGE-GROUP PRESENTATION

(PRETEEN sits at desk or table, finishing math; picks up phone and calls friend.)

Hi, Jennifer. Yeah, I just finished my math. Are you done? I thought it was easy. It was mostly review from last year but Mr. Evans explains it way better than Mrs. Reed did. So, anyway, I was going to take a break before I did my spelling. Want to come over and watch cartoons with me?

MORE TO DO

(Responds to Jennifer.) Oh no! SOCCER practice! I forgot all about it! And my mom left me a note, too! *(Looking through papers.)* Where IS it? Here it is. I thought I was going to have PLENTY of time to get everything done. Rats! I gotta go. Bye. *(To self.)* I can't BELIEVE I forgot!

(Reads note aloud.) "Good morning, (your name)! Don't forget that you have soccer practice at 4:30 today. Jen's mom will be by to pick you up at 4:15, so be ready."

(Looks at clock) What time is it now? 4:10! Oh, NO! "Make sure to have a snack before practice. We won't be eating dinner until after 7 tonight. Also, put on sunscreen so you don't get sunburned. See you tonight! Love, Mom

P.S. Feed the cat."

MORE CHORES

Oh, great! NOW I've got to study my SPELLING WORDS before practice! OK. What ELSE do I need to do? Oh, yeah. Feed the cat. OK. *(Pours Cheetos from bag into cat dish while studying spelling words.)* Have a snack, kitty. Rhythm. R-H-Y-T-H-M, rhythm. *(Reaches into cat-food bag and eats pieces of cat-food, spits it out in trash can.)* Oh, that's SICK! I can't believe I just ate CAT FOOD. GROSS!

(Grabs toothpaste, begins to put it on face while rereading note.) Sunscreen, sunscreen. *(Goes back to reading spelling words.)* Article. A-R-T-I-C-L-E, article. Is it L-E, or E-L? ACK. I have cat-food breath! *(Puts sunscreen on toothbrush, looks in mirror to brush teeth, screams.)* AAAHHH!!!!! I have TOOTHPASTE all over my face! I almost brushed my teeth with SUNSCREEN! I ate CAT FOOD! *(Sits down dejectedly.)*

TOO MUCH!

How am I EVER going to get EVERYTHING done? I have a LOT more homework this year. I have SOCCER. I have GUITAR lessons. And on top of all THAT, now I'll have a bunch of VERSES to memorize—and Bible reading to do every day!

Other kids probably just have their regular homework to do, but I'll have all this OTHER stuff, too. With everything I have to do, is it REALLY that important to be memorizing Bible verses? Somebody tell me, WHY should I study GOD'S WORD? WHY should I memorize SCRIPTURE? You guys see if you can figure it out. I'm LATE! *(Exits.)*

SMALL-GROUP DISCUSSION TIME

Provide one "Time for God" Discussion Sheet (p. 220) to each student. Invite students to find verses and discuss answers to questions on the sheet. Invite interested students to talk more with you about joining God's family (see "Leading a Child to Christ" on p. 11).

GRAND FINALE

(PRETEEN returns.)

Whew. I still have a lot to do this year. But SOME things are SO important that I am going to MAKE time for them—because being BUSY is just not a very good excuse. EVERYONE is really busy!

I think studying the book that GOD wrote should be important! After all, GOD MADE me. He LOVES me. He knows what's BEST for me! I know I'll have more free time if I play on the computer less and don't watch as many TV shows. God should come first, BEFORE those things.

It's going to be TOUGH sometimes, though. I don't always FEEL like memorizing verses. Do you feel like that sometimes, too? *(Looks around at audience.)*

I've got an idea. Why don't we PRAY for each other? Our small-group leaders will be praying for us, too. Sometimes we all want to do what's easy or we want to quit. But I'm sure glad JESUS didn't give in and quit! If He had, we'd ALL be in BIG TROUBLE! It's worth my time and effort to memorize verses. I'll try if you will! You know, I actually think this is going to be FUN! *(Exits.)*

Leader invites a student to read Psalm 119:11,105 from the Key Verse Card. **There's an old saying: "If the devil can't make you bad, he'll make you busy." Sometimes being busy with even GOOD things can keep us from the things that really are the BEST things. Let's begin to pray for each other right now!**

Close in prayer, asking God to help each person put Him first by planning and making time for Bible reading, memorization and prayer.

Time for God

DISCUSSION SHEET

What are some reasons to study God's Word and memorize Scripture? **Find Psalm 119:9-11.**

How do we know the Bible is really worth studying? **Find 2 Timothy 3:16.**

(God "breathed" the words so we would read it and do what it says.)

What's a good use for those Bible verses once you know them?
Find 1 Peter 3:15-16.

What are some things God promises us about knowing His Word?
Find James 1:22-25.

KEY VERSE CARD

Psalm 119:11,105
"I have hidden your word in my heart that
I might not sin against you. Your word is a lamp
to my feet and a light for my path."

INDEXES

CHARACTER INDEX

INDEXES

SCRIPTURE MEMORY INDEX

SEASONAL INDEX

More Great Resources from Gospel Light

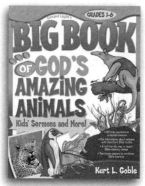
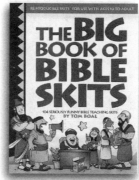

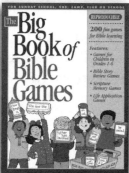

How to Teach Children to Think and Act Like Jesus

"If people do not embrace Jesus Christ as their Savior before they reach their teenage years, the chance of their doing so at all is slim."

George Barna
Transforming Children into Spiritual Champions

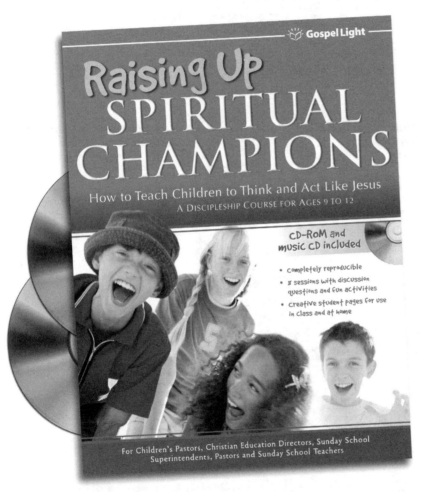

Raising Up Spiritual Champions
How to Teach Children to Think and Act Like Jesus
A Discipleship Course for Ages 9 to 12

Help kids answer the big questions about what it means to think and act like Jesus every day of their lives! This eight-session discipleship program provides the tools teachers need—from meaningful discussion questions to creative activities, from student pages to parent pages—to nurture lifelong spiritual growth in their students. Because most children's spiritual beliefs are in place by age 13, it's crucial that they acquire a biblical foundation for how they view themselves and the world. This program will help leaders teach God's truth during these all-important preteen years!

ISBN 08307.36638
Reproducible Manual
with CD-ROM and Music CD

Raising Up Spiritual Champions Includes

- CD-ROM containing everything in this book, including awards, **Student and Parent Pages**, publicity flyers, customizable forms, clip art and more!
- 8 reproducible sessions with discussion questions and fun activities
- Reproducible music CD with 12 praise and session-related songs
- How-tos for setting up the program
- 12 teacher-training articles
- **Student Pages** for use in class and at home to build discipleship habits
- **Parent Pages** that support parents in their role of spiritual teachers
- Teaching resources, including skits, discussion cards, games and more!

To order, visit your local Christian bookstore or www.gospellight.com

Gospel Light
God's Word for a Kid's World!™
www.gospellight.com